'MY GOD, SOLDIERS'

PATRICK HOWARTH

'MY GOD, SOLDIERS'

FROM ALAMEIN TO VIENNA

HUTCHINSON

London Sydney Auckland Johannesburg

To
MICHAEL AND PAMELA LIS

This edition first published in Great Britain by
Hutchinson, an imprint of Century Hutchinson Ltd,
Brookmount House, 62–65 Chandos Place,
London WC2N 4NW

Century Hutchinson Australia Pty Ltd, 20 Alfred Street,
Milsons Point, Sydney NSW 2061, Australia

Century Hutchinson New Zealand Ltd,
PO Box 40-086, Glenfield, Auckland 10, New Zealand

Century Hutchinson South Africa (Pty) Ltd,
PO Box 337, Bergvlei, 2012 South Africa

British Library Cataloguing in Publication Data

Howarth, Patrick, *1916–*
    'My God, soldiers' from Alamein to Vienna.
    1. World War 2. Army operations by Great
    Britain. Eighth Army
    I. Title
    940.54'12'4

ISBN 0-09-173554-8

Printed and bound in Great Britain by
Butler & Tanner Ltd, Frome, Somerset

CONTENTS

LIST OF MAPS

ACKNOWLEDGEMENTS

I am deeply grateful for the help given me and the under-standing shown by the Italian State Tourist Office and, in particular, by Paola Greco in London, Filippo Calandruccio and Aldo Bonaventura in Taormina, Signor Nicolini and Silvia Cordella in Pesaro, Angelo Lorizzo in Ravenna and Mietta Shamblin in Trieste.

I am also much indebted to the National Association of Italian Partisans and, in particular, to its Bologna branch, where I was fortunate enough to meet Dr Francesco Arnoaldo-Veli, Susanna Boltonelli, Professor Luciano Bergonzini, Lino Michelini and Magli Umberto. Other members of the Association who were kind enough to help me were the brothers Cicoria in Pescara and Alessandro Severi in Pesaro. The Italian Military Attaché in London, Colonel Alberto Ficuciello, also gave me valuable help.

The Austrian National Tourist Office helped me greatly, in particular Barbara Greul in London and Sabina Eggar, Dr Kurt Broer and Evelyn Miksch in Vienna.

Among British officials who helped me I am much indebted to the Defence Attachés in Rome and Vienna, Brigadier Michael Hague and Lieutenant-Colonel Michael Ledger; Christopher Woods of the Foreign Office; and Jeremy Larner, Commercial Secretary and Consul in Tunis.

I find it difficult to express adequately my thanks to those who were good enough to send me their diaries and allow me to quote from them, in particular Ricky Hall, Ernest Kerans, Harry Ramsbottom and Ernest Stephens.

I wish too to thank all those who were good enough to write to me, to talk to me or to help me in other ways. They include K. Akula, Jim Allan, Joseph Anderson, Carlo Baldini, Kenneth Best, I. R. Brindley, G. Broadbent, Bill Brotherton, Dr Michael Brown, N. Cassoni, Marchese Raimondo Marini Clarelli, W. Chrzczonowicz, Dr Anthony Clayton, Richard Clogg, Lieutenant-Colonel George Colchester, K. T. J. Czelny, Samir Darwish, Sydney Davis, Walter Drzewienicki, Harald Eggar, Alan Gibbs, Arnold Graves, Dr Francesco Griccioli della Griggia, Andrew Grochowski, Dr Gruber, T. Harland, Ernest Harrison, T. W. Harrison, Denis Hills, Mark Hyatt, Leslie Jackson, M.W. Japp, Peggy Jones, J. W. Juszczyk, Dr V. Kapetanyannis, Jo Kenney, T. Korzeniewicz, Martyn Lloyd-Davies, Ludwik Lubienski, J. Mahally, Rachid Mardassi, R. L. Middleton, Captain W. Milewski, John Miller, Nicholas Nikon, Felicjan Pawlak, General Sir Thomas Pearson, Robert Perrin, the Pierini family, Marina Polydoras, Terence Price, John Reid, Edmond L. de Rothschild, Edward St Maur, Maurice Sarfati, H. T. Shergold, Diana Skene, Philip Swaddling, M. Szwedziuk, Lieutenant-Colonel Jerzy Szymanski, P. A. A. Thomas, S. W. Wall, James Whitton, James Wilkie, Sir Peter Wilkinson, Sir Edgar Williams, Theo Williams and D. A. Yorke. I hope I have not omitted any. If I have I trust those inadvertently left out will forgive me.

I received valuable help from the Public Record Office in Kew, the National Army Museum, the Special Forces Club Library, the Richmond Public Library, the Burroughs Library, the India Office Library, the Sikorski Institute Library, the Institut Français Library, and the libraries of the High Commissioners for Australia, Canada and New Zealand and of the South African Embassy in London. For this I want to thank, in particular, Dr D. M. Blake, Dr Peter Boyden, Colonel J. A. Combrinck, Alfred Knightbridge,

Colonel D. R. Lawrence, Peter Lee, Colonel George Van Niekerk and Andrzej Suchicitz.

My thanks are due to *New Crusader* and the *Polish Daily* for helping to put me in touch with so many former members of the Eighth Army.

Transcripts of Crown-copyright records in the Public Record Office appear by permission of the Controller of H. M. Stationery Office.

Finally I would add that my principal helper was my wife, who made most of the journey with me and offered valuable suggestions at all stages in the preparation of this book.

Prologue

INVITATION TO A JOURNEY

At the end of October 1942 a cosmopolitan force under British command began one of the great military journeys in history. The force was known as the Eighth Army.

The journey began in the desert which links Egypt with Libya, continued along the North African littoral to where Carthage once stood, took the form of a seaborne and airborne invasion of Sicily, and, after the mainland of Italy had been traversed from south to north, ended in Vienna, at the heart of central Europe.

The men who made up this army were drawn from a variety of nations. Many of them came from countries which at that time were coloured pink on English maps, for the creation of the Eighth Army was one of the last cohesive actions of the constituent parts of the largest empire known to man, an empire which shortly afterwards was to disintegrate. There were units from the self-governing dominions of Australia, Canada, New Zealand and the Union of South Africa. There was a strong force from the Indian Army formed by troops from Great Britain, from the countries which later became known as India and Pakistan, and from Nepal. There were units too from Cyprus, Mauritius, Rhodesia and the Sudan.

There was a large Polish contingent and a smaller Greek one. There were troops fighting under the flag of France, most of them drawn from the French colonial empire. Also,

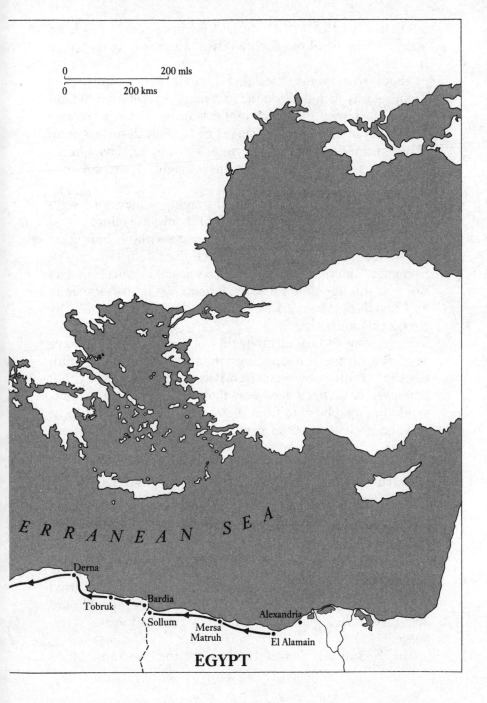

after an armistice with Italy had been signed in 1943, an appreciable part of the Eighth Army was made up of Italian troops.

There were some specialist United States units. The Eighth Army included too the first regular formation to fight under the Jewish flag since biblical times. There were also some Libyans. In the later stages of the war deserters from German conscript and other armies – Soviet citizens, Czechoslovaks, Yugoslavs and Austrians – fought in partisan units under Eighth Army command.

Various honours fell to the different elements in ways now largely forgotten. Indeed, today only a well-informed military historian would be able to state without hesitation the nationalities of the troops which liberated the cities of Bologna, Rimini, Ravenna, Florence and Venice. In fact Bologna was liberated by Poles, Rimini by Greeks, Ravenna by Canadians, Florence by South Africans, and Venice by New Zealanders.

In the long and colourful history of Venice there can have been few stranger happenings than its liberation in mid-twentieth century by motorised Pacific islanders. Nor could it readily have been foreseen that the city of the Medici would be freed by men from the southernmost tip of Africa, and the ancient imperial capital, Ravenna, by men whose country extended to the Arctic Circle.

The journey of the Eighth Army from Egypt's Western Desert to Vienna lasted rather more than two and a half years. During this time the Army was engaged in desert warfare, in mountain warfare and in street-by-street and house-by-house fighting. It was confronted by enemy forces which were commanded with great skill and which defended and counter-attacked, delayed and withdrew with exemplary discipline in conditions which frequently strongly favoured the defence. In consequence the Eighth Army suffered heavy losses in killed and wounded. Yet in its journey it did not lose a battle.

The Eighth Army was the first of the Western Allied

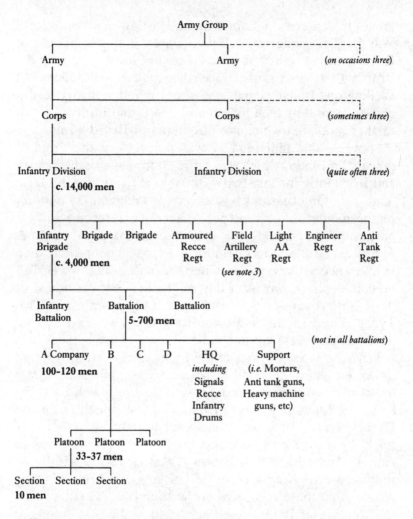

Notes

1. This is the basic organization. There were many variations.

2. Divisions would sometimes have a medium artillery regiment; Corps and Army would have additional heavy and medium artillery and/or heavy mortars.

3. By 1944 Infantry Divisions had *three* field artillery regiments and in some cases an armoured brigade (or three regiments) instead of simply one armoured regiment.

4. The Infantry Divisions shown above all included logistic units – transport, signals, ordnance, workshops, etc. which are not shown on the chart.

(Chart provided by Dr. Anthony Clayton, RMA Sandhurst.)

armies to achieve any significant and lasting victory in World War II. This understandably endeared it to the people of Britain, and in time it acquired a greater prestige among the British than any army since the time of the Duke of Wellington. It had a panache too, an individuality and a corporate pride which may readily be found in divisions or smaller units, but which are rare in major British armies.

Some of this individuality was reflected in the dress of officers and men, which was variegated, sometimes bizarre and frequently inconsistent with what is meant by the term 'uniform'. On occasions this variety was dictated by military requirements or convenience. There were reconnaissance parties in the desert, for instance, to be seen in Arab headdress and sandals. But it was panache rather than military necessity which ordained the garb of the two British officers depicted day after day by the brilliant cartoonist of the *Eighth Army News*, Cyril James, and known as the Two Types. Even in the snows of Italy the Two Types wore desert boots and silk cravats.

When reviewing troops of the Eighth Army after they had advanced as far as Tripoli, Winston Churchill said: 'After the war when a man is asked what he did it will be quite sufficient for him to say, "I marched and fought with the Desert Army."' He went on to suggest the Army's deeds might be a source of song and story 'long after we who are gathered here have passed away'. Rather less fancifully he then wrote to King George VI: 'I suppose Your Majesty realises that these two corps of the Eighth Army comprising together about 160,000 men are perhaps the best troops in the world.'

The book which follows is an account of the campaign which the Eighth Army fought, and I have chosen to present its progress as a journey rather than as a series of military actions.

More than forty years after the Eighth Army finally reached Vienna I have recently retraced its route, but in my descriptions I have tried to present it as it was seen by the soldiers or as it affected their battles and their rest periods, their pleasures and their discomforts. The route itself is richly rewarding scenically, architecturally and in the ease with which history, both ancient and modern, can be sensed and evoked. My own impressions of it have been formed partly by the journey I made in the spring and summer of 1988, and partly from my memories as a serving officer of the Special Operations Executive in North Africa and Italy from August 1942 onwards. It is therefore a travel book, yes. But it is not a guidebook, and it is intended primarily as a tribute to an army whose full achievements have never yet been adequately chronicled in a single work.

I hope others, including those who were not yet born when the events described in this book took place, will also decide to make at least some part of this journey. Sadly, for British travellers, at least, there is one section which cannot at present be recommended. This is the passage through

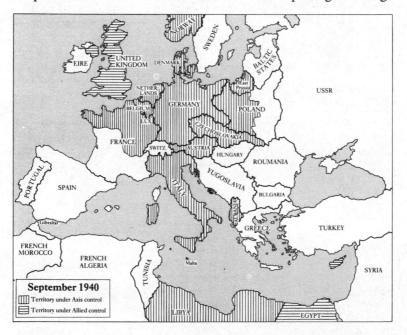

September 1940
||||| Territory under Axis control
≡ Territory under Allied control

Libya, a country which owes its freedom from colonial rule entirely to the Eighth Army, but in which the men who served in that army and their descendants are now not welcome.

The journey of the Eighth Army as a steady progression forwards began only after a decisive battle had been fought at El Alamein in the last days of October and the first days of November 1942. But before that event there had been more than two years of campaigning in the Western Desert. The nature of this campaigning and the reasons why it took place have to be understood in some measure before it is possible to appreciate how the battle of El Alamein came to be fought and how the journey which followed it was made possible.

PART ONE: EGYPT

(September 1939 – November 1942)

BACKGROUND TO A JOURNEY

When war broke out in 1939 Britain had a small military force in Egypt. Its primary purpose was the defence of the Suez Canal.

In the neighbouring country of Palestine there was also a British military presence. This was in fulfilment of the mandate to administer Palestine which Britain had been granted by the League of Nations in 1923. By 1937 the members of a British Royal Commission had come to the conclusion that the mandate should be terminated and the territory of Palestine divided between Jews and Arabs. But before any such advice could be followed war threatened and then broke out, and the troops remained.

By British soldiers a posting to Egypt was generally regarded as good fortune. The climate of the country is excellent, and although the heat is considerable in the summer, the air is always dry. The only really disagreeable climatic condition is the *khamsin*. This is the hot wind from the south, which raises dust everywhere and sometimes in the desert will create a wall of grit some hundreds of feet high. The *khamsin* can blow for several days at a time.

The *khamsin* and the flies apart, Egypt offered peacetime soldiers many delights of open-air life. Some became fascinated by the Western Desert, which occupies more than two-thirds of the territory of Egypt. The desert consists mainly of sandy plains and rocky limestone ridges and

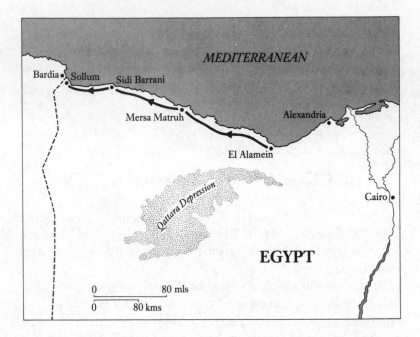

plateaux. At sunrise and sunset these take on shades of pink
and brown which cannot be seen in any cultivated landscape.
The Sinai Desert, where a mirage taking the form of a large
inland lake is a common occurrence, has comparable attrac-
tions. Those soldiers who had ready access to Alexandria,
the principal naval base, or to Cairo, where a huge headquarters was to be built up in World War II, were particularly fortunate. Both cities were delightful in themselves,
and much of their life was regulated to suit the tastes of the
British occupying forces.

    The Cairo of most British officers, in war or in peace – a
scene I came to know well – was not the Cairo of the
mosques and mausoleums, the citadel and the early Coptic
churches, nor that of the nearby sphinx and pyramids. They
were of course familiar with the street sights of Cairo: the
dozens of figures in white *galabiyahs* clinging to the outsides
of trams; the sallow men in grey flannel suits and red

tarbooshes sipping strong coffee from tiny cups and flicking the air with fly-whisks. But the Cairo the British made their own was the Cairo of Shepheard's Hotel and Groppi's Café, the Turf Club and, perhaps principally, the Gezira Sporting Club.

Gezira, set in a green suburb, offered sportsmen virtually everything they could wish, including a large polo field, an excellent cricket ground and a race track. Its social centre in the daytime was a swimming pool, around which girls from embassies and airlines and military offices could be seen sun-bathing while black, smiling, imperturbable Sudanese waiters brought out gin fizzes and cold lunches.

The Egyptian who arguably commanded the greatest respect among British officers was the Gezira squash rackets professional, a tall, handsome, courteous man known as Mahmoud, who gave every defeated opponent the impression that the match had been a close one. After the war he was to emerge, under the name of Mahmoud el Karim, as the acknowledged champion of the world.

A treaty made between Britain and Egypt in 1936 had specified that a British garrison of 10,000 would be stationed in the Canal Zone. But as the threat of war grew in 1938 and 1939 and Mussolini made no secret of his aggressive intentions, particularly in North Africa, the terms of the treaty were interpreted more and more freely. Some reinforcements were sent from Britain, largely in order to improve the anti-aircraft defences of Egypt. In the event Egypt was to be happily free from aerial bombardment. There was also some talk of building an imitation Maginot Line to prevent an invasion from Mussolini's Libya, but nothing came of it.

Then in the summer of 1939 a mobile British force was assembled near Mersa Matruh, about 180 kilometres from the Libyan frontier. It consisted of units of the Royal Horse Artillery, the 7th, 8th and 11th Hussars, the Royal Tank Regiment, the Royal Army Service Corps and a Field Ambulance. This body was known at first as the Cairo

Cavalry Brigade. It was to be the nucleus around which the Eighth Army eventually grew. The brigade was poorly equipped. It did have some armoured cars, but they had seen service in World War I. In general, in the words of the historian of the 7th Armoured Division, of which these units would later form part, the equipment was 'lamentable and out-of-date'.[1] In Tripolitania at that time there were nine Italian divisions. The Italians also had numerical superiority in aircraft.

The effect on life in Egypt of Britain's declaration of war on Germany in September 1939 was for some months muted. The Egyptian government broke off diplomatic relations with Germany and declared a state of siege, which amounted in effect to imposing martial law. Both actions suited British administrators, but the more perceptive among them nevertheless felt some concern about certain groups and individuals who were helping to shape Egyptian policy. One of these was King Farouk who, nearly three years earlier, at the age of seventeen, had succeeded his father, King Fuad. Farouk, who soon revealed himself as a young man of gross appetites matching his gross appearance, was strongly under Italian influence, both female and male. His *chef de cabinet*, Ali Maher, also had pro-Axis sympathies.

There was too the National Moslem Party, which had recently changed its name from that of the Young Egypt Party. This body was receiving money from Italy and had sent a delegation to a Nazi Nuremberg rally. Its official policy was 'complete and definite liberation of Egypt of all limitations on her sovereignty'. Its leader, Ahmed Hussein, addressing King Farouk as 'the centre of hope in all Arabic countries', called on him to act as leader of the Arab bloc in 'liberating all its parts and lifting it high and assuring its place under the sun'.[2]

The task of the British Embassy – of considerable import-ance to the conduct of military operations from Egyptian

bases – was to ensure the presence of an Egyptian government friendly to Britain, and strong enough to quell dissent.
This task the Embassy was to perform with skill over the
next few years. Early in 1940, for example, after Egyptian
police had seized the National Moslem Party's printing
press, the British Government, for its part, agreed to buy
the entire Egyptian cotton crop at a generous price of £30
million.[3]

The speed with which the Dominions joined Britain in
declaring war allowed troops to be sent very quickly to the
Middle East from Australasia. These included a New Zealand division, units of which were immediately stationed on
the Gezira racecourse to provide protection against
parachutists.[4]

The commander of the New Zealand division, Bernard
Freyberg, had an extraordinary military record. He was
awarded the Victoria Cross in World War I for an action in
which he was twice wounded. He was officially listed as
wounded nine times in that war and was mentioned in
despatches six times. Although perhaps too unhesitatingly
gallant to be an altogether shrewd strategist – in World War
II Field-Marshal Montgomery spoke in rather patronising
terms about his ability as a commander – he was an inspiring
leader, and would play a distinguished part throughout the
campaigns in North Africa, Greece and Italy. It was in Italy
that he was awarded the third bar to his DSO in 1945.
Freyberg was to end his working days as Lieutenant-Gover-
nor of Windsor Castle.

The New Zealand division included an appreciable
number of Maoris. They became much respected soldiers,
but during their early training the customs of their culture,
particularly their sharing of property, caused certain problems. The official historian of the Maori battalion was to
write: 'To be charged for shortages discovered in kit inspection when the article was probably being put to good use by
somebody else was, in the opinion of the Maori recruit, an
erratic *pakeha* custom.'[5]

An Australian infantry division and a cavalry division were also promptly despatched to the Middle East, but not at first to Egypt. One of the principal preoccupations of the Middle East Command in 1939 was still the policing of the mandated territory of Palestine, and assisting in this was the first task allotted to the Australians.

Another body which was to play a major part in the battles ahead, and which was also an early arrival in the Middle East, was the 4th Indian division. This included both British and Indian infantry brigades and a Gurkha battalion. Signals and administration were partly in British, partly in Indian hands. The sappers were all Indians.

The Sudan was at that time administered as an Anglo-Egyptian condominium, with its own Defence Force. This was strengthened by the raising of an additional battalion.

By the early summer of 1940 the British and Common-wealth military force in the Middle East numbered nine divisions. Six were based in Egypt and three in Palestine.[6] They all came under the command of General Archibald Wavell, Wykehamist, anthologist of distinction, and the possessor of perhaps the best mind of any senior British soldier of his time.

On 10 June 1940, with the collapse of France imminent and Germany already the master of much of Europe, Italy declared war on Britain. Early in September an Italian army began to invade Egypt on a narrow front along the coast, and succeeded in capturing the small Arab township of Sidi Barrani. A month after the invasion Hitler and Mussolini met at the Brenner Pass. Hitler offered to send German mechanised and other troops to support the Italians in North Africa. Mussolini, with characteristic vanity and misjudgement, turned the offer down.

Wavell waited until December to launch his counter-attack. When it came it was devastatingly successful. The counter-attacking force was commanded by Major-General Richard O'Connor and consisted of the 7th Armoured

Division, later to be known as the 'Desert Rats', and the 4th Indian Division, with the 6th Australian Division in reserve. Within a week 40,000 Italian troops had been captured and all Italian forces removed from Egypt. The advance continued, and the Australians captured Bardia and Tobruk in Libya, towns with which the Eighth Army would later become painfully familiar. In his diary the Italian Foreign Minister, Mussolini's son-in-law, Count Ciano, wrote: 'Something is wrong with our Army if five divisions allow themselves to be pulverised in two days.'

This was the clearest lesson to emerge from the brief campaign. There was much wrong with the Italian Army. Its equipment was even worse than that of the British, and its soldiers for the most part showed little interest in fighting. The Royal Air Force, although inferior in numbers, gained ascendancy in the air, and the Royal Navy was able actively to support the troops by bombardment.

Wavell had planned the attack as a limited one, with the sole object of securing the Egyptian base against an attack from Libya, since he had to be wary of other neighbouring parts of Africa where Italian troops were present in considerable numbers. These included Eritrea and Ethiopia. Offensive operations were carried out in these territories also, and with overwhelming success. When they were concluded a number of formations, including units from the Union of South Africa, became available for service on the Egyptian–Libyan front.

Major-General O'Connor's force in Libya had advanced 500 miles. Men whose previous experience of fighting had been limited to trench warfare could reasonably regard this as an astonishing distance. To the more thoughtful it opened up new possibilities. To those in charge of supplies it revealed new difficulties. The campaign was indeed an early illustration of the truth later to be enunciated by the German panzer commander, General von Ravenstein, when he said that the desert was 'a tactician's paradise and a quartermaster's hell'. A lesson learnt on the Axis side was expressed in a directive issued by Hitler in January 1941. In this he wrote: 'For strategic, political and psychological reasons Germany must assist Italy in Africa.'

The advance into Libya revealed with startling clarity the importance of mobility and armoured formations in desert warfare. Major-General Patrick Hobart, who had largely formed and trained the nucleus of the 7th Armoured Division, had long and vocally been aware of this, but his views had not been well received by some of his superiors, and in November 1939 he had been relieved of his command.

About a year and a half later Wavell's successor, Auchinleck, was to inform Churchill: 'Infantry divisions, however well trained and equipped, are no good for offensive operations in this terrain against enemy armoured forces.'[7] About the same time the commander of the South African forces in the Middle East, Major-General Brink, was to inform Smuts that, in his opinion, two South African armoured brigades would be of much greater practical value than the two large South African infantry divisions then under his command.[8]

At a lower level there were imaginative men in the Middle East Command who had novel ideas on how the peculiar qualities of the desert could be turned to military advantage. One of these was Ralph Bagnold, an officer in the Royal Corps of Signals and brother of the well-known novelist Enid Bagnold, one of a group of young officers who in the 1930s became fascinated by the adventure of driving motorcars over long distances through the desert. He designed a sun compass, developed a condenser for conserving water in car radiators, and, with others, set about disproving the common military belief that large areas of the desert were impassable by motorised formations.

Having no claim on any Army transport, Bagnold began by obtaining what vehicles he could from the Chevrolet Company in Egypt and the Egyptian Army. From this modest start the body known as the Long Range Desert Group came into being. It consisted of small, self-contained parties able to find their way over areas for which no maps existed and carry their own water and food supplies. They would disappear into the desert for weeks at a time and, sometimes wearing Arab dress, would take up positions far behind enemy lines and from there report by radio details of the movements of enemy vehicles, guns and troops.[9]

Wavell was among the first to encourage Bagnold. Freyberg too was attracted by the concept of the Long Range Desert Group, and he readily gave consent to the secondment of a number of New Zealanders to it. An officer who worked closely with the LRDG later wrote: 'The New Zealanders, farmers in civil life, took easily to a roaming life in the desert.'[10] The LRDG also had a Rhodesian squadron and one drawn from the Brigade of Guards.

Other more or less independent military formations came into being in response to the demands of the desert. One of these was the creation of David Stirling, an officer in the Scots Guards, who also believed in the use of small groups of highly-trained, highly-qualified men. Stirling originally envisaged his men going into action after being dropped by parachute, and his small force was given the name of L Unit of the Special Air Service Brigade. But he then reached an agreement with David Lloyd Owen, who commanded the Long Range Desert Group, that the LRDG would provide land transport, and that there would be an accepted division of duties, the LRDG concentrating primarily on intelligence and Stirling's men on action, particularly sabotage.[11]

Yet another irregular unit was wholly the creation of a Belgian citizen of Russian parents named Vladimir Peniakoff. After being educated at Cambridge, Peniakoff served for a time in the French Army, but he regarded England as his country and, in his own words, 'loved it with a somewhat ridiculous fervour'. He settled in Egypt in 1924 and worked in the sugar business. He was forty-two when the war broke out.

In October 1940 Peniakoff was posted to the Libyan Arab Force in Egypt as a second-lieutenant. This body consisted of Libyans who had escaped to Egypt as refugees from the repressive regime imposed by the Italian colonising power. The British High Command was inconsistent and unimaginative in its use of these men, and after a time they were placed under the command of the 4th Indian Division. Peniakoff thought some of them could be employed to advantage in building up an intelligence network in Libya. He was given permission to try to form his own unit for this purpose. As some British staff officers found the name Peniakoff rather a mouthful, one of them suggested Popski instead. (Popski had been the name of a bearded, bomb-throwing bolshevik in a popular strip-cartoon in the *Daily Mirror* in the 1920s and 1930s called *Pip, Squeak and Wilfred*. Pip was a dog, Squeak a penguin and Wilfred a rabbit.)

In the event the unit came to be officially designated Popski's Private Army. It was to continue to take part under this name in various irregular operations through the Italian campaign, the Libyans in it being discarded before long and carefully selected British soldiers taking their place.[12]

Campaigns of the kind waged in World War II were won by bringing superior firepower to bear at the right places at the right times and by the subsequent occupation of territory by regular troops. Private armies and irregular formations could have only a peripheral influence. But some of these were able to make contributions far out of proportion to their manpower and equipment, and to achieve results which could not be – or at least had not been – attained in other ways. They also served to break down rigid official thinking and to point lessons for the future.

A reconnaissance carried out by a New Zealand member of the Long Range Desert Group, Captain Nick Wilder, was at a later stage in the North African campaign to help change the course of a decisive battle. David Stirling's L Unit would be the genesis of the SAS Regiment, which three or four decades later was to become arguably the most elite in the British Army and certainly the one which commanded the greatest international reputation. Popski's Private Army was abiding evidence that the Eighth Army command was more than usually flexible in its thinking.

The Long Range Desert Group also made contact with an Allied force which was to play an important role in the desert campaigns and would eventually become a part of the Eighth Army. This was a body of French colonial troops commanded by a young, fair-haired colonel called Leclerc, whose real name was the Vicomte de Haute-Cloque. After the fall of France he had escaped to England, taken the name of Leclerc out of consideration for his family in France, and been sent by de Gaulle to the Cameroons. From there he had made his way to Chad and taken charge of the garrison after its commander had been killed. From Chad he brought his force to Kufra, an oasis in the desert where the frontiers of Egypt, Libya and the Sudan converge. There he made contact with the LRDG. Kufra was to be used as a base by the LRDG for some two years. Leclerc's distinguished military career had barely begun.

The individuality of dress which was characteristic of the Eighth Army derived in part from the experiences of those irregular units. In Britain the belief still persisted early in the war that it was dangerous to expose oneself to the Middle Eastern midday sun. Before leaving for West Africa and Egypt in 1942, for example, I was advised to purchase a solar topee. I did so and never had occasion to wear it.

Once troops had become used to the desert it was commonplace for them to wear nothing but shorts and whatever covered their feet. In the Long Range Desert Group the growing of beards was found helpful. This eliminated the use of water for shaving, and beards afforded some protection to the face from sun and wind, an asset to those driving long distances in trucks without windshields.[13] Various devices were used in different units to protect the eyes, nose and mouth from sand and grit. The commonest of these was the tying of a handkerchief across the face.

In short, regulation uniform – and even regulation shaving – was largely dispensed with. Ernest Kerans, a private in the Durham Light Infantry, wrote in his diary soon after reaching the desert: 'In the first month we learned that if we were going to live we had to ignore all Blighty soldiering. No blancoed webbing. No polished brasses. Dirt was camouflage (at the front at least). It is smart not to be smart.'[14]

Ernest Kerans is one of a number of Eighth Army soldiers whose first-hand impressions I have had the privilege of reading. These impressions were recorded in diary form and in words which I found both deeply moving and uniquely informative. The diaries came to me through the good offices of *Crusader*, the Eighth Army magazine, which continues to be published today.

Unfortunately the territory captured as a result of O'Connor's advance into Libya in the winter of 1940–41 did not remain in Allied possession for long. Events in Europe were to have the effect of gravely weakening Allied forces in the Middle East, and in the desert itself a new enemy was encountered.

Rather more than a month after the unsuccessful attempt to invade Egypt Mussolini's Italy committed another act of aggression. This was an attack on Greece. It too had little success, not least because it aroused minimal enthusiasm among the troops who were committed to it. The Greeks resisted strongly and were defeated only after considerable German forces had become engaged.

While Greece had still been resisting, the British government felt obliged to send military forces to her help. These had to come from Wavell's command, and the decision Churchill made was that Wavell's main task now was to help Greece and, possibly, Turkey. It was a decision which could be justified morally and politically, but hardly militarily.

On the very day that Wavell received his instructions a man arrived in Tripoli who was to play a major role in the desert battles. This was General Erwin Rommel. With him came elements of a German armoured division. Rommel was nominally subordinate to the Italian commander, Marshal Bastico, but he tended to interpret their respective roles much as he chose. His impact on the desert war was felt almost immediately.

In spite of the depletion of his forces Wavell went on the attack in the desert, but combined German-Italian counter-attacks followed, and Wavell's forces had to retreat to the Egyptian frontier. This process of an allied advance westwards, followed by a retreat eastwards, was to continue over nearly the next two years. Because of the frequency with which the town of Benghazi, in particular, changed hands it became known by racing enthusiasts as the Benghazi Handicap. In the course of this oscillation the 11th Hussars, also known as the Cherry Pickers and Prince Albert's Own, crossed the Egyptian frontier into Cyrenaica no fewer than four times.[15]

Even more decisive than Rommel's leadership was the German 88-mm gun, designed for anti-aircraft defence, but used in the desert primarily in an anti-tank role. Its effect on the British tanks of the time was devastating. In spite of this, Axis successes in the summer of 1941 were limited. In particular the attack which Rommel launched on Tobruk was successfully repulsed, largely by the Royal Artillery and by Australian infantry.

The Australians were not to remain in Tobruk for long. The Australian government was becoming increasingly convinced that the proper task of the Australian army was the defence of Australia. After a fairly acrimonious exchange of telegrams at a high level it was agreed that the Australians in Tobruk would be withdrawn, and in September 1941 a complicated naval operation was carried out to effect their relief. The replacements for the Australian Division consisted of the British 7th Division and a new force in the desert warfare, the Polish Carpathian Brigade, so-called because the great bulk of those who formed it had escaped across the Carpathian mountains to continue the fight after Poland had been overrun in 1939.

Wavell's failure to carry out a successful offensive campaign in 1941 with depleted forces led to his removal from the command. His successor was General Claude Auchinleck, who had made his career in the Indian Army.

In September 1941 the body of men Auchinleck commanded acquired a new name. Originally called the Cairo Cavalry Brigade, the Allied forces operating on the Egyptian–Libyan front had become known as the Western Defence Force. On 1 January 1941 it had been renamed 13 Corps, but in the summer Auchinleck came to the conclusion that he needed a more flexible command structure.

He therefore decided to have two corps headquarters, one of which would control the infantry divisions which operated mainly in the coastal areas, and the other the armoured divisions. The corps commanders would be responsible to an army commander in the desert. This plan was put into effect, and the reorganised force came to be known in September 1941 for the first time as the Eighth Army. Its first commander was General Alan Cunningham, whom Auchinleck appointed because of the success he had gained against Italian forces in Ethiopia. He was not to remain in command for long.

Auchinleck launched an offensive commanded by Cunningham in November 1941. Rommel's forces were driven back; the Eighth Army advanced as far west as El Agheila, and the campaign was popularly regarded as a victory. But the success was limited, for the enemy retreat was carried out in excellent order. As in naval warfare, victories in the desert can be measured only in terms of enemy forces destroyed, not of surface areas covered.

As had happened before, a counter-attack followed, led by Rommel, and this time it seemed likely that the decisive breakthrough would be made. In June 1942 the British public, long inured to news of defeat and resilient in the face of it, was profoundly shocked to learn that the defences of Tobruk had been overrun with astonishing speed, and that its garrison had surrendered. Around 25,000 men had been taken prisoner, some 10,000 of them South Africans. Large quantities of valuable equipment had been seized.

Auchinleck had General Cunningham replaced by General Neil Ritchie. Finally he decided to take over direct operational command himself. Rommel was now thinking in terms of advancing not only to the Suez Canal, but of driving much further east to link up with the German armies as they advanced through the Caucasus.

Mussolini's ambitions were more immediate. He arrived in Derna, piloting his own plane, his intention being to enter Alexandria riding a white horse. Later he planned to enter Cairo in the same way.[16] He had good reasons for thinking both these ambitions would be fulfilled.

With Rommel's army posing a direct threat to Cairo, British administrators were concerned to prevent panic from developing. The Egyptian government shared their anxiety and was consistently helpful. That there was a helpful government in office was attributable, to a surprising extent, to the activities and personality of Sir Miles Lampson, the British Ambassador.

King Farouk had continued to pursue a policy which he no doubt believed would enable him to retain his throne no matter which side won the war in the desert. At the insistence of Sir Miles, he dismissed his pro-Axis *éminence grise*, Ali Maher, from office. He remained discreetly in contact with Maher, however, maintained links with Italy, and openly declared at banquets, and on other occasions, that Rommel was winning the war in the desert. Then, early in 1942, after elections had been held, he provoked Lampson's anger by trying to form a coalition government which wholly ignored the party with clearly the greatest popular support. This was the nationalist party known as the Wafd, whose leader was the well-known lawyer politician, Nahas Pasha.

Lampson, a heavily built man of unprepossessing appearance but formidable personality, decided to take action. At nine o'clock on the evening of 5 February 1942 he drove up to the King's residence in the Abdin Palace together with, in his own words, 'an impressive array of stalwart military officers armed to the teeth', and demanded to see the King.

This was swiftly arranged. Lampson then read out a document listing what he considered to be the King's principal misdemeanours and ending with the words: 'Such recklessness and irresponsibility on the part of the Sovereign endanger the security of Egypt and of the Allied forces. They make it clear that Your Majesty is no longer fit to occupy the throne.'[17]

The King seemed ready to sign an instrument of abdication. Then he pleaded for one more chance. This Lampson decided to give him, and the King agreed to invite Nahas Pasha to form a government. As an exercise in diplomacy it was unorthodox, particularly as it is now clear from the Foreign Office papers that Lampson acted entirely on his own initiative. But in the event Nahas Pasha's government provided stability when the war crisis came in the summer, and a run on the banks, which at one time had seemed imminent, did not in fact take place.

During the early years of the war British prestige in Egypt rose and fell in direct relation to advance or retreat in the desert. Now, in the summer of 1942, crowds could be heard in the streets of Cairo crying, 'Long live Rommel.'

In a quieter way various members of the community sought some kind of reinsurance. My own first night in Egypt was spent in Shepheard's Hotel in August 1942, and I was slightly disturbed to hear two Sudanese waiters teaching each other German. (*'Das ist ein Glas.'*) Nevertheless Lampson was able to write in a despatch to the Foreign Office: 'The present tranquillity and lack of hostility among the Egyptian population is a remarkable example of what can be done by a friendly government even in adverse circumstances.'[18]

Militarily, however, the immediate need was to halt the retreat. Churchill had wanted it to be halted inside Libyan territory and at one stage had insisted that Tobruk must be held. This had not been feasible, but a delaying action was fought in the area of Mersa Matruh, where the New Zealand rearguard resisted effectively. Finally a halt was called at what was known as the Alamein line.

This, in the visual sense, did not exist. It had no evident features and was virtually indistinguishable from the rest of the desert. But it was well chosen because of the difficulty of outflanking it. To the north was the Mediterranean, and to the south the huge area of soft sand known as the Quattara Depression, generally considered impassable by heavy vehicles. Admittedly David Lloyd Owen had claimed that he could lead a brigade group of all arms through the depression, but the experiment had never actually been carried out.[19] Auchinleck had had the Alamein line prepared in advance for defensive purposes, and there for a time the enemy was halted.

Churchill continued to favour offensive action, and when Auchinleck informed him in August that there was no immediate prospect of breaking Rommel's front or turning his southern flank, and that no British offensive could be considered before mid-September, he described the report as 'a depressing account'.[20] The truth was that German fighting forces, supported by Italians, had shown themselves to be superior to the Eighth Army.

A number of explanations can be offered of why this was so. Rommel himself stated that the British soldier was characterised by 'tremendous courage and tenacity combined with a rigid lack of mobility'.[21] There was much truth in this. The notion that the tank was not a fighting arm in its own right, but merely an adjunct to infantry, was laid to rest in the desert, but it died hard.

Lieutenant-General Sir Francis Tuker, who took over command of the 4th Indian Division in December 1941 and later became a most thoughtful commentator on the desert war, was scathing also about some of the methods of supply. Petrol, for example, was brought up in flimsy kerosene tins with the result that much of it was lost before being put to use. The only discernible advantage of the method was that the tins could easily be pierced with a bayonet and used for the constant desert ritual known as 'brewing up'.[22] This consisted of producing the peculiar British concoction arrived at by boiling several spoonfuls of tea-leaves in a metal container and adding large quantities of sugar and condensed milk. In the Eighth Army brewing up occurred almost whenever an opportunity presented itself.

In a number of respects the Eighth Army soldiers also were less well trained than their German counterparts. Auchinleck realised this, and no doubt he annoyed Churchill when he sent him a signal stating: 'We are trying to train an army and use it on the battlefield at the same time.'[23] The need for more training was fully accepted by Auchinleck's successor.

There were deficiencies, furthermore, in the high command. Wavell and Auchinleck were both men of outstanding ability, and Wavell in particular was later to serve with distinction as Viceroy of India. But neither had been an ideal commander of the fighting forces in the desert. Wavell had an imagination to match the quality of his mind, but he did not communicate easily except on paper. Lieutenant-General Sir Brian Horrocks, who was to command a corps in the desert, stated that Wavell had an expressionless, poker face and 'never spoke at all if he could help it'.[24] Such men, however able, do not inspire fighting soldiers.

Auchinleck, once he had assumed direct command of the Eighth Army, had conducted the final stages of the retreat and the holding of the line with much skill. His principal weakness was a curious inability to choose the right men for the higher command and staff posts. To some extent this was a consequence of his Indian Army background. Senior officers in the British Army tend to know each other. They may well have attended staff courses together and are aware of each other's strengths and weaknesses. Montgomery even kept a little book in which he noted the personal details of officers who might prove useful later.[25] Auchinleck, coming from India, had no such advantage when choosing officers from the British Army. He had to rely on reputation rather than personal knowledge, and all too often his judgement was proved wrong.[26]

By the beginning of August 1942 Churchill had decided that Auchinleck must be replaced, and that other changes must be made in the higher command. He was not alone in holding this view. The Eighth Army in general had largely lost confidence in its commanders. It was not a demoralised army, but it was a disillusioned one, and men had ceased to assume that the orders they received and obeyed were the ones which should have been given. By contrast Rommel had acquired among Eighth Army troops a disturbing reputation for infallibility. Rigidity of thinking, primitive methods of supply, inadequate training and uninspiring leadership all contributed to the disheartening record of the Eighth Army in the spring and summer of 1942. But the principal shortcoming was still the inadequacy of equipment. In this significant changes were about to be made.

In June 1942 a huge convoy of ships sailed from Britain bringing reinforcements to the Middle East. I was on board one of them on my way out to serve in North Africa. Looking out from the deck of our ship as we made our way slowly westward and southward, I was continually impressed by the scale of the enterprise. The ships came unmolested to Freetown, where I left the convoy to make my way to Cairo by flying-boat. They then sailed round the Cape, calling at Durban. There the troops were, as one of them expressed it, overwhelmed by hospitality and oranges.

The convoy arrived safely and brought enough men and materials to transform the balance of strength in North Africa. The manpower included the 51st (Highland) Division, including three battalions of the Black Watch to join

the 2nd battalion, which had been in the Middle East since
the outbreak of war.[27] In all, the number of reinforcements
the Eighth Army received in the months of August, September and October was about 41,000. About 1,000 tanks were
added to the Army's strength during the same period as well
as some 9,000 other vehicles.[28]

Almost as important as the numbers were the improve-
ments in equipment. The Eighth Army received its first
consignment of the American Sherman tanks, which were
far superior to any tank produced until then in Britain. A
new 17-pounder anti-tank gun also came into service, and
new equipment was to increase greatly the accuracy and
value of the work of units of the Royal Corps of Signals
engaged in intercepting enemy messages, pinpointing
positions and decoding.[29]

Rommel's intelligence had for some time been superior
to that of the Eighth Army, not least because the Germans
had been able to read all the enciphered messages sent by
the United States Military Attaché in Cairo. But in the
latter part of 1942 valuable information emanating from the
Government Code and Cipher School at Bletchley was now
being passed to the Army Commander, and thus helped to
swing the advantage strongly towards the Eighth Army. No
less important was the greatly improved interception service
in the battle area. Before long indeed intelligence officers at
Eighth Army headquarters felt they had failed if they had
not already acquired for themselves most of the information
which reached them from Bletchley.[30]

The benefits of new equipment were not confined to the
Army. The Desert Air Force was also greatly strengthened,
enough to alter the balance of power in the air decisively.

Churchill came to Cairo in person to make the changes
he had decided upon in the high command. His choice for
C-in-C Middle East was General Harold Alexander and, to
command the Eighth Army, General William Gott.
Churchill found Gott inspiring. General Sir Alan Brooke,
the Chief of the Imperial General Staff, considered him

tired. While Churchill was still in Cairo an aircraft which was bringing Gott there was shot down, and Gott was killed. The man who replaced him was General Bernard Montgomery.

Churchill's instructions to Alexander as the theatre commander were unequivocal. They began: 'Your prime and main duty will be to take or destroy at the earliest opportunity the German–Italian Army commanded by Field-Marshal Rommel, together with all its supplies and establishments in Egypt and Libya.'[31]

PRELUDE TO A JOURNEY

Montgomery imposed his personality on the Eighth Army as a deliberate act of policy. He believed a commander must know his men and the men must know their commander as closely as the circumstances of war permit. While he was adept at delegating staff work, he insisted on talking directly to gatherings of officers and men and telling them what his intentions were. Not everyone in the Eighth Army welcomed his arrival. There were old desert hands who did not relish being placed under the command of men whose conspicuous whiteness of knees proclaimed their recent arrival from England. Not only was Montgomery a new arrival; so was Horrocks whom Montgomery had sent for to command a corps, and there were others.

In particular the old hands resented being told that their troops, some of whom had known two years of desert warfare, were inadequately trained. There were staff officers who were disturbed in the comfortable rhythm of their days by Montgomery's insistence on physical fitness. There were also commanders who were not attracted by the personality of this short, slight man with his abrupt manner, his resemblance to an underfed terrier, and his abundant self-assurance.

One such was the commander of the 4th Indian division, Francis Tuker. In his memoirs he refrained from much adverse comment on Montgomery, but he also refrained

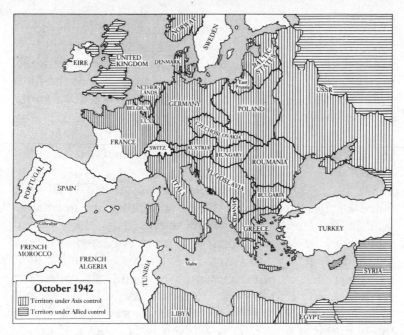

October 1942

Territory under Axis control
Territory under Allied control

from praise. He did however reveal his feelings clearly enough when he wrote that in his opinion the first two requirements for a commander to gain the trust of his officers and men were that he should be victorious and that he should be modest.[1]

Most of the resentment against new men and measures began to fade as it became clear that Montgomery knew exactly what he wanted and intended to get it. He also made an excellent impression when he ordered that all plans for further withdrawals should be scrapped. It had been prudent to make such plans, but after the long retreat their very existence was inclined to induce defeatism. Montgomery realised that the Eighth Army now had the advantage in both manpower and firepower, and that for these reasons alone all thoughts of retreat could, and therefore must, come to an end.

Montgomery's first battle in the desert was forced on him.

The line had been stabilised during August, and Montgomery took up the defensive positions which Auchinleck
had prepared. On the last day of August Rommel returned
to the attack, concentrating at the southern end of the line,
which was dominated by the Alam Halfa ridge. The battle
which followed, and which has come to be known by the
name Alam Halfa, was the first in which the two greatest of
the desert generals, Rommel and Montgomery, confronted
each other.

All attempts by the German armour to break through
failed against the Eighth Army's anti-tank guns and tanks
used in a defensive role. A major reason for the German
failure was the support which the Desert Air Force was now
able to give the Eighth Army. This far exceeded anything it
had been able to offer before. At the end of a week the
battle was over and Rommel had suffered a serious defeat.

One significant order which Montgomery issued during
the battle of Alam Halfa was given to Horrocks, who was
then commanding 13 Corps. This instructed him that in no
circumstances was he to allow his armour to become
involved in close fighting. Montgomery wanted this armour
to be preserved for pursuing a beaten enemy after the
Eighth Army had moved over to the offensive.

After Alam Halfa Montgomery concentrated primarily on
training and on generally raising the spirit and morale of his
army. The training was intensive. 'We dug trenches,' Ernest
Kerans wrote in his diary, 'as under fire, lying on one's
stomach, using the entrenching tool. Taught to pinpoint
enemy guns from compass readings, back bearings and, 120
paces counting as 100 yards, to make maps. To find our way
by varying readings, our only light the luminous dial of our
compass, over long distances . . . We easily and quietly cut
"Dannet" wire and learned to wriggle over the body of a
mate lying on it . . . Taught how to find mines with a forty-
five degree sloping bayonet, to render them safe by putting
a nail in the hole of its detonator . . .

'There were also tips from the desert warriors, the veterans. When in convoy and attacked from the air to go as far as opportunity allowed away from the vehicles, and not to shelter under them, with the bombs aimed at the vehicles and not the ground round about . . . Not to clench the teeth or tighten the muscles, let the jaw sag . . . Taught us that if you were lying at the base of a three-foot slit-trench it would take a direct hit to kill you, but crouching it might take your head off . . .

'Not all tips,' Kerans went on, 'were concerned with enemy action. We were taught how to wash in a mug full of water, to shave in it, to filter it through a handkerchief, then save it to wash underclothes and socks. Taught us that the monotony of hard-tack biscuits can be alleviated somewhat by soaking them the night before and frying for breakfast.'[2]

An Australian summed up the training programme more succinctly. In a normal rest area, he wrote, 'you either dug holes all day and guarded dumps all night, or you trained all day and guarded dumps all night.' He added: 'This rest area was different. You trained all day and then you trained all night.'[3]

Montgomery's insistence on night training served a clear purpose. He had decided that when he launched his main offensive the first attack would go in by moonlight. Some ten years earlier, when serving in Egypt, he had studied the possibility of night attacks, and he had come to understand their advantages.[4] By day in the desert infantry could attack only under the cover of thick smoke-screens fired by artillery, and against well-defended positions the carnage was likely to be horrific. Night attacks clearly favoured the attackers, but for a well-coordinated attack by night a particularly high level of discipline and training was required. By and large this level was achieved. When Montgomery went to inspect New Zealand troops he was told by their commander, Brigadier Howard Kippenberger, that every man present was a veteran. Montgomery's comment was: 'Yes, trained to kill in the moonlight.'

During this period of intensive training morale rose steadily, and Montgomery's standing rose with it. The admirable military historian Ronald Lewin, recalling his own period of service in the desert as an artillery officer, wrote: 'Old hands and new shared a sense of elation: it was as though 8 Army believed in itself again.'[5] Montgomery's talks to officers and men contributed much to the change of mood. He exuded optimism wherever he went, and he gave those under his command the impression that he was taking them into his confidence. This indeed he did, and on one occasion at least to an extent that might have had disastrous consequences for the Allied conduct of the war.

Just before the battle of El Alamein the Eighth Army had benefited even more than usual from the achievements of the code-breakers at Bletchley, where through the process known by the code-name Ultra messages sent in German high-grade ciphers could be read. Four days after Montgomery assumed command in the desert a detailed summary of Rommel's intentions was sent to him and, to the consternation of the Chief of the Imperial General Staff, General Sir Alan Brooke, he passed this on in talks to those under his command, explaining not only how Rommel was going to be defeated, but what Rommel's plans were.

The German High Command was already puzzled, as well as disturbed, by the high proportion of losses which its convoys in the Mediterranean were sustaining, and had begun an enquiry to ascertain whether its ciphers were really secure. Only a rigid refusal to believe that the high-grade ciphers used for the enciphering machines could be broken eventually prevented the right conclusion from being reached.

Churchill had wanted Montgomery to launch his main attack in September. Montgomery was adamant that the army would not be ready by then. The date he chose instead was 23 October, which was during the full moon period. In the personal message which he sent to the Eighth Army on that day he wrote: 'The battle which is about to begin will be one of the decisive battles of history. It will be the turning point of the war.' It was an accurate assessment of what has become known as the Battle of Alamein.

The Eighth Army had a considerable preponderance of strength, but for an offensive action against a well-prepared defensive line such a preponderance was needed. It had some 195,000 troops against approximately 50,000 Germans and 54,000 Italians. Its advantage in tanks and guns was approximately two to one. The Eighth Army Command also knew, through Ultra, the enemy's general intentions. It knew that Rommel was in Germany on sick leave and that he had been temporarily replaced by General Stumme, who had come from the Russian front. It also knew that the enemy was suffering from a worrying shortage of fuel for its tanks and other vehicles.

As part of the preparations for battle, where possible, men were given short breaks in rest camps before being called upon to go into action. Private Kerans was sent to a camp near Alexandria, where he had, in his own words, 'the most wonderful three days of the time spent in the Middle East.' On their first day of rest he and a friend each had four eggs, bacon and sausage for breakfast in the Springbok Club in Alexandria. Their final meal was at 2 a.m. in a Greek restaurant. The next day they lunched off chicken, egg and chips followed by fruit salad and ices at the Jewish Club and in the afternoon had tea and cakes at the YMCA. They had their photographs taken near the Mohammed Ali statue, teamed up with two New Zealanders, visited the zoo, and saw two ATS girls on the arms of Egyptians, giving the impression that they had found the sheikhs of their imagination.[6]

Montgomery, who himself had a reputation for austerity, impressed on his senior commanders the need to make their working conditions for the battles that lay ahead as efficient as possible and as comfortable as could reasonably be expected. He gave instructions for his own headquarters to be moved from what he described as 'dung-strewn camel tracks' to some pleasanter place in close proximity to the headquarters of the Desert Air Force.[7]

Divisional commanders were now provided with caravans. Tuker found as a result that he could sleep on a mattress instead of an ambulance stretcher, and that he could transfer his books from an old grenade box to a table. The books he had chosen to bring with him were the Bible, *Alice in Wonderland* and *Alice Through the Looking Glass*, Surtees's *Handley Cross*, the *Pickwick Papers* and a verse anthology. He had also brought paints, but found, as he put it, that 'desert war impelled one to words, often hard words, but never to line, form or colour.'[8]

During its preparations for the battle the Eighth Army suffered one setback. Thoughout the first two years of campaigning the health of the Army in the desert had been remarkably good, with no epidemics. Now there was an outbreak of hepatitis or, as it was then called, jaundice. Some units suffered severely. In one battalion of the Royal East Kent Regiment, more commonly known as The Buffs, fifteen officers were at one stage out of action because of the disease.[9] This apart, the general physical condition of the Army, partly as a consequence of the intensive training, was as good as it had ever been. The attitude of mind was now such that a number of senior officers were convinced that the morale of the Eighth Army was superior to that of the Germans.[10]

It was known almost everywhere that a major battle lay immediately ahead, and Montgomery emphasised this wherever he went. Every soldier knows that major battles mean heavy losses. Another admirable diarist who served in the ranks in the desert, Sergeant Harry Ramsbottom of the 4th County of London Yeomanry, noted: 'For our part there were no false illusions as to the struggle that lay ahead.'[11] But there was general confidence about the outcome, and men felt not only a readiness but a compulsion to go into battle.

Keith Douglas, poet and graphic artist, had a comparatively safe position as a camouflage officer. He abandoned this, together with his batman, in order to rejoin his old unit, which was to go into action as part of the 7th Armoured Division (the Desert Rats).[12] After Brigadier Kippenberger gave a final talk to the New Zealand troops under his command they gave three loud cheers. Someone present commented that their first objective was as good as taken.[13]

There were three corps within the Eighth Army, the 10th, 13th and 30th commanded respectively by the British Lieutenant-Generals Brian Horrocks, Herbert Lumsden and Oliver Leese. 30 Corps, which was on the right or northern flank, comprised the 51st Highland Division and a British armoured brigade as well as an Australian, an Indian, a New Zealand and a South African division. 13 Corps, on the left or southern front, was a predominantly British formation. So was 10 Corps, which was initially to be in reserve but, under the ex-cavalry commander Lumsden, was now intended as the main pursuit force once the enemy line had been broken.

To create further diversions the Special Air Service Regiment, which included a Special Boat Section, was to make raids behind the enemy lines, and the Royal Navy was to carry out a bombardment and feign a diversionary landing.

In addition to the Commonwealth forces there were two French brigades and one Greek brigade in the Eighth Army at this stage. These formed part of 13 Corps under Horrocks. The French brigades had fought a defensive action in the desert at Bir Hakeim with distinction. The Greeks were mostly men who had escaped when the Germans overran their country in 1941.

The Desert Air Force cooperating with the Eighth Army had been strengthened by the addition of six United States squadrons, three of fighters and three of light bombers.[14] A number of American tank crews had also been included in the armoured formations, largely to enable them to gain combat experience.[15]

Montgomery's plan was essentially simple. 13 Corps on the left or southern front was to make thrusts to the north-west, giving the impression that this was the main attack. In fact the main attack was to be in the north on a four-division front. Once two corridors had been made through the enemy minefields there, 10 Corps was to pass through, their main task the destruction of the enemy armour. Montgomery foresaw heavy losses, and his foresight was borne out by events. Commanders have terrible responsibilities which those who have never had the duty of condemning men to the near-certainty of death can never know.

The enemy's strategy was defensive. German units had been deliberately mixed with Italian units to provide a stiffening force, for it was generally accepted that only in the Folgore Division was Italian morale at all high. The armoured groups were all placed under German commanders.[16]

On the evening of 23 October, after the rumble of the Eighth Army's transport moving into position had died down, there was a period of silence scarcely broken by either of the opposing armies. Then at exactly 9.40 p.m. a barrage from 800 guns opened up, with a line of lights flashing across the desert.[17] Some measure of tactical suprise was achieved, for the enemy had not expected the attack to begin so soon.

In the days that followed the power of the artillery was supplemented by that of the Desert Air Force. Sergeant Ramsbottom noted in his diary: 'Today formidable formations of Bostons, shepherded carefully by weaving fighters, so like hens fussing round their chickens, continually flew over, to drop their devastating loads on Rommel's supply lines and troops. So different to the early days when very little of our aircraft was seen.'[18]

The first phase of the attack was what Montgomery

euphemistically called both 'a crumbling process' and 'wearing down the enemy's infantry'. By the third day some doubts were beginning to be felt about the success of this hard, costly, but necessary operation. Horrocks stated that by 25 October 'the first enthusiasm had waned. People were beginning to ask whether we should ever break through the deep crust of minefields which protected the German positions.'[19]

Doubts about the correctness of the strategy had been felt earlier by some of the senior commanders. The Australian, New Zealand and South African divisional commanders, Morshead, Freyberg and Pienaar, did not believe that 10 Corps would be able to break out as intended until the strong enemy anti-tank screen had been neutralised. They conveyed their doubts to Oliver Leese, the commander of 30 Corps, under whom they were serving. Leese, lacking their experience of desert warfare, was inclined to accept their opinions and, on telephoning Lumsden, gained the impression that he thought the same.[20]

Leese decided Montgomery must be told of the doubts felt, and he informed Montgomery's Chief of Staff accordingly. It was now well into the night of 24–25 October. The Chief of Staff was Brigadier F. W. (Freddie) de Guingand, an independently minded soldier, who had caused something of a sensation when giving a lecture at the Staff College in Haifa in May 1940, in which he forecast that France would be defeated within three weeks. Montgomery had hesitated before appointing him. 'He liked wine,' he later wrote, 'gambling and good food. Did these differences matter? I quickly decided they did not.'[21]

On his own initiative de Guingand decided that the two corps commanders, Leese and Lumsden, must attend a conference at Montgomery's headquarters. Montgomery was in the habit of going to bed about 9.30 or 10 p.m. even at the height of battle, and he did not expect to be disturbed during the night. On this occasion de Guingand woke him at 3.30 a.m. After hearing what his corps commanders had to say Montgomery insisted that his original plan should be adhered to. He told Lumsden that his armoured formations must do their best to break out that night.[22]

Montgomery's decision was not due to a lack of flexibility. On other occasions he did decide to change his original plans as news of how the battle was progressing reached him. On the day following his night-time meeting with the corps commanders, for example, he came to the conclusion that a further attempted advance by the New Zealand Division would be too costly and that the main thrust of 30 Corps should be in the coastal area. The next day, too, he informed his corps commanders he would carry out a major regrouping of forces in order to launch a second offensive, but after discussions with Freyberg he decided that he would postpone the launching of the offensive from 1 to 2 November.[23] This second offensive, like the first, was a costly one. Ernest Kerans, serving in a battalion of the Durham Light Infantry in 50 Division, saw serious action at Alamein for the first time. At the beginning of the battle he wrote: 'I could not help saying, "This is my first real battle, I only hope I don't let you fellows down."'

Later he recorded: 'I sat on the sand on the top and got sizzling sausages and bacon going (bought at the South African mobile canteen). Ignoring the scores of dead bodies, with the flies heaped up on their eyes and wounds, pretending they were just part of the scenery. If I'd but thought, with feeling, I wouldn't have wanted my breakfast. Then four shells exploding within an area of 25 square yards did no harm to me but shattered our breakfast in a shower of sand. Picked up the bacon and sausage, covered with sand, and dived back with it into our trench. Even as I collected the sandy breakfast a huge, two-foot long shell landed within a yard of me without exploding, adding force to my legs taking me to our trench . . .

'About noon I risked a glance over the trench-top. The only living things I could see were the heads of Big Bill (the second-in-command) and the Padre. The area was littered with the dead of both sides and their flies. Many I had known, at least by sight, and I wanted to cry when I saw them lying in all sorts of angles, a meal for myriads of flies.

'About 50 yards to the rear the MO, an American, Captain Stone, did wonders for the wounded in a hastily dug dug-out. Unheeding the flying shrapnel, aided by Bill Ryde from Gateshead, his sergeant, they tended the many wounded. When it was suggested he take more cover he just smiled and said: "When is this damned war going to start anyway?" He was at work when he was killed by a shell. The same shell also killed his sergeant. All that was left of the latter was his head and shoulders.'[24]

On the night of 2–3 November intercepted wireless messages made it clear that the Germans were planning a withdrawal in the northern sector. Their original commander, General Stumme, had been killed on the first day of the battle, and Rommel had meanwhile returned to resume command. By the evening of the 3rd it was known that the enemy was withdrawing in both the northern and southern sectors and that an Italian corps was planning a withdrawal which would have to be conducted almost entirely on foot. By 4 November there was no further doubt that the Alamein line had been broken and that the enemy was in full retreat.[25]

Within the Eighth Army, particularly among those in armoured formations, there was a feeling of exhilaration as the defeated enemy was pursued. But the exhilaration was soon dampened and the pursuit hampered by an unforeseen event. On 6 and 7 November there was a heavy downpour of rain. Rommel took full advantage of the respite afforded him by the effect of the rain on the desert sand. Although constantly attacked from the air and largely dependent on a single coastal road, he was able to bring out the German forces in relatively good order. He left the Italians largely to their own devices, which meant in practice surrendering. The Eighth Army took 30,000 prisoners in all, including nine German generals.

Whether Montgomery could, or should, have cut off Rommel's retreat has long been argued by military strategists. No doubt the arguments will continue. The certainties are that the decisive battle and the turning point of the war had occurred just as Montgomery had forecast, and that the victory had been won at a heavy cost in human life.

The Eighth Army's losses in killed, wounded and missing were 13,500. Of the casualties, 55 per cent came from the United Kingdom, 22 per cent from Australia, 10 per cent from New Zealand and 6 per cent from South Africa. The remainder was divided between the Indian division and the French and Greek contingents.[26] In the Alamein cemetery today the graves of 7,500 Allied soldiers are marked with crosses. On the surrounding walls are the names of thousands whose bodies were never found.

Churchill was later to say that before Alamein Britain never had a victory in World War II, and after Alamein she never had a defeat. The statement was not strictly accurate, but it strayed only marginally from the truth. For the Army which had won the victory, the battle of Alamein marked the beginning of a journey which was to last more than two and a half years.

PART TWO: LIBYA

(November 1942 – February 1943)

JOURNEY INTO LIBYA

After the battle of El Alamein the Eighth Army's progress to the Egyptian–Libyan frontier was rapid. The first important objective was Mersa Matruh, which had a minor harbour. It was also designed by nature to be a seaside resort, since the sands are brilliantly white, and the dunes, built up by the winds to some six or seven metres, offer a variety of colours and an even greater variety of shapes. John Verney, painter, writer and tank commander, described the beach as 'a giant tray of creamy *millefeuille* pastry floating in cream and with more cream poured over it again'.[1]

The road along which the bulk of the Eighth Army's transport had to advance was, in origin, the Roman road which had once connected the great cities of Carthage and Alexandria. Over the centuries thousands of pilgrims from the coastal regions of North Africa had walked or ridden along it on their way to Mecca.

Mersa Matruh was captured by the 8th Armoured Brigade on 8 November, that is to say only four days after the enemy line at El Alamein was finally broken. Sollum and Bardia fell shortly afterwards. By 11 November Egypt was finally cleared of all enemy troops. A railhead was established at El Alamein, which was soon receiving three supply trains from the east per day, and the port of Mersa Matruh was opened up. Liberated Egyptian territory was swiftly restored to the control of the Egyptian Government, but Libya,

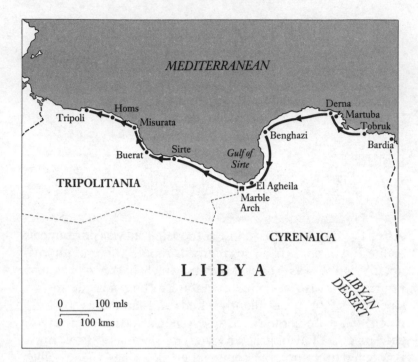

being an Italian colony, would require some new form of
administration if any large part of it came under Allied
control. As an optimistic first step a political officer was
attached to the Eighth Army's rear headquarters.[2]

It was not at once clear how much cooperation would be
received from the indigenous population. Large numbers of
Libyans in exile in Egypt had volunteered for service on the
British side, and valuable intelligence continued to be
obtained from local sources as the Army advanced. On the
other hand there were reports early in December that Arabs
working in the enemy's interests had been pulling down
telephone poles at places along the Eighth Army's advance
route.[3]

In general the Arab population of Libya was bitterly
opposed to Italian rule. This was understandable. In 1911
the Italian government had issued an ultimatum to Turkey,

which was then still nominally in control of Tripolitania and Cyrenaica, the two provinces constituting modern Libya. The ultimatum gave Turkey twenty-four hours in which to accept Italy's intention of invading and occupying the provinces.

The invasion which followed seems to have been the first military operation in which aircraft were actively engaged.[4] Arab opposition was overcome, and Italian settlers began to be introduced. The main opposition to the Italians had been provided by members of the Senussi sect, founded in the eighteenth century by Mohammed ben Ali ben as-Sanusi, who believed that the Bedouin had strayed from the strict requirements of Islam. The order he founded was puritanical, and imposed bans on both coffee and tobacco. Total commitment to faith was also demanded. The founder himself had two sons, whom he ordered to climb extremely high palm trees and then jump, depending solely on the protection of Allah. Only his younger son, aged fourteen, accepted the challenge. He fell to the ground unharmed and was thereupon appointed his father's successor.[5]

Under the Fascist regime created after World War I the policy of colonisation was carried through with new ruthlessness. In each of the years 1930 and 1931 it was estimated that 12,000 people were executed in the province of Cyrenaica alone, and the most fruitful land belonging to the Senussi and other Arabs, which was in the coastal areas, was expropriated – some compensation being offered to those deemed not to have taken part in rebellion. The Governor at that time was Pietro Badoglio, who was later to play an important role on the Allied side in World War II, though personal responsibility for the worst excesses did, it is true, rest with his deputy, Rodolfo Graziani.[6]

Large numbers of the Senussi became refugees in Egypt, including the man who emerged clearly as their leader, Mohammed al Idris. Many of those who remained in Libya lived in tented villages, tending their flocks, occasionally trading animals, but otherwise doing little gainful work.

Peniakoff described the Senussi he encountered as 'a small isolated group whose mode of life had remained little changed since the Arab conquest, 1100 years previously; an anachronistic self-contained community, nearly cut off, not only from the Western but even from the Muslim world.'[7]

Although Rommel was the effective commander of the Axis forces in North Africa, Hitler recognised that Libya was a part of the Italian Empire, and no attempt was made to impose German political control there. Consequently, in the absence of administrators and of policemen, secret or otherwise, the war was fought wholly as a soldier's war. This and the fact that so much of the campaigning took place in the open desert, with virtually no civilian population involved, must in part account for the high level of chivalry in the desert war and the relative lack of animosity between the Eighth Army and the Germans.

After General von Thoma had been captured at Alamein Montgomery invited him to dinner and to spend the night at his headquarters.[8] Horrocks expressed the opinion that there had never been less hate between two opposing sides.[9] Keith Douglas wrote of soldiers inhabiting 'a dangerous, but not wholly terrible world, having to kill and be killed, and yet at intervals moved by a feeling of comradeship with the men who kill them and whom they kill, because they are enduring and experiencing the same things.'

He learnt that the few men of his regiment who had been taken prisoner early in the Alamein battle had been well treated by the Germans, and insisted that German prisoners should be treated in the same way. Some of them were even photographed exchanging chocolate for bully beef with British soldiers.[10]

There was even a suggestion of comradeship in the way in which the men of the Eighth Army adopted as their own a song they had heard German soldiers singing. This was a sad little ballad about a girl waiting outside a barracks. With slightly anglicised spelling and an almost literal translation of the words it became known as *Lily Marlene*. There were other songs developed by the Eighth Army, such as *I'm dreaming of a white mistress*, but *Lily Marlene* was the song they were to sing at Alamein reunions decades later.

Towards the Italians the Eighth Army in general did not feel great respect. Respect would come only later when Italian qualities of courage and loyalty were to be revealed in very different circumstances.

The first place of importance captured by the Eighth Army as it advanced into Libya was Tobruk. To the administrative staff the most welcome sight in Tobruk was a large Italian medical store, which was found to contain much needed drugs and dressings. It was also gratifying to find that the water supply was intact, for the enemy had evacuated Tobruk hurriedly and had had little time to carry out demolitions. For the rest, there was little to please the eye in this town: it had changed hands more than once and its harbour had been made temporarily unusable by the Desert Air Force.[11] The South Africans entered it on 12 November, the first Eighth Army troops to do so.[12] Garrison duties were shortly afterwards undertaken by the Sudan Defence Force.[13]

As the Eighth Army continued its advance its next important task was dictated by the requirements of the Royal Navy and the Royal Air Force and was directly concerned with the defence of the beleaguered garrison of Malta.

Near a small place called Martuba, about twenty kilometres south-east of Derna, there were some landing grounds for aircraft. A convoy was to sail for Malta from Alexandria on 15 November, carrying petrol, food, ammunition and other badly needed supplies. Its safe arrival was considered vital for Malta's continued defence, and once the Martuba airfields had been taken adequate fighter cover could be provided.

At eleven o'clock on the morning of 15 November a flying

column of the 4th Light Armoured Brigade reached the
landing grounds and reported them free of the enemy and
in good working order.[14]

The capture of Benghazi followed within a week. Here
the harbour was in better condition than had been expected.
There was uninterrupted passage into the inner harbour for
ships drawing up to about eight metres, and there was
berthing accommodation for three ships. Elsewhere the
damage was grave. Benghazi's central power station had
been wrecked by air bombardment, and the town was
without piped water, electric light or sewerage. Among the
population who remained there were virtually no
Europeans.[15]

An ancient Greek settlement, Benghazi had long been
well-endowed with mosques and minarets, and the Italians
added a cathedral, which untypically was found to be
scarcely damaged. Montgomery came to Benghazi shortly
after its capture and acted, de Guingand stated later, 'more
like a tourist than a victorious commander', as he walked
among the white, square buildings of the town.[16] Benghazi
was to be for a time the site of the Eighth Army's rear
headquarters.

To the west of Tobruk lies the hilly, fertile land of the
Djebel Akhdar. Soldiers of the Eighth Army, accustomed
to the sands of the desert, were astonished to find carpets of
purple and gold and crimson, which on closer inspection
were seen to be flowers. P. A. A. Thomas, then an acting
unpaid lance-corporal in the Royal Army Ordnance Corps,
recorded more than seventy different species.[17]

It was November, and the same wealth of flowers could
be seen on the road beyond Benghazi towards El Agheila.
General Tuker was able to identify cranesbill, anemone,
ranunculus, cornflower, iris, poppy, spurge, borage, great
marguerite, daisy, marigold, charlock, rockrose, fritillary,
stock, thyme, sage and ladslove. There were, he stated,
about a hundred more. His Pathan driver was so overcome

by the spectacle that he could not speak above a whisper, and then all he said was 'lovely, lovely'.[18]

Not only were there flowers. There were olive groves and wooded hills and red earth. There were also prosperous looking farms with the word 'DUCE' painted on most of the buildings in large capitals. To this, Sergeant Ramsbottom commented in his diary, 'there were many instances of additions by troops, rude and otherwise, anything but complimentary to the Duce.'[19]

As the Eighth Army's advance through Libya began, important changes were made in the formations which composed it. These were the result of political pressures.

Nearly a week before the battle of Alamein the Australian Prime Minister, John Curtin, asked Churchill for the early return of the Australian 9th Division because he did not think the forces available to defend Australia were adequate. The substance of this request was conveyed to the commander of the division, Leslie Morshead, the day after the battle began. He replied that Alexander had told him that of all the formations in the Middle East the Australian division was the one he could least afford to lose. Once the battle was over the Australian division was withdrawn to Palestine, and soon afterwards it returned to Australia.[20]

A similar request was made for the return to its homeland of the 1st South African Division. This was not for the purpose of defending South African territory, but to enable the force to be converted into an armoured division. Montgomery agreed to the South Africans' release in a signal which he sent to Middle East headquarters on 7 November.[21]

Freyberg asked senior New Zealand officers whether they considered their division should return home also, once Egypt was freed of enemy troops. The general opinion was that it should stay. Brigadier Kippenberger was to write later: 'It was only a small Eighth Army that took Tripoli and, at the least, it would have been difficult without us.'[22] The New Zealanders were to remain a part of the Eighth

Army until the end of its campaign. South African forces were to rejoin it in Italy. But the Australian association with the army of which it had formed such a distinctive part, had come to an end. Also, the bulk of the Greek Brigade returned to Egypt following an order issued by Montgomery.

Rommel was right to make no attempt to defend either Tobruk or Benghazi. The direct route from El Alamein to the Gulf of Sirte runs well to the south of both towns and of the Djebel Akhdar desert. Any garrisons left behind would therefore have been doomed. Benghazi had always fallen fairly easily as one army or the other approached it, and only because supplies were brought in by sea had the British, the South Africans and the Poles been able to defend Tobruk for so long, an option not now open to the Germans.

What was not immediately clear was where Rommel could most effectively make his next stand. At one time it seemed possible that this might be at El Agheila, the furthest point westward reached in earlier advances, where there was a naturally strong defensive position. But the German withdrawal continued. Rommel had in fact decided to shorten his supply lines, and it would be along a line running south from Buerat that the next battle would have to be fought. The distance between Tripoli, his main port of supply, and El Agheila was roughly 800 kilometres. From Tripoli to Buerat was about half that distance.

As Rommel shortened his supply lines, so inevitably those of the Eighth Army became extended. Even so, the advance continued to be extraordinarily fast, certainly as fast as was compatible with the taking of reasonable precautions. Ports were opened; engineers worked to improve the roads and railways; and a bonus was provided by the presence of American Douglas aircraft, which ferried supplies from Egypt to the forward areas.[23] Nevertheless the danger of outrunning supplies was ever-present.

When advancing through the desert a brigade group

would move forward as a large, flexible square. The battalions of the brigade, themselves protected by their anti-tank guns, would provide the front and flanks of the square, and the artillery the rear. The headquarters and the administrative services would be in the middle.[24]

The main dangers were mines and enemy aircraft, including Stuka dive-bombers. As a precaution vehicles moving by day would keep a distance of two hundred metres between them. Nevertheless, in spite of this disciplined advance, there was a period towards the end of November when the Eighth Army headquarters lost touch with forward units and was not fully aware of what was happening.[25]

An addition to the supplies to be sent to all units was made by a personal decision of Montgomery's. Christmas Day 1942 was, he decided, to be observed so far as possible as a day of rest, and all troops were to have a proper Christmas dinner. As a result men as far as 1,200 miles from Cairo were supplied with turkey, pork, fresh vegetables, a bottle of beer and a rum ration.[26]

The contrast with normal rations was startling. Tank crews on the whole were better fed than others because certain extras could more easily be transported, so that for them tinned sausages, bacon and, occasionally, eggs bought from Arabs were not uncommon.[27] But for infantrymen and others, bully beef – or, as it is known outside the Army, corned beef – was likely to be relieved only by hard biscuits and fig jam. Some enterprising units employed Italian prisoners of war, who were professional chefs, to make what they could of these materials, but the results were still meagre. The basic rations supplied to Eighth Army troops were at all times inferior to those of American soldiers.

There were occasional windfalls. Keith Douglas recorded finding an Italian store replete with Chianti and brandy, cigars and cherries. 'We shared out the plunder,' he wrote, 'with the immemorial glee of conquerors.'[28]

Rest periods too offered opportunities. During one of them a unit of the County of London Yeomanry briefly took cooking seriously. A competition was held, and, 'it was nothing exceptional,' Sergeant Ramsbottom wrote, 'to see troops smeared with flour, kneading a large lump of dough and furtively trying to pick out cigarette ash or other foreign matter from the composition. . . . An oven was prepared from an old ammunition box, with the result that potato pie, Lancashire hot pot, roast meat and jam tarts frequently appeared on the menu.'[29]

During their December advance, also, troops of the Eighth Army were confronted by a strange spectacle. This was a massive and isolated stone arch rising out of the desert. Its correct name was the Arco dei Fileni, and it had been constructed in the late 1930s, on Mussolini's orders, to mark the completion of a new highway linking Benghazi and Tripoli. To the Eighth Army it became known immediately as Marble Arch. The location of the arch was near the border between the provinces of Cyrenaica and Tripolitania.[30] It attracted so much attention that Montgomery found it necessary to issue orders that it was not to be destroyed or defaced.

With Marble Arch behind it the Eighth Army had completed the conquest of Cyrenaica. Now only Tripolitania remained of Mussolini's crumbling overseas empire.

On 8 November 1942, when its advance units were entering Mersa Matruh, still well inside Egyptian territory, the Eighth Army had received encouraging news from the outside world. This was that Allied troops under American command had landed in French North Africa near Casablanca, Oran and Algiers. With no immediate prospect of an invasion of France across the English Channel, this had seemed the swiftest and easiest way of bringing additional forces into action in a manner which would affect the war in Europe. From North Africa they could help to exercise control of the Mediterranean and threaten both southern France and Italy. The newly landed forces were still far away from Libya, but a meeting with the Eighth Army somewhere in Africa was not difficult to imagine.

Montgomery's own opinion, on receiving the news of the landings, had been that the meeting-point should be somewhere east of Tripoli. The easiest way to capture Tripoli, he considered, would be from the west. Lines of communication from the main ports were shorter, and the road and rail services were better.[31] By the beginning of the year 1943 he knew from the reports he received of what was happening in French North Africa that it would be the Eighth Army, not the Anglo-American forces, which would have to capture Tripoli, and he made his plans accordingly.

A setback occurred on the night of 3–4 January, when a violent storm did extensive damage to the port of Benghazi. The outer mole was breached by heavy seas, which swept into the harbour, drove three ships ashore, and damaged others. For a time supplies which would have come to Benghazi by sea had to be added to those being sent from Tobruk by road. The gales continued through much of January.[32] Nevertheless by the middle of the month the Eighth Army was ready to give battle along the defensive line which Rommel had established in the Buerat area.

The Eighth Army was now reorganised into two corps, 10 and 30, which were commanded respectively by Horrocks and Leese. After the Alamein battle Montgomery had described Leese as 'first class' and Horrocks as 'very good'. Montgomery's loyalty to his subordinates once they had gained his confidence was limitless, but that confidence was not easily won. He did not have a high opinion of Lumsden as a corps commander and had decided to send him home. There had undoubtedly been a clash of personalities of a kind which Montgomery would not tolerate, and there was even some evidence that at times Lumsden had deliberately kept out of contact with his Army Commander during operations in order to be able to act on his own intiative.[33]

Leese was later to succeed Montgomery as Eighth Army

commander. Harold Macmillan then described him as 'a very nice fellow, a big burly, efficient, solid Guardsman'.[34]

Horrocks was a highly imaginative soldier, who after the war was to emerge as something of a television star. He was also to hold the largely ceremonial post of Black Rod. In World War I he had been a prisoner of war. This he considered an excellent apprenticeship for what he called 'the difficult business of command' in that it taught him self-reliance. Soon after that war he became a prisoner of the Red Army. The title he gave to his autobiography, *A Full Life*, was well merited.[35] Lumsden did not survive World War II. He was killed by a Japanese kamikaze pilot while on board USS *Mexico*.[36]

A road leading to Buerat had been built by the Italians near the coast. For most of the way it ran along an embankment slightly higher than the surrounding desert. There were a number of salt marshes on both sides of the road, and the bridges over several wadis, or dried up river-beds, had been blown up by the retreating enemy. For these reasons the terrain was not easy for an advancing army to cross.

Montgomery decided to launch an offensive against Buerat on 15 January. His plan carried the assumption that ten days later his forces would be able to enter Tripoli. If they did not, he expected to have to order a retreat, for he considered the Army could not be maintained indefinitely so far west of Benghazi without having control of another port. His final instructions to subordinate commanders were that 'a due measure of caution' must be exercised by formations at the sea end of the front in order to avoid heavy losses of tanks.[37] In the event it became clear by the evening of the 16 January that the enemy was already withdrawing. Rommel did not think the time had yet come for a major defensive battle to be fought.

Montgomery continued to be worried by the slow pace of the advance which the nature of the ground now necessitated, and he later recorded that it was at this time that he experienced his first 'real anxiety' since assuming command of the Eighth Army.[38] Nevertheless an important stage on the road to Tripoli was reached with the capture on 19 January of Homs.

Homs is a seaside town near the site of the ancient Roman city of Leptis Magna, where the Italians had carried out some important excavations. The British occupation authorities soon allowed this work to continue, leaving the enthusiastic Italian supervisor in charge. He impressed not a few of the visiting military by vehemently informing them that the Emperor Severus was not well enough known and that the reign of Pertinax had been all too short.[39] Inland from Homs is the plateau of Mizda, the end of which slopes upward to a huge escarpment. In the hilly country primitive Berber people live. The escarpment dominates the final plains leading to Tripoli.[40]

Although no major battles were fought in the approaches to Tripoli, enemy rearguard action was continually effective, and among the wounded was Major-General Harding, the commander of the Desert Rats, or 7th Armoured Division. This was one of the most distinguished soldiers of his time, a man who, unusually for a senior British commander, had begun his military career in the Territorial Army.

John Harding had left school at the age of fifteen. His first job was as a clerk in the Post Office Savings Bank, and while working there he joined the County of London Yeomanry. He saw service in the Middle East in World War I, winning the MC at the battle of Beersheba, which led to the capture of Jerusalem. In 1940 he came to the Middle East from India and before long was appointed Brigadier (General Staff) in the Western Defence Force. The citation for the DSO which he won in the 1941 campaign described him as 'that invaluable asset, a fighting staff officer'.[41]

Harding was badly wounded near Tripoli, but recovered in time to rejoin the Eighth Army during the Italian campaign. He eventually reached the rank of field-marshal and became Governor of Cyprus and Chief of General Staff.

Tripoli had long been envisaged by the Eighth Army as a journey's end, a promised land. Once it had been captured the conquest of Libya would be virtually complete, and until the Anglo-American landings later in 1942 the countries to the west and north-west, Algeria and Tunisia, being under the rule of the French neutralist government in Vichy, were not regarded as combat zones. Tripoli moreover would be the first major town to be reached by the Eighth Army west of Alexandria.

As a foretaste of what the soldiers might encounter when Tripoli was reached *Crusader*, the weekly newspaper published by and for the Eighth Army, included an article in its issue of 21 December 1941: 'Hundreds of miles of small oases with clean-looking native villages and great olive-groves,' the author wrote, 'will be your prelude to Tripoli.' He went on: 'You will find that Tripoli is one of the cleanest towns you have visited in Africa.' Of the promenade Lungo Mare Conte Volpi he wrote: 'Never in the south of France or anywhere else in Europe have I seen anything to compare with its magnificent sweep and its little gardens.'

The climax was a paragraph which read: 'Very refreshing after the wastes of Cyrenaica will be the sight of the Tripoli girls. Dark-eyed and lush-figured, many of them are daughters of Italians who married Arab women before the Fascists forbade mixed marriages. There are many beautiful Italian and Maltese girls too. None of them are standoffish.' The article was accompanied by a drawing with the caption 'Not standoffish.' The girl in the drawing was unquestionably dark-eyed and unquestionably lush-figured.

Montgomery's hope of being in Tripoli within ten days of giving battle at Buerat was fulfilled. On 22 January about 5 a.m. an advance party of the 11th Hussars, the Cherry Pickers, veterans of all the Middle East campaigns, entered the city. The streets were deserted. Then, as daylight grew, people began to emerge from the houses. The troops, they discovered, were British, and soon wonder gave way to wild enthusiasm.[42] It was a foretaste of the kind of welcome which would be received in city after city, village after village, in Italy, a welcome which perhaps only those who have experienced it can find easily credible.

Soon after the 11th Hussars came advance elements of the Highland Division. They had brought their bagpipes with them and gave the inhabitants of Tripoli their first experience of a sound with which they would soon become familiar.

At noon on 23 January Montgomery himself made a formal entry into Tripoli, where he received the surrender of the city from the Vice-Governor of Tripolitania. It was three months to the day since the opening of the battle of Alamein. During those three months the Eighth Army had advanced 1,400 miles, an achievement which Montgomery, in a personal message to all troops, described as 'probably without parallel in history'. In his message he called due attention to the part played by the Allied Air Forces and stated: 'I have always maintained that the Eighth Army and the Royal Air Force, Western Desert, constitute one fighting machine, and therein lies our great strength.'[43]

However, in contrast with what had happened in Tobruk and Benghazi, in the Tripoli port area the retreating Axis forces had carried out thorough demolitions. The harbour was completely closed by eight sunken ships, eleven craters had been blown in the Spanish Quay, and all moles had been partly demolished. Plans were immediately drawn up for reopening the harbour. Within two days four landing craft were operating in it, and a salvage ship arrived outside the next day.

Meanwhile a headquarters was established in the Comando Piazza building; anti-aircraft defences were organised, and the policing of the city was put in hand. A slight foretaste of what was later to be found in Europe was given when a camp containing 2,500 Jews was liberated.

It was estimated that there was enough food to last the

civil population about two months. The banks had virtually
no money, and there was a severe shortage of fuel. It was
therefore decided that the only troops to be billeted in the
city would be those whose presence was clearly necessary.
The old town was placed out of bounds, and all troops were
forbidden to eat meals in civilian restuarants.

The dream picture of Tripoli as another Cairo or Alexandria, which had been held by so many, began to dissolve.
Sergeant Ramsbottom commented: 'One visit to Tripoli was
enough . . . Taking a tin of bully and a packet of biscuits on
a day trip is itself discouraging.'[44] By way of slight compensation the NAAFI (Navy, Army and Air Force Institutes)
took over a local brewery, and a club for other ranks was
opened which had a library, a games room, a cinema and a
chapel. A canteen was added only later.

For the inhabitants of Tripoli the principal entertainment
provided was the changing of the guard. This was watched
by large numbers, particularly when Highland regiments
were participating. Other troops wondered how the Highlanders had found space for their kilts in the journey across
the desert.[45]

Another spectacle which may have puzzled the people of
Tripolitania was provided by the New Zealanders, who were
at last given a rest period in the Tripoli area. There they
received their first reinforcements. Inevitably a rugby football competition was staged. It was won by the Maori
battalion.[46]

Tripoli had a theatre large enough for the staging of fairly
ambitious concert parties. One of these gave rise to an
extraordinary occurrence. Montgomery himself attended
the show, and when the curtain came down the troops
spontaneously began to chant: 'We want Monty. We want
Monty.' Such a demonstration of loyalty must surely have
been without precedent in the annals of the British Army.[47]

Early in February 1943, while it was still in the Tripoli area,
the Eighth Army received some unexpected reinforcements.

These were 3,000–3,500 troops, many of them Senegalese, under French officers. Their commander was the Vicomte de Haute-Cloque, alias Jacques Leclerc, who had been promoted to the rank of General. After operating for some two years in the Libyan desert Leclerc's force set out from Lake Chad to join the Eighth Army near Tripoli.

It was a journey of some 2,000 kilometres across rocks and sand and over the Tibesti mountains, whose summits are about 3000 metres high.[48] For some it was an exhilarating experience. Yves de Danuvar, who commanded one contingent within Leclerc's force, a group of Tibesti nomads mounted on camels, wondered if he would ever again find the same independence and the same pleasure of command.[49]

Leclerc's force was not well-equipped for the kind of battle which the Eighth Army was fighting, and he showed warm gratitude for such supplies as could be made available to him. In general he created a most favourable impression on his fellow commanders. Montgomery described him as 'magnificent'.[50] Tuker also admired him and described him as 'alert and sinewy and a fine soldier'. When Leclerc was woken in the morning, he added, he 'sprang to life as though he never slept, quick and aware.'[51]

At the end of its journey across Libya the Eighth Army too was in peak condition. Montgomery reported to the War Office that the sick rate was one man per thousand per day, adding: 'You cannot want anything better than this.'[52] Once the jaundice epidemic had died down the principal scourge had been the ubiquitous flies. Not only did they find their way into eyes and mouths and nostrils, but they produced sores and dysentery. The menace was sufficiently serious for the Eighth Army to create a body officially known as No. 1 Fly Control Unit. It was formed from troops from an infantry base depot and from the Mauritius Pioneer Corps.[53]

Morale remained as high as it can be in any army. Montgomery was to define this memorably when he wrote

some years later: 'They knew that they were fine soldiers
and they looked it; every man an emperor.'[54]

Eccentricity of dress was no less evident after the Libyan
campaign came to an end than it had been in the desert. A
discussion was arranged at a hotel in Tripoli on the tech-
niques of modern warfare, at which Montgomery gave an
address. Senior officers from the force which had invaded
French North Africa were invited. They included the distinguished American soldier, General George S. Patton.
Describing the event, the New Zealander Kippenberger
wrote: 'The visitors were correctly dressed in serge and Sam
Brownes, with gleaming buttons and even some field boots
and spurs . . . The Americans were particularly smart.' By
contrast, he wrote, the Eighth Army representatives looked
like 'a gang of pirates'.

There was however one occasion on which the Eighth
Army decided, almost spontaneously, that its turn-out must
be of impeccable smartness. This was a visit of inspection
by Winston Churchill, of which advance notice was given
late in January.

'The majority of us,' Sergeant Ramsbottom wrote, 'had
no cleaning materials . . . and frenzied searches and appeals
produced boot and metal polish from most unusual
quarters.'

The results were spectacularly successful. On 3 February
Churchill took the salute in the main square of Tripoli with
tears running down his cheeks.[55] Later he was to inform the
House of Commons that never in his life, although he had
from youth been much concerned with military matters, had
he seen troops march 'with the style and air of the Desert
Army'.[56]

Of the event Ramsbottom wrote: 'It was the nearest thing
to glamour and fanfare of war I had yet experienced. So
different to the smoke, grime and disorder of the
battlefield.'[57]

On 11 January Montgomery had announced that Libya
would be administered by British military government until

the end of the war.[58] The governing of Tripolitania proved to be rather more complex than that of Cyrenaica because of the varied nature of the population. But in November 1949 the General Assembly of the United Nations agreed that Tripolitania should form part of the independent and sovereign state of Libya. In December 1951 the Senussi leader, Mohammed al-Idris, who since 1946 had been recognised by the British government as Emir of Cyrenaica, was proclaimed King Idris I.

This was the final stage in the freeing of Libya from foreign colonial rule, a liberation brought about exclusively by the efforts of the Eighth Army and the naval and air forces which supported it. Sadly this fact seems unlikely for some years to be acknowledged in the textbooks from which the young of today's Libya learn the history of their country.

For the Eighth Army Tripoli, which had long been seen as the terminal point of the African campaign, had become instead a staging post. The Germans had responded to the Allied invasion of French North Africa by landing troops, virtually unopposed, in the French protectorate of Tunisia, and it was now apparent that the task of ousting them would be every bit as much the responsibility of Montgomery's army as of the force which had landed in North Africa in November.

PART THREE: TUNISIA

(February – May 1943)

JOURNEY THROUGH THE MATMATA HILLS

Tunisia, the country through which the Eighth Army's advance was to continue, is slightly larger than England and Wales together. Its coastal area in the north-east is exceptionally well favoured by nature, enjoying a Mediterranean climate and having numerous underground aquifers. Together they give rise to a glory of blossom and a wealth of fruit. Off the coast lies the island of Djerba, the land of Homer's lotus-eaters, where it was always afternoon. Much of the rest of the country is desert or the kind of semi-desert known as steppe. There is also a relatively parched area inland from the coast called the Sahel, which is covered with olive groves.

Tunisia served as a granary for imperial Rome, and Roman ruins are still abundant in various parts of the country. The coastal areas provide the clearest evidence of the numerous conquerors and occupiers who succeeded the Romans: the Normans in the twelfth century, the Moroccan caliphs who followed, the Spanish and the Turks in the sixteenth centuries.

Like Tripoli, Tunis, with its surrounding territory, was for long dependent largely on piracy for its revenue. There was a period in the latter part of the nineteenth century when a British protectorate seemed likely to be established. Concessions for building railways, lighthouses and waterworks were

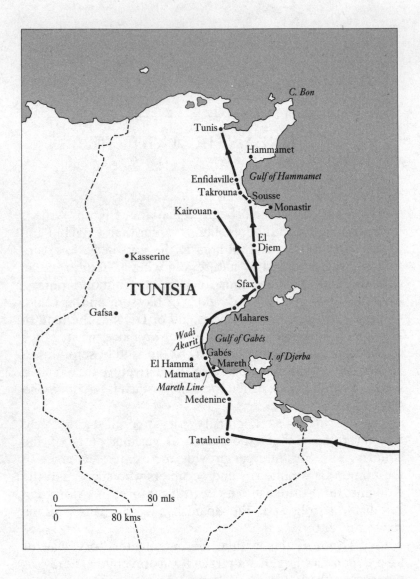

indeed granted to the British. But, in a manner characteristic of the time, the fate of Tunisia for three-quarters of a century was in fact settled at the Congress of Berlin in 1878. In return for French acceptance of Britain's lease of Cyprus Lord Salisbury agreed to allow France a free hand in Tunisia.

What the French then did was to invade Tunisia from Algeria, in 1881. The Arabs of Tunisia resisted – quite effectively for a time around Sfax – but they were defeated, and France was able to establish a so-called protectorate. Until 1956 when Tunisia was to gain full independence, the French were to be, as a Tunisian of my acquaintance has happily put it, the guests of Tunisia on full *pension*.

Of the many works which the French undertook in Tunisia one was of particular concern to the Eighth Army. This was the construction of a strongly fortified defensive line, intended to prevent an invasion of Tunisia from Italian-occupied Libya. It was known as the Mareth Line and was clearly a formidable obstacle.

Another legacy of French rule was an Arab population whose antagonism was directed, not towards the Italians, but towards the French themselves. There was no tradition of hostility to Germans, furthermore, and Rommel was among those who were impressed by the friendliness which the Germans encountered in Tunisia.[1]

The Allied force that had landed in French North Africa in November 1942, and towards which the Eighth Army was now advancing, had two main constituent parts. One was the United States 2nd Corps. The other was the British First Army, which consisted of two infantry brigades, part of an armoured division, three parachute battalions and some commandos.

The Americans were not seasoned troops. Nor for the most part were the British. Some of the generals too were undistinguished. The commander of the First Army was a Scotsman, Lieutenant-General Kenneth Anderson, whose name was to become irretrievably linked with Montgomery's tactless description of him as 'a good plain cook'. This unfortunately gained wide circulation.

After some time Patton took over command of the US 2nd Corps; of his predecessor, Major-General Lloyd Fredenhall, he said: 'I cannot see what Fredenhall did to justify his existence.'[2]

The landing force had at first advanced rapidly and had moved into the northern coastal area of Tunisia as early as mid-November 1942. There it was checked, and a German counter-attack drove it out of one town, Tebourba, which it had earlier captured. Heavy rains had fallen in December, and the Allied advance had been effectively halted. In short the campaign had not gone according to plan, and worse was to follow.

The Eighth Army's advance into Tunisia began in mid-February 1943 and was led by the 7th Armoured Division. In the semi-desert country there were few villages. One of them, Tataouine, was captured on 18 February and another, Medenine, two days later. From Medenine Montgomery was able to plan his attack on the Mareth Line. No serious opposition had been offered to the Eighth Army's initial advance, for Rommel's attention was directed elsewhere. On 14 February he launched a major offensive against the US 2nd Corps in the Kasserine area in western Tunisia. It was largely successful, and constituted a threat to the lines of communication of the Allied forces advancing from the west.

This was a setback serious enough to require a major change in the command structure that had allowed it. General Alexander was put in operational command of all the Allied military forces in North Africa, including the Eighth Army, the Americans and the British First Army. The combined body became known as the 18th Army Group. One of Alexander's first actions in his new capacity was to send an urgent message to Montgomery, calling on him to exert maximum pressure on the enemy and so force him to withdraw troops from the Kasserine area.[3] This was done, and before long a signal was deciphered through Ultra, which transmitted orders to Rommel to break off the attack at Kasserine and turn against the Eighth Army.[4] By the end of February the enemy was withdrawing in the face of attacks both by the Eighth Army from the south and the First Army from the west.

The employment of the Eighth Army to relieve pressure on another allied force in the same operational area was a sound strategic measure. But its success was to fortify Montgomery's belief in the superiority of the troops under his command and, by implication, of their commander. This belief he was, unfortunately, all too ready to express. After an early meeting with Eisenhower he wrote to Alexander: 'I should say he was good, probably on the political line; but he obviously knows nothing whatever about fighting.'[5] Seeds of Anglo-American discord were already being sown.

Montgomery was not alone in making assumptions of superiority after the action of February 1943. Another excellent diarist, Sergeant E. G. (Ricky) Hall, who served in the Ammunition Echelon of the 2nd Armoured Brigade, recorded informatively: 'Originally our goal was Tripoli and old desert sweats did not bargain for being drawn in to help First Army. Attitude was: "Let those rookies and Yanks have a basinful."'[6]

But Rommel's withdrawal on the southern front was only temporary, and on 6 March he launched a new attack on the Eighth Army's position at Medenine. Both his intentions and his strength were clearly revealed by Ultra and by signals intercepts. He planned to attack with three panzer divisions, and he had a total strength of 160 tanks and some 200 guns.[7] The attack was launched under cover of fog. The Eighth Army forward units could hear the rumble of the enemy tanks long before they could see them. Then suddenly the sun broke through, and the advancing tanks became targets for anti-tank guns. Devastating fire forced the tanks to withdraw, but they came on again three times.[8]

That was the end. By the afternoon Rommel's forces had lost more than fifty tanks. The Eighth Army lost none, and indeed only one squadron of tanks was engaged. As Montgomery himself recorded, it was a victory for infantry and the anti-tank gun.[9]

The battle of Medenine was the last which Rommel fought in Africa. A few days later he flew back to Germany. By then he had noted in his diary that for the German forces to remain in Africa was 'suicide'.[10] The Allies were now confronted by Juergen von Arnim as supreme commander of German forces in Tunisia. Experienced soldier though he was, von Arnim did not enjoy the peculiar mystique which for so long had been attached to the name of Rommel.

The Mareth Line extended from the sea to a point some twelve miles inland in the Matmata Hills. Before it lies a wadi which served as a natural anti-tank obstacle. The landscape of the Matmata Hills consists of fold after fold of brown, conical, pock-marked shapes, some of which can at a distance be mistaken for slag-heaps. There is little vegetation other than esparto grass. A few goats somehow find pasture of a kind.

Among the more remarkable features of the region are cave-dwellings occupied by a tenacious Berber people who to this day survive in this barren region. Herodotus called their ancestors Libyans. The Romans called them Barbarians, a name which has persisted in little altered form. When the Arabs overran Tunisia in the seventh century the Berbers accepted Islam, modifying its tenets somewhat to fit their own established practices. They have never been wholly absorbed in the Arab world.

The cave-dwellings in the Matmata Hills are designed for protection against extremes of heat by day and of cold by night. They have a courtyard outside and, inside, a small entrance hall with a granary above it. The living rooms are dug deep into the hillside. When I visited these dwellings I was somewhat startled to see television aerials sprouting from them and motor-cars parked on the flat surfaces above them. It was in this territory that the Eighth Army was to fight the second of its two great battles in Africa.

The battle of Mareth began on 20 March 1943. There had been cloud and rain for three days beforehand and air photography had been barely possible. But on the 20th the weather was fine. After a massive artillery barrage the main attack on the Mareth Line front was made by the 50th Division. An enemy counter-attack followed, and after two days the Eighth Army had made no progress.

One of the units in the 50th Division was the 7th Battalion of the Durham Light Infantry, in which Ernest Kerans served. As a member of an advance party he was given the task of laying tapes to guide the platoons in their advance.

The start line was within the fortifications built by the French, and in one of the bunkers Kerans found some bread. It had evidently been there for a long time, for it was mouldy and full of grubs, but as it was the first bread he had seen since his days in Alexandria he ate it. The deep trenches provided some protection against the enemy shelling, but already on the first day the medical staff were, in Kerans's words, 'doing a roaring trade'.

On one flank of the Durham Light Infantry was a battalion of the East Yorkshire Regiment. The men of both units were virtually queueing up to go through a gap. While he crouched waiting his turn Kerans found beside him an old friend from Birkenhead named Jimmy Bridges, now serving in the East Yorks. Bridges gave him forty cigarettes and wished him luck in the battle. As they went through the gap dead and wounded were lining the sides. Another friend of Kerans's named Bill Jones was manning an anti-tank gun. Blood was dripping from a rag roughly tied round his hand, but he continued firing.

Of the enemy Kerans wrote: 'At Alamein, thanks to the barrage, when you got anywhere near, the Germans would put their hands up, but not early Mareth. It was them or you right up to the last moment. It was a lot of Durhams for one enemy. Even the Italians fought like the devil when they thought they had a chance of winning.'

The company Kerans was serving in failed to cross the wadi on the first night, and in the morning they buried their dead. He himself brought a corporal in the Royal Engineers, who had had a foot blown off, to an armoured car which was acting as an ambulance. The armoured car was hit by an enemy shell and burst into flames. Kerans and some others filled their tin hats with sand, threw the sand on to the fire, and succeeded in putting it out.

Kerans was then told to man an observation post. From there he saw men going forward from the trenches. 'There seemed,' he wrote, 'to be more dropping than running, but they got there, a few of them. The same thing must have been happening all along the Brigade's front.'

Kerans's commanding officer, a small man known as Nobby Clark, was with him and showing remarkable coolness. 'To anything I said he just grunted and pretended it wasn't important . . . That is until a screaming, running, high-ranking 8th battalion officer came round the extreme left-hand edge of our particular trench. Nobby left me and with his little legs ran like the wind to pull the 8th's officer down and sit on him.'

When night came Kerans hoped for a little sleep. A bren-gunner passing him tore off a blazing jacket and threw it away. Kerans picked it up, put out the flames and placed the jacket round his shoulders as a protection against the cold. Then, after saying a prayer, he slept for a time in a slit trench. So the battle continued for one who, at its outset, had described himself as 'a rather scared 24-year-old private who wanted to live'.[11]

The failure of the Eighth Army's initial assault on the Mareth Line was a serious setback, and once again it was deemed necessary to wake Montgomery in the middle of the night. The time on this occasion was 2 a.m. on 23 March. When the extent of the setback was explained to him he was reported to have lost for once something of his

normal composure.[12] By the next morning his confidence
had returned and he had a plan clearly formulated. It was
to be based on the principle of the left hook. There was
nothing new in this strategy. Indeed it had been forced on
Montgomery continually because the sea had been on his
right, and lack of suitable vessels had precluded any large-
scale seaborne landings in the enemy's rear. Now however
there was a particular circumstance of which the enemy was
unaware. Contrary to the common military belief, first
accepted by the French designers of the Mareth Line, that
because of the terrain the line could not be outflanked at its
western end by motorised forces, one of the Long Range
Desert Group's New Zealanders, Captain Nick Wilder, had
found a pass through the Nefusa Hills which armoured
vehicles could negotiate. It was to become known as Wilder's Gap and would provide the means by which the Eighth
Army could outflank the enemy.

Montgomery decided to use the 50th, 51st Infantry and
7th Armoured Divisions to contain the enemy along the
Mareth front, while the 10th Corps under Horrocks made
the long march to the west to join the New Zealand Corps
in an outflanking movement by way of Wilder's Gap. A
heavy dust storm served for some time to conceal this
transfer of forces from the enemy. Thus the strategy succeeded, and because of it the battle of Mareth was won.

That the corps which Horrocks commanded contributed
so greatly to the success was, in his judgement, attributable
in no small degree to the fighting qualities of the New
Zealanders. He afterwards wrote: 'This 2nd New Zealand
Division commanded by General Freyberg was unquestionably the most experienced and formidable fighting machine
in the Eighth Army. No man was considered for a commission unless he had been in at least six actions, and a high
proportion of the men had been wounded two or three
times.'[13]

Like other Eighth Army formations, the New Zealand

Corps which Freyberg commanded at Mareth was a somewhat polyglot force. It included Leclerc's troops, who at
that time were generally known as the Fighting French
rather than Free French, as they later came to be called,
and also the Greek Sacred Squadron. Of those who escaped
from Greece after the country was overrun in 1941 a high
proportion consisted of officers. The Sacred Squadron was
formed in August 1942 largely to enable many of them to
serve in the ranks. It was the least politicised of the Greek
army units and the one most highly regarded in British
military circles. Elsewhere in the Greek forces in the Middle
East politics were so obsessional that they even gave rise to
mutiny.[14]

In the outflanking operation at the battle of Mareth the
Eighth Army had its first introduction to the problems of
mountain warfare. The one formation which was properly
trained for this was the Indian Division, and as the campaign
progressed the special skills it had learnt would be more and
more needed. Now a number of Madrassi and Sikh sappers
were required to clear minefields before the advance of 30
Corps. This they did under heavy enemy fire, and when
they had completed their task one of their officers, Lieutenant-Colonel Blundell, suggested to them that if they ran for
cover it might have a bad effect on other troops. So they
strolled back casually, laughing and chatting.[15]

Discipline of this quality among the Indians was not
confined to the fighting troops. In the division there were a
number of non-combatants, who were predominantly of low
caste: the *boberjees, bhistris,* barbers, *dhurzis* and sweepers.
James Whitton, who as an officer in the Queen's Own
Cameron Highlanders served in the 4th Indian Division,
wrote of them: 'In the fluidity, especially of desert battles,
their units were often outflanked or surrounded and they
endured the same strafing and bombing and shelling; had
the same general discomfort.' He added: 'They had deeper
family responsibilities than us and their pay was sent home
unfailingly.'[16]

*   *   *

Montgomery described Mareth as 'our toughest battle since Alamein'. Harry Ramsbottom, as a sergeant, held the same view, but he found that a number of those in the 51st (Highland) Division judged the Mareth battle to have been the fiercer of the two. Both were unquestionably victories for the Eighth Army. The withdrawal of the German and Italian forces after the battle opened up the way into most of Tunisia. It also made possible the meeting of the Eighth Army with the American and British forces invading Tunisia from the west, a meeting which had been looked forward to for nearly five months.

'You know — the things we used to wear in England.'

STEPPE, SAHEL AND RICH
COASTAL PLAIN

The advance of the Eighth Army from the Mareth Line brought it to Tunisia's principal oases. The largest of these enabled the town of Gabès to come into existence. At first sight the oases seem to be carpets of green covered by palm-trees. Some of the palms are stunted and look like sprawling pineapples. Others suggest slim young negresses with extravagant hair-dos. The total number of date-palms in the Gabès area is said to exceed 300,000.

Gabès is both an oasis town and a port. An appreciable proportion of its population when the Eighth Army arrived was French, and on entering it the New Zealanders were greeted enthusiastically. 'The population crowded round us in high excitement,' Kippenberger wrote, 'French police-men, elderly men and some astonishingly nicely dressed girls whom we looked on with relish.'[1]

It was a foretaste of the welcome which was to be received wherever the French were present in large numbers. Peniak-off, on being embraced by a French girl in Tunisia, was told: *'Vous êtes de la huitième armée. Alors vous êtes des héros.'*[2] The reception by Arabs was more muted.

Another oasis town captured was El Hamma, the site of hot sulphurous springs which have been used for the treat-ment of rheumatism since the time of the Roman occupation.

Meanwhile there was a second good defensive position north of the Mareth Line to which the German and Italian forces retired. This was the fairly narrow neck of land which lies between the sea on the east and the Shott el Fejej on the west. The *shotts*, which virtually traverse Tunisia to the west of the Gulf of Gabès, are expanses of sand interspersed with water and salt, whose appearance suggests that nature has deposited huge quantities of scummy detergent. They are effective barriers to motor vehicles.

The enemy's main defensive line rested on the deep Wadi Akarit, which is dominated by a huge outcrop of rock nearly 300 metres high.

Montgomery launched an attack on the Wadi Akarit position in the early hours of 6 April. It met with almost immediate success, a success he attributed largely to surprise. He had decided not to adopt his usual practice of attacking by moonlight, because he did not want to wait for the next full moon, and chose darkness instead.[3] Certainly the enemy was surprised. Leese recalled later that large numbers of prisoners were taken with their boots off.[4] Horrocks, on the other hand, pointed out that the bombardment of enemy positions from the air was 'on a scale never attempted before'.[5]

Tuker too had his own version of events. The rocky *massif* dominating the front was, he considered, no more puzzling at night to the Gurkha battalions under his command than parts of London would be 'in the blackout to a Cockney'. Remembering a night in 1937 when thirty Gurkhas had ambushed 600 Pathans on the north-west frontier of India, he expressed the opinion that the massif would be taken by 4.30 a.m.

The Gurkhas attacked in silence with the knives known as *kukris*, which in the hands of Gurkhas are peculiarly frightening weapons. German machine-gunners, no doubt experienced soldiers, were reported to have fled for safety, and the Gurkhas reached their objective two and a half hours earlier than Tuker had forecast.

Tuker's summary of events was: 'It is scarcely too much to say that the battle of Wadi Akarit was won single-handed several hours before the formal attack began.' Every commanding height that mattered had, he pointed out, been taken by first light.[6]

On the following day, 7 April, patrols of the Eighth Army came into contact with the United States 2nd Corps, which was advancing eastwards from Gafsa. Other meetings between the two forces which had crossed North Africa in different directions followed.

The contrasts between the armies, between the Eighth Army and the British First Army as much as between the Eighth Army and the Americans, were immediately apparent. They were memorably expressed by a tank crew of the 9th Queen's Lancers, veterans of the desert campaigns, who, on seeing some First Army troops in regulation battledress and steel helmets, exclaimed: 'My God, soldiers!'[7]

One of the best of the many good war correspondents of the time, the Australian Alan Moorehead, had left the Eighth Army shortly after the battle of Alamein. Now he met it again when advancing with the First Army through Tunisia. The impact which the Eighth Army troops made on being seen again was powerful.

'The British desert soldier,' Moorehead wrote, 'looked like no other soldier in the world. He looked at first sight like a rather rakish and dishevelled boy scout, the effect, I suppose, of his bleached khaki shorts and shirts and the paraphernalia of blackened pots and pans and oddments he carried round in his vehicle which was his home. He practically never wore a helmet, and he had a careless loose-limbed way of walking which came from living on the open plains.'[8]

Moorhead went on to claim that the Eighth Army was no longer a European army. Cut off from Europe for years, it had become an overseas army, based on Cairo. It had developed private habits and even its own slang language.

It had been encouraged by Montgomery, he wrote, to consider itself as invincible, even to the point of becoming 'a private expeditionary force knowing no law except its own'. Those who did not belong to the Eighth Army were inevitably outsiders. To Eighth Army veterans the British First Army appeared a parade-ground army. First Army soldiers found the men of the Eighth Army loud and over-confident. The poet Keith Douglas even likened the differ-ences between the two to those which separated Gaullists from Vichy French.[9]

These were immediate impressions. As experiences were shared, differences became blurred, particularly when ele-ments of the First Army became integral parts of the Eighth Army. In rest areas too, and when otherwise thrown together accidentally, Allied soldiers easily establish com-radeship. Abiding evidence of this is to be found in the private notebooks or scrap-books which a number of sol-diers kept.

One such was preserved over the years by N. L. Mallins, an Eighth Army veteran, who rose to the rank of regimental sergeant-major in the Royal Tank Regiment. Among the entries in his book is an American one which reads: 'To a swell English soldier that I met in the NAAFI the best of luck. If you ever come to America look me up.' An address in Hazleton, Pennsylvania, follows. Another entry reads: 'With very best wishes to one I am privileged to call a mate.' There are signatures from Italian prisoners of war and pressed poppies from Tripoli. There is also a characteristic Eighth Army comment: 'When in doubt brew up.'[10]

Many of the entries are in verse, for the war evoked poetry from thousands. A substantial anthology was later produced consisting largely of poems written in North Africa and Italy during the war years.[11]

Alexander's immediate requirement, once the junction of the armies had been effected, was to assure adequate supplies, particularly of petrol, for the Eighth Army. 'I had decided,' he wrote in a despatch, 'to employ 2 US Corps in a limited operation. The objects of this were to build up confidence after the earlier setbacks . . . to exert pressure on the right rear of the enemy . . . and to be ready to open an alternative line of supply for 8 Army after they had broken through the Gabès gap.'

The Eighth Army's task after the battle of Wadi Akarit was to advance north and north-east in the direction of Tunis. This it now did with remarkable speed.

The first terrain to be crossed is sterile land with a high salt content. Among the villages on the way are Limadou, inhabited largely by the descendants of black slaves; El Aouilet, north of Gabès, whose name is the Arabic term for *the eyes* and whose houses nearly all have small peep-holes in lieu of ordinary windows; and Mahares, which has a harbour and brightly coloured Mediterranean fishing boats. Next comes Sfax, a port that had been of major importance to the Axis powers, and in consequence had been largely destroyed by attack from the air. Montgomery had had a bet with Eisenhower who did not believe Sfax could be captured before 15 April. Montgomery bet him that it could, and in fact Eighth Army troops entered it on the 10th. As the country's second-largest city Sfax has the blend of the European and the Arabic which Tunisia's few large towns acquired during the French occupation. It is part citadel – or *kasbah* – with minarets and ramparts dating back to the ninth century, and part a pleasing example of European town-planning with a regular pattern of streets and solid bourgeois houses.

As in Gabès the reception from the French was enthusiastic. One soldier received a bouquet from an elderly Frenchwoman and, as he was driven on, handed it to a military policeman, who continued to direct traffic with one hand while holding the bouquet in the other. Then the sound of bagpipes could be heard, and more military police arrived, trying to clear the streets.

The pipes were those of the 51st (Highland) Division.

The streets were being cleared for Montgomery, who, to roars and clapping and waving of flags and throwing of flowers, drove through. Then came the Highlanders with, in the words of one observer of the scene, 'kilts swinging, webbing white, metal gleaming, every rifle at the same angle, a triumph of military perfection,' as 'the pipes drowned every other sound and the drummers crashed their sticks from eye level to drum.'

The observer, E. M. Spalding, who described the scene in a letter home, also wrote of 'destruction and ruin, great holes, smashed buildings, wrecked homes, engines and coaches at all angles, bent iron, twisted rails, hanging wires and broken mains . . . the inevitable result of the bombing of military objectives in a city.'[12]

This kind of destruction was a comparatively new spectacle to many members of the Eighth Army. They were to see much of it later. After soldiering in Italy Peniakoff was to write: 'We had had a foretaste in Tunisia of what war in inhabited countries could be like – and we hadn't liked it. In the desert we had fought a clean conflict between soldiers, with nothing to ravage. We had left no trail of piteous burnt houses and devastated fields; there had been few civilian casualties, no refugee women and children.'[13]

The advance was on a broad front. The day after Eighth Army troops entered Sfax, Kairouan was captured. This was Tunisia's holiest city and regarded, certainly by Muslims in North Africa, as ranking only after Mecca, Medina and Jerusalem. It is a walled fortress town, whose defence had clearly been considered of the greatest importance by Arabs through the centuries. To the Eighth Army soldiers the inhabitants displayed, as they have displayed to travellers through the ages, their rugs and carpets, perpetual reminders of how long and how skilfully the Arab world has exploited a tradition of the abstract in art.

Kairouan was a point of convergence for the invading forces, and it was there that members of the United States

Second Corps and Leclerc's Fighting French met for the first time.[14]

Up the east coast the advance continued even more rapidly. As the army moved northward it returned to steppe country, where stunted vegetation and stone give colours to the landscape ranging from sedge-green to dusty brown, from oatmeal to near-pink. In these areas flocks of sheep can occasionally be met, driven by semi-nomads. Every third year, perhaps, after a good rainfall, they will settle for a time and cultivate some grain or some olives before returning to the road.

Suddenly, as the advance continued, an astonishing structure appeared on the horizon, the amphitheatre of El Djem, reputed to be the largest constructed by the Romans apart from the Colosseum. It is thought to have held 30,000 spectators. Seen from down in the arena those who occupied the top rows would have appeared hardly larger than ants.

After El Djem had been passed cultivated areas appeared again. Here in the Sahel olives and almonds dominate, but there are also eucalyptus trees, introduced from Australia by the French to check the spread of the desert. The cactus is cultivated also, partly to provide a kind of hedgerow, and partly for its fruit, known variously as the Barbary fig and the prickly pear.

Sousse lies about 100 kilometres north of Sfax, yet it was captured only two days later. It too was subjected to heavy bombardment. Alan Moorehead described its port area immediately after the arrival of the Eighth Army as 'a frightening sight'. He saw a grand piano on a housetop and the roof of an apartment block on top of another building. The palm-trees on the seafront looked like those to be seen in photographs of Florida after a hurricane. Some ships had been hit and sunk. Some had been beached by near misses and had then been broken up by the waves. Some had disintegrated. The Arab quarter, Moorehead wrote, 'had been split open and the midday sun poured in over all its tawdry and shabby secrets; the labyrinthine brothels, the sweet-vendor's shops, the miserable fetid courtyards.'[15]

Happily the new town, unlike the port area, was little damaged, and again the welcome from the French was wholehearted. One French girl even had the temerity to fling her arms round Montgomery's neck. Montgomery's response was not recorded.

The combined Allied force under Alexander's command was now a formidable body. Numerically, and in tank power and artillery, the Eighth Army formed a relatively small part of it.

In the French colonial territories which had come under Allied control conscription had been introduced, and this added appreciably to the Army Group's strength. As a result the total number of infantry battalions under Alexander's command was 156. Of these only forty-three were in the Eighth Army. There were thirty-eight French and twenty-two American; the remaining fifty-three were in the British First Army. Similarly, of a total tank strength of 1,193, the Eighth Army had only 460. Opposing the 156 infantry battalions were 90 German and Italian ones. The discrepancy in tank strength, 1,193 against 143, was even greater.[16]

The distribution of his forces being what it was, Alexander now decided, reasonably enough, that the burden of the fighting should be shared rather more evenly than it had been in the past between the Eighth Army, on the one hand, and the American and French forces and the British First Army on the other. The nature of the terrain also afforded good reasons why he should do so. 'I decided,' he wrote in a despatch, 'for topographical reasons, to make my main attack on the western front of this perimeter. My intention was to break through to Tunis from the west and thereby split the enemy forces in two. I would then leave the smaller body of enemy to the north to be mopped up by the Allied troops on the spot and, turning southwards with

the greater part of my forces, drive the larger body of enemy
on the right flank of the penetration against the line firmly
held by the Eighth Army.'[17]

Before any such plan could be put into operation further
battles had to be fought on the Eighth Army front. Over-
looking the coastal road which leads northwards from
Sousse to Enfidaville is a hill which rises almost perpendic-
ularly, on top of which is set the village of Takrouna,
normally with about 500 inhabitants. It was a natural
strongpoint for the Germans.

The task of capturing Takrouna was given to the New
Zealand Maori Battalion. At the top there is a flat space
some thirty metres square largely occupied by an Arab
tomb, and below this a sheer drop of perhaps ten metres
with an overhang at some points. The platoon commander
who led the attack on the night of 20–21 April was wounded
early on, and there were a number of other casualties. When
daylight came only two sergeants and seven other men
remained, but they continued to make their way up the hill
and somehow the Maoris not only succeeded in reaching the
top but also took seventy German prisoners.

Horrocks visited the site later and wrote: 'It was all I
could do physically to get to the top. How the Maoris did it
wearing full equipment and facing such tough opposition I
simply do not know.' He, like others, was deeply disap-
pointed when the recommendation of a Victoria Cross for
Sergeant Manahi, who led the attack, was not accepted.[18]

Enfidaville was entered shortly before Takrouna was
captured, but north of the town enemy resistance grew
stronger. On 29 April Montgomery was forced to the
unwelcome conclusion that a body of troops under his
command was not fighting well, and in the evening he sent
a signal to Alexander which read: '56 Div gave very bad
showing today.' He also had misgivings about the general
strategy which was being applied, and he invited Alexander
to come and see him the next day. Alexander replied that
he would do so at 7.30 in the morning.[19]

The meeting took place at Monastir, where today a new town of rare beauty is to be seen. The result of the meeting was a change in the plans for the capture of Tunis and for the conclusion of the North African campaign.

ENTRY INTO TUNIS

In Alexander's new plan the First Army was still given the responsibility of capturing Tunis, but it was temporarily to have under its command the best formations which Montgomery could spare. Montgomery agreed to release the 7th Armoured Division, the 4th Indian Division and 201 Guards Brigade. Reporting this, Alexander wrote in a despatch: 'These were both the freshest and most experienced formations in Eighth Army. They were indeed the nucleus around which Eighth Army had grown up, for in 1940 they made up the whole of the Western Desert Force.' He added: 'It was particularly appropriate that the two divisions which had won our first victory in Africa at Sidi Barrani should be chosen for the main role in our last victory, the Battle of Tunis.'[1]

In the new plan the New Zealand Division would have a holding role on the Enfidaville front and would carry out local operations to help the French 19th Corps. The formations of 30 Corps and 51st Division had already been withdrawn to rest and to prepare for the Eighth Army's next major campaign. The fighting north of Enfidaville was severe, and significantly it is in Enfidaville that the principal British war cemetery in Tunisia is to be seen today.

Even heavier fighting was expected in the near future. Harry Ramsbottom recorded in his diary: 'Whisperings of a coming offensive, with Hammamet the coastal town as the first objective, began to be heard. It was ominously stated that it would be a costly affair and 50 per cent casualties officially anticipated.' He added: 'The cancellation of that attack was almost a relief . . . The division was to join the 1st Army immediately.'

Among those giving medical help to the Eighth Army on this front was an American Field Service Ambulance Unit, which had come out as a body of volunteers to the Middle East long before the United States entered the war. It was shelled near Enfidaville and lost a number of its members. Harry McDonald, a New York ambulance man, whose grandfather was transported from Scotland for stealing and became a missionary in Hawaii, was one of the survivors. He found that most of his patients were Indians, French or Senegalese, but he told the Eighth Army newspaper *Crusader* of a badly wounded British gunner, who said to him: 'Don't let me die. I must get back to my gun. I've got to get to Tunis.'

It was clearly desirable that the transfer of two divisions and a brigade from the Eighth Army to the First Army front should be concealed from the enemy. Assuming the presence of many local Axis informers, it was recognised that this could be achieved only if Eighth Army soldiers changed their habits and appearance.

A remarkable order was therefore issued, which read:

1. A soldier of the Eighth Army is more sunburnt than his counterpart in the First Army. Little can be done to overcome this difficulty other than keeping in leaguer areas and keeping the locals out.
2. Personnel of the Eighth Army are in the habit of using the 'V' sign. The First Army have not cultivated this habit. All troops are therefore to refrain from using it.
3. First Army troops are trained to sit at attention in vehicles when on the move. It is therefore not hard

for a trained observer to identify Eighth Army vehicles.

4. Eighth Army personnel have some knowledge of Arabic expressions, whereas the First Army use only French. Troops should refrain from using Arabic.

5. It is felt that our troops will be rather apt to talk of the achievements of the Eighth Army. They should be warned not to do so.

Security was clearly not the only reason why this fifth paragraph was included, for in the paragraph which followed it was stated that 'formations in the First Army are very sensitive.'[2]

As an instruction to victorious troops not to behave as they normally would, the order may well be unique in military history.

Alexander's strategy was successful. Within a few hours of each other the US Second Corps were able to enter Bizerta and the First Army, reinforced by divisions from the Eighth Army, entered Tunis. This was on 7 May 1943, just six months after the Allied landings in North Africa. As in Tripoli, among the first to enter Tunis were the Cherry Pickers (11th Hussars).

The entry into Tunis took place in heavy rain and in the face of continued resistance in the streets. A battalion of the 1/7 Queens was in the vanguard, and in his official report its commanding officer wrote:

The sight as the battalion entered the town was an unforgettable one. Despite the pouring rain dense crowds of wildly enthusiastic French men and women lined the streets, throwing flowers over the vehicles, attempting to jump on them and in many cases throwing their arms round the troops and kissing them. In the midst of this was the smoke and flames from burning vehicles and buildings and the noise of rifle and machine-gun fire from the enemy still holding out in various buildings.

Later in his report he wrote:

> Throughout the night a steady flow of enemy transport
> was intercepted . . . The Germans in most cases either
> tried to turn round and get away or jump out and run off
> in the dark. Some were killed or wounded, the remainder
> gave themselves up. By 0500 hours the position . . . was
> clear and no further enemy appeared. The collection of
> POWs continued.[3]

Sergeant Ricky Hall described the scene rather more lacon-
ically in his diary: 'Wogs, froggies clap like hell. Kiss backs
of squaddies' hands. Climb on tanks and kiss commanders.
Free wine. Free food. Everything free. Jerries take a dim
view. Spit and hiss. Iti women and French fight.'[4]

Enemy resistance indeed continued as long as it could
serve any purpose, particularly in the hills to the north-west
of Enfidaville. Montgomery himself had earlier written: 'In
Tunisia the Italian is fighting desperately; he has never done
so before; but he is doing so now.' In acknowledgement of
this, after Field-Marshal Giovanni Messe had been taken
prisoner, Montgomery invited him to dinner.[5]

Nevertheless within a week of the entry into Tunis the
North African campaign was effectively concluded. On 13
May Alexander sent a signal to Churchill which read: 'It is
my duty to report that the Tunisian campaign is over. All
enemy resistance has ceased. We are masters of the North
African shore.'[6] About a quarter of a million enemy troops
surrendered. Less than 700 are thought to have escaped.

Mopping-up operations brought Eighth Army troops to the
Cape Bon Peninsula and the shores of the Gulf of Hammamet. In Hammamet itself Rommel, earlier in the campaign,
had established a headquarters in a villa built by a Rouman-
ian named George Sebastian and much admired by the
architect Frank Lloyd Wright. It has white colonnades, a
swimming pool and a sunken marble bath and is approached

along an impressive avenue of cypresses and palms. I found
it in striking contrast with the caravans which had housed
Eighth Army commanders, and observed that it is regarded
by Tunisians today as a suitable setting for a great soldier.

The sands here are near-white and extensive. A little
inland from them oranges and lemons, oleander and tamar-
isk, bougainvillaea and marigolds flourish. So along the road
from Tunis to Hammamet do vines, which the French
introduced, and olives. In the hills to the west wild boar
abound. Before long a boar hunt was organised by officers
in the Coldstream Guards. An account of this event even
found its way into the pages of the *Field* magazine.[9]

Among the townships through which Eighth Army units
passed is the so-called Andalusian village of Sidi bou Said,
which was created largely by Spanish Jews. The whole
village is a brilliant display of light blue and white, colours
which were chosen not for aesthetic reasons but for protection against flies and heat. Flies, it was discovered, would
not land on a blue surface, the presumption being that they
could not see anything coloured blue. Hence the light blue
doors, window-frames and shutters on the white houses.
The effect is delightful.

In Libya the Eighth Army had served as an army of
liberation. In Tunisia it was an army in transit. After it had
fought its battles French occupation of the country was
resumed, a condition which was to continue for a decade
after the end of World War II.

PART FOUR: SICILY

(July – September 1943)

PLANNING AN INVASION

When Churchill and Roosevelt met at Casablanca in January 1943 they agreed that once North Africa had been cleared of the enemy an invasion of Sicily must follow. In doing so they acted against the advice of the Anglo-American Planning Committee.[1]

Churchill, with his rare ability to summarise strategy in a single sentence, had spoken of Italy as 'the soft under-belly of the Axis'. There were good reasons for believing that landings in Sicily or southern Italy would strengthen the resolve of those Italians who had no wish to continue an increasingly unpopular war. There was the important strategic consideration that control of Sicily would remove most of the dangers to Allied shipping in the Mediterranean. In addition, an attack on Italy would certainly force the Germans to withdraw some divisions from the Russian front.

Questions still disturbed the doubters: in particular, whether an attack on Italy should have a limited objective and, if not, where it would lead; what ultimate purpose it would serve, and to what extent it would absorb forces which could otherwise be used in the invasion of France the following year. Decisions on all these points were postponed for the time being. A precedent for compromise was thereby established, the kind of compromise which was to influence Allied strategy in the Mediterranean and the fate of the Eighth Army for the next two years.

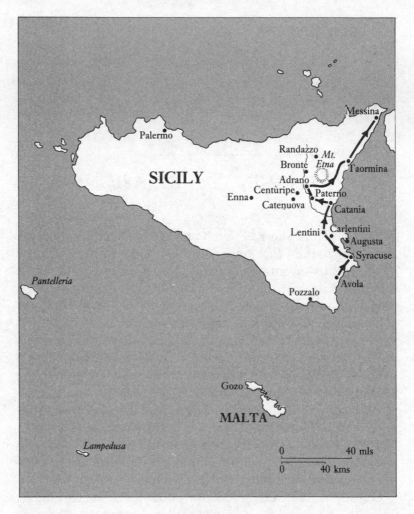

The main planning of the invasion of Sicily took place at the headquarters in Algiers of General Eisenhower, the Supreme Commander of the Allied forces. Montgomery did not feel at home there, and he did not have a very high opinion of the staff. This was not conducive to good feeling, nor were the consequences of a visit which he paid to Britain.

When Montgomery had arrived in the Middle East he had been little known outside military circles, and he had not

even been Churchill's first choice as commander of the
Eighth Army. After the North African campaign was over,
he found himself acclaimed in Britain as a national hero. He
was neither prepared for such an immense change of status
nor altogether well equipped to deal with it.

Montgomery's performance in North Africa had been
magnificent. Latter-day critics have arisen and complained
of his failure to exploit the break-through at Alamein. The
adjective 'dawdling' has even been used. These have been
expressions of post-operational perfectionism. They cannot
detract from Montgomery's achievement in transforming an
army and leading it a distance equivalent to that between
London and a point some 200 miles east of Moscow in only
six months.[2] He had been the victorious general in two
major battles and had transformed British military tactics
by the closeness of his cooperation with the Commander of
the Desert Air Force, Air Vice-Marshal Harry Broadhurst.
By the time of the Tunisian campaign RAF officers in
armoured cars were controlling air strikes from positions
alongside the forward troops.

After the North African campaign Montgomery's career
entered a new phase, one in which political skills were
increasingly required. In these he was regrettably deficient.
Superb as he so often was in handling subordinates, he could
be inept in dealing with those whom he was expected to regard
as equals, particularly if they were of foreign nationality, and
the adulation he received in Britain did nothing to improve
his capacity for showing tact. What it did instead was to fortify
his propensity for the theatrical. This had never been far
below the surface. He had often used it to advantage in his
communication with troops, but on one occasion when I
myself was in his company for some length of time after the
war I gained the impression that he was parodying himself. In
other words, he had found a role which he enjoyed playing,
and he played it inordinately well.

When Eisenhower had made his bet with Montgomery

about the date of the capture of Sfax he had said that if he lost he would give Montgomery a Flying Fortress aircraft for his own use. Montgomery held him to this. But since there was no shortage of aircraft in North Africa at that time, and an Army commander's requirements could always have been met, Montgomery's use of a Flying Fortress bomber as a private transport aircraft was seen by Americans as flaunting his success, and it was resented as such. As it happened, he did not have the Flying Fortress for long. It was to crash when he visited Patton in Sicily and was replaced by a much more suitable Dakota carrying a jeep.

The use of the Flying Fortress was only a minor irritation. Relations between the Allies were more severely strained when Montgomery received the plans for the invasion of Sicily and briskly expressed his unfavourable opinion of them. The parallel he drew was with a flock of birds alighting on an island, nowhere in strength.[3] As so often in his views on strategy however, Montgomery was right. Eisenhower later wrote: 'On 3 May we stopped tinkering and completely recast our plan on the sound strategic principle of concentration of strength in the crucial area.'[4] For this change the Allied armies owed Montgomery a debt of gratitude, but unfortunately he had managed to be right in a way which did not improve relations.

In his discussions with Eisenhower about the invasion of Sicily Montgomery understandably suggested that full use should be made, not only of the Eighth Army's resources, but of the mystique of its title. Eisenhower was wise enough to agree. Of his army at the end of the North African campaign Montgomery wrote to Alan Brooke, the Chief of the Imperial General Staff: 'The high morale of my soldiers is almost unbelievable. I sometimes wonder whether it is a bit too much, and possibly dangerous; they believe that this Army is invincible and can do nothing wrong.'[5]

Eisenhower's decision was that the Eighth Army under Montgomery would invade Sicily from the south-east and south. Quite independent of it would be the United States

Seventh Army under Patton, which would be responsible for the western sector. Alexander was to have an overall military command. With the personalities involved this was probably the wisest decision which could have been made, but it did establish the principle of dividing Italy into a western and an eastern front, with American control in the west and British control in the east, a division which was not always successful either militarily or politically.

Under his own supreme command Eisenhower appointed Admiral Andrew Cunningham and Air Marshal Arthur Tedder, both British, to command the naval and air forces respectively. This meant that Eisenhower's personal control from Algiers was somewhat tenuous, for Cunningham had his headquarters in Malta, and Tedder had his in Tunis. Nevertheless, as Montgomery had forecast, in his appointments Eisenhower was showing himself to be 'good on the political line'.

Eighth Army troops were widely dispersed for their periods of rest and training before embarking for Sicily. Elements of the 50th Division, for example, found themselves near Ismailia on the banks of the Suez Canal.[6] Montgomery was assiduous in visiting as many units as possible. Sidney Kirkman, who was later to command a corps in Italy, commented on the visits: 'It's like in the Peninsular War. A glimpse of Wellington's nose, and they knew all was well.'[7]

The ports of embarkation too were widely scattered. In addition to Tunis, Sfax and Sousse they included Tripoli, Malta and Haifa. Airborne forces were assembled near Kairouan.

The ports used were not confined to the Mediterranean. Additional forces were sent direct from Britain to take part in the landings, including two formations which were to play major parts in the Eighth Army campaigns during the next two years, the First Canadian Division and a Canadian tank brigade.

Canadian troops had been in the United Kingdom for

nearly three years. Units of the Canadian Second Division had been involved in the largely disastrous raid on Dieppe, but the rest had seen no fighting. Concern had begun to be expressed in Canada about their lack of action, so much so that Brooke wrote to Montgomery: 'Both political and military grounds make it essential that Canadian forces should be brought into action this year.'[8]

The Canadian 1st Division, which was selected to be sent to Sicily, consisted of three infantry regiments of the Permanent Force. These were the Royal Canadian Regiment, Princess Patricia's Canadian Light Infantry and the Royal 22ème Régiment. The man who was due to command them in action, Major-General H. L. N. Salmon, was killed in an air crash near Barnstaple when leaving to take part in a conference in the Middle East. His replacement was Major-General Guy Simonds.

The Canadians had one serious disadvantage in relation to the other units in the Army of which they were about to become a part. They had no experience of campaigning in summer conditions in Mediterranean countries, and the invasion of Sicily was planned to take place in July.

A hundred and twenty-five vessels transported the Canadians and their equipment from British ports. The convoys came as far as Oran without incident, but between Oran and Algiers two of the ships were torpedoed. Fortunately the loss of life was not great.

The south-west coast of Sicily is only about 140 kilometres from the north-east coast of Tunisia. For this reason alone it was easy for the enemy to deduce that the Allies would decide to invade Sicily rather than any other part of southern Europe. It was therefore necessary to devise a cover plan which would direct his attention away from the obvious. Because everyone likes a really good story the belief has grown up that this deception was achieved almost entirely by a single hoax involving the use of a corpse.

The corpse was that of a young man who had died in England of pleural pneumonia. It was kept frozen in the

mortuary and was later dressed up in the uniform of a major
in the Royal Marines. The supposed major was then given
two confidential letters, one written by General Sir Archibald Nye, the Vice-Chief of the Imperial General Staff, and
the other by Lord Louis Mountbatten, who at that time was
Chief of Combined Operations. The body was then released
from a submarine so that it would drift ashore on the
Spanish coast.

The whole enterprise was planned by a body known as
the London Controlling Section, which had been created to
devise and put into effect methods of deceiving the enemy.
A number of statements in the letters placed on the corpse
were true and verifiably so. But there was also a clear
indication that any landings in Sicily would be by way of a
feint intended to draw off troops, and that the main Allied
attack would be launched in Sardinia. Mountbatten's letter
even contained a heavy-handed joke involving the use of
the word 'sardines'.[9]

The hoax, since made famous through book and film,
achieved its purpose, and information received through
Ultra made it clear that the Germans had accepted the
documents on the corpse as authentic. This was an unqualified success, but even so the use of the putative major was
only one part of a complex deception plan, and, arguably,
not the most important. An elaborate bogus strategy was
worked out involving attacks against both Greece and
southern France. Dates for each stage of the imaginary
operations were chosen. Western Crete, for example, was
supposed to be attacked on 26 July, Sardinia and Corsica on
the 31st and the mainland of France on 4 August. For the
attack on Greece a non-existent force called the British 12th
Army was created, its presence being suggested to the
enemy largely by the signals traffic in which it appeared to
be engaged.[10]

The routing of convoys was organised to strengthen belief
in these operations. Under the guidance of the chief British
Liaison Officer with the Greek resistance forces, Brigadier

E. C. W. (Eddie) Myers, guerrilla bands were called upon to make attacks on communications and other targets of the kind which would be expected to precede an invasion.

Perhaps most convincing of all, strategic bombing was carried out of areas which would not in fact be invaded. In war innocent people are killed not only because they happen to live in towns and villages which invading forces intend to capture, but also at times because they do not.

Montgomery, however, was not altogether confident of success in Sicily. Before the invasion he wrote: 'I consider that if we are to succeed we must have average luck, and probably 60 to 70 per cent luck.'[11] Churchill described the whole operation involving the landings as 'our greatest venture so far'.[12]

Damned good job there were no walls in the desert!'

ACROSS THE MEDITERRANEAN

Before any landings were made on Sicily it was thought necessary to eliminate the Italian garrisons of two offshore islands. One of these was Pantelleria, a volcanic outcrop of 83 square kilometres which, during the Roman empire, had served as a place of banishment for people of prominence and even members of the imperial family. Mussolini had had it fairly strongly fortified for defence. Lampedusa, the other island, is at most some three kilometres wide. But it had a harbour from which motor torpedo boats could operate, and Mussolini's government had had an airfield built. Pantelleria had a population of about 10,000, Lampedusa about half as many.

Both islands were effectively conquered from the air. During the third week in May heavy bombardment began, and altogether 5,258 air sorties were flown against Pantelleria alone. These, it afterwards became clear, had been several thousand more than were needed. Landing parties from the Eighth Army on both islands were required to do little other than accept the surrender of the Italian garrisons. Pantelleria had been largely devastated. There were countless corpses under the rubble, and the landing parties found dogs roaming in packs and searching for bodies. They were also aware of an extraordinary abundance of fleas.

One unorthodox benefit from the landings was derived by a guardsman named Butterfield, who strained a ligament.

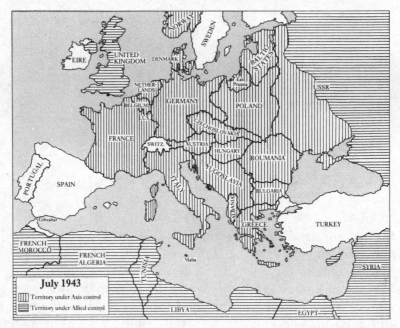

He was to find himself before long in a hospital in New York, as the only available hospital ship happened to be bound there.

Pantelleria was surrendered on 11 June. The surrender of Lampedusa came the following day. Here too the port had been wholly destroyed, and there were huge craters to be seen. But the Italian governor retained a sense of theatre and dignity to the end. He was much concerned that the ceremony of raising the Union Jack should be properly conducted, and he even persuaded an officer of the Coldstream Guards that he himself should be allowed to take the salute after the British guard had presented arms.[1]

A number of raids on Sicily also took place before the main landings. Pilotage parties were taken in by submarine to examine the beaches.[2] The SAS and the Special Boat Service also mounted raids, both to destroy enemy installations and to bring back reports.[3] Intelligence gathered in these ways and topographical studies showed that there are numerous beaches in south-east Sicily, most of them sand, some of them shingle, and that they range in length from a hundred metres to several kilometres. The sand is fine and soft, and was likely to be an impediment to tanks and to motor transport generally.[4]

There were a number of airfields and landing grounds in the south-east, including an important group round Catania. Of the ports, Syracuse has a natural harbour in a wide bay. It had at that time five quays and moles. The invasion plan did not provide for the immediate capture of any sizeable port, and a substantial force would therefore have to be maintained for several days from open beaches. This was certain to be hazardous, and to result in a slow build-up of supplies.

The Allies did however have one new and valuable asset, which was yet another example of the benefits of American technology. This was a two and a half ton amphibious vehicle named DUKW. It had six wheels, which were power-driven, but when it entered the water the motive power was transferred to a propeller. Its name was derived from serial initials in the factory which first produced it, but, the purpose of the vehicle being what it was, it naturally became known as the 'duck'.[5] Like the jeep it was one of those inventions which seem indispensable as soon as they have been made available.

The most encouraging of the intelligence reports concerned the enemy forces in Italy. The deception plan had clearly been effective, and the German forces on Sicily were limited to two German divisions, two works battalions, a fortress battalion and some Air Force personnel.

The first formation the Eighth Army would meet after the landings would be the Italian 206 (Coastal) Division. This had not been in action before; its equipment was known to be poor; and its morale was thought to be low.[6]

The date chosen for the main invasion force to set out for Sicily was the night of 9–10 July 1943. The weather forecast

was discouraging, and Eisenhower, as Supreme Commander, was faced with a problem similar to the one which
would confront him nearly a year later on the eve of the
Normandy landings. On both occasions he made the same
decision. The invasion would go ahead as planned. During
the evening the winds rose to near gale force, a surprising
but not unknown occurrence in a Mediterranean July.
About 260 vessels sailed from the various ports. Some were
unable to keep up with the convoys. A few foundered.

Many of the soldiers in the crowded vessels were horribly
seasick. A lance-corporal in the Black Watch even died
from seasickness.[7] Joseph Anderson, another Black Watch
lance-corporal, who came from a fishing village in Fife and
so took to the sea easily, remembered later wondering how
many of the troops would be in a condition to fight if they
met with determined opposition on landing.[8]

For those who were not seasick there was the blend of
anxiety and tedium in being transported by others, unable
to do anything themselves. Ronald Cox, a lieutenant in an
Anti-Aircraft Regiment, who had sailed with the Canadians
from the Clyde and had first made contact with the Eighth
Army off Gozo on the way to Sicily, described the period of
waiting in verse:

> Bound for the Isle of Sicily
> Soldiers sit shorted and shirt-sleeved,
> Smoking, coughing, laughing, cursing;
> Peering at maps and oiling guns.[9]

Large numbers were certainly smoking, for in World War II
tobacco was accepted as a prime necessity. Huge amounts
of scarce dollars were spent by the British government in
obtaining it and the lives of thousands were risked in
transporting it. Space in all the vessels making for Sicily was
severely limited, but no one would have countenanced a
shortage of tobacco.

During the night the wind abated. It was blowing from

the north, and as the convoys approached Sicily the land provided some lee and the sea moderated. With naval guns providing a barrage, troops were transferred from ships to landing craft. Then they began to come ashore.

As he landed Ernest Kerans heard the sound of machine-gun fire from the shore. He later wrote: 'I was much too seasick to care. There was only two foot of pebbles between sea and low cliff at Avola . . . I got awful wet going under the low cliff the same time as a big wave. We climbed the bank, cut the wire and ran across a vineyard. Occasional rifle or machine-gun fire did nothing to slow us down.'[10]

In this way the Eighth Army gained a toehold in Europe.

ADVANCE TO MOUNT ETNA

The Allies invaded Sicily from the air as well as from the sea. The 82nd (US) Airborne Division and the 1st (British) Airborne Division used both gliders and paratroops for the assault. Losses were heavy. Half the British glider force landed in the sea, including the gliders of the divisional commander and a brigade commander. The powered aircraft and gliders used in the operation, which were mostly American, had been hurriedly assembled in North Africa. Bad weather, faulty navigation and anti-aircraft fire, not a little of it from Allied troops, all contributed to the difficulties.[1]

As Kerans's battalion of the Durham Light Infantry made their advance they passed a wood, where, in his words, 'from every tree hung a dead Para.' But at first there was little firing. As a result the paratroops who reached the ground in safety were obliged to operate largely as small, independent units. This they did with considerable success in spite of being faced by German troops of high quality. Montgomery, like most soldiers, sparing in his references to bravery, wrote that airborne forces held one important bridge 'with remarkable heroism for nearly eighteen hours'.[2] He estimated that the action of the airborne forces accelerated the Eighth Army's advance by about seven days.[3]

The Eighth Army troops who came by sea met less fierce opposition at first. The Italians manning the coastal defences did not believe the invasion would take place in the wind and sea conditions prevailing on the night of 9–10 July and were clearly taken by surprise.[4]

Nor were many of them inclined to fight. The Canadians were particularly surprised by the reception they had in what they had reasonably assumed to be hostile territory. One of their first objectives was the capture of the small coastal town of Pozzalo. When they entered it they heard the sound of singing and learnt that this was in celebration of their arrival.[5] They also found that Italian prisoners whom they had taken were volunteering to help unload stores. Among the stores which other Italian prisoners helped bring ashore was the ammunition for a squadron of the Royal Tank Regiment.[6]

When Kerans called at a farmhouse to fill his water-bottle, 'for a start there was just one elderly lady, with tears rolling down her cheeks, watching our attack on the pill-box. Then one man came out, kissed me on both cheeks, took my water-bottle off to fill and showed me into a cellar, where there were only young girls. They made a fuss of me, gave me glasses of wine, showed me photos of relations in America and told me that the old lady was crying because *suo figlio* (her son) was in the pill-box, by now under fire from our six-inch anti-tank gun. As I made conversation first one and then another man came out, some old but most of them of possible soldier age.'[7]

It was a measure of the light opposition they faced that a few hours after dawn on 10 July some eight Allied divisions had come ashore. In the early fighting British casualties amounted to about 800. Of these 500 were in the 1st Airborne Division.[8]

In Libya and Tunisia the impact of local politics on Eighth Army troops had been negligible. Italy was altogether different, for just two weeks after the invasion of Sicily the structure of the Italian state began to collapse.

On the night of 24–25 July the Grand Council, which was

the only body to which Mussolini considered himself in any way answerable, met for about ten hours. Towards the end of the session Count Dino Grandi, ex-Ambassador to Britain and ex-Foreign Minister, put down a motion condemning Mussolini's conduct of the war. This was carried by nineteen votes to seven. A day later King Victor Emmanuel III informed Mussolini in a twenty-minute interview that he had been dismissed and that a new government would be headed by Marshal Badoglio. In this astonishingly simple way a dictatorship which had lasted for twenty-one years was brought to an end. The invasion of Sicily had been the decisive factor.

As the invading armies increasingly came to realise, although Fascism had exercised an immensely powerful stranglehold, it had not enjoyed a deep popularity among the people of Italy. Mussolini had come to power as the leader of a minority cult, with no clearly defined political policy other than colonial expansion, the essence of his economic system being state control through so-called corporations, whose heads he personally appointed.

Much of the appeal of Fascism derived from Mussolini's well-developed sense of theatre. In fact the black shirts, the salutes, the marching, even the use of the term 'Duce', had all been introduced by the colourful adventurer and poet, Gabriele d'Annunzio, when he had seized Fiume in September 1919 and had governed it autocratically for some sixteen months, but Mussolini quickly saw the attraction of all this and adapted it to a wider Italian audience.

To a people who had seen large numbers of their friends and relations emigrating to the United States and elsewhere in order to escape from perpetual poverty, Mussolini's colonial policy had an obvious appeal. But for the most part Fascism meant oppression by policemen and other servants of the state, who to a large extent were above the law. As a system it had little attraction after three years of a war which was clearly being lost and which had been begun altogether unnecessarily. Hence the phenomenon, which at first puzzled the invading armies, of a people who greeted their supposed enemies with flowers and wine and kisses and spontaneous offers of help.

Change of heart was evident too on the walls of towns and villages. The Fascist slogans *credere, obbedire, combattere* (believe, obey, fight) and *Mussolini ha sempre ragione* (Mussolini is always right) were soon eliminated, as were the ubiquitous words *Viva Mussolini*. But indulgence in political graffiti being such a deeply ingrained habit among the Italian people, they were soon replaced by *Viva il Rey, Viva Badoglio, Viva Roosevelt, Viva Churchill* and, increasingly, *Viva Stalin*.

In Sicily the roots of Fascism were even shallower than in most other parts of Italy. The island had a long tradition of opposition to authority, even before the famous rising on Easter Day in Palermo in 1282, when the French rulers were massacred in the so-called Sicilian Vespers. The tradition never died, and in 1860 Sicilians, inspired by Garibaldi, drove 15,000 Bourbon troops off their island to seek refuge in the Kingdom of Naples.

The clearest expression of the tradition of resistance to external authority was to be found in the secret society which bears a number of names but is most commonly known as the Mafia. The essence of its creed is the so-called *omertà*, or obligation never in any circumstances to apply for justice to the legally constituted authorities, nor to assist in the official detection of crime committed against oneself or others.

In World War I a number of Italian deserters had been protected, and later exploited, by the Mafia. Now in World War II Italian soldiers in Sicily were encouraged by members of the Mafia to return to their families, and were told that they could be supplied with civilian clothes and whatever else they might need to enable them to do so.[9] Advantage was taken of these and other opportunities to escape from war, and as a result Sicilian villages suddenly seemed devoid of Italian troops. Robert Perrin, a young officer in the 24th Field Regiment, Royal Artillery, while looking for a gun site, came upon a village which was not marked on his map. Here he was met by a man of evident authority. He did not discover whether the man was the mayor, the local head of the Mafia or, possibly, both, but he did learn that he was being encouraged to capture the village single-handed.[10]

The opportunities to lay down arms and return home being what they were, there was a growing tendency among Sicilians to feel that the war was largely over. But for the Eighth Army this was manifestly not so. Under the unremitting July sun four infantry divisions of the Eighth Army marched some forty miles in forty-eight hours after coming ashore.[11]. Kerans's battalion passed through Carlentini and Lentini, where the villagers lined the route and cheered and clapped. Then 'back on the road, hot and weary, up hill and down dale, mile upon mile. Feet raw, bodies too weary to lift them off the ground. Darkness fell, still we marched. The column straggled, the strong carried the rifles of the weak. Had the enemy stopped and given fight we would undoubtedly have got the worst of it. Apart from the fruit we had got at Lentini we had had nothing since early-morning breakfast.' Then they halted. They were some two miles from their next objective, the bridge at Plimsole.

When they came to the river they were met with devastating fire from a German parachute battalion. There was fierce hand-to-hand fighting with rifles and bayonets. This continued throughout the day. The river was crossed, and the Durhams continued to advance under constant shell-fire. In the engagement the 151st Brigade of the 50th Division, consisting of three battalions of the Durham Light Infantry, lost approximately one-third of its total strength.[12]

During the following night there was a pause, and Kerans and another man were sent searching for water. In the moonlight they found a huge barn. 'The floor,' he wrote, 'was six inches deep in liquid. We tasted it and found it was *vino*. There, wrecked by the enemy, were huge vats with the bungs knocked out. . . . We had half filled our can from one that had a little left in when suddenly there was a snore. We dropped the tin and pointed our weapons at a very, very drunken goat staggering round in the corner.'

In a letter to John Harding, who was still recovering from the wounds he had received in North Africa, Montgomery wrote: 'The initial phase was an unqualified success. The enemy was thrown off his balance by the strength, speed and violence of our attack and it took him some time to recover.'[13]

With the capture of Syracuse, which was effected without serious fighting, the Eighth Army reached its first European city of importance.[14] Although there had been some Allied bombing, the destruction within the city was not great. Loss of life too was limited, partly by the very antiquity of the town, which had been described by Livy as the noblest and most beautiful of Greek cities. Established by the Greeks as a colony in the eighth century BC, at one time it had had about half a million inhabitants.[15] In the process of discovering its past glories a number of catacombs came to light, and these in 1943 provided the inhabitants of Syracuse with excellent ready-made shelters.

One of the exceptional features of the Syracuse region is the presence of the papyrus, which does not grow elsewhere in Europe. Libraries at one time depended on the papyrus for their books, and it may well be that its cultivation was an important factor in making Syracuse, the city of Archimedes, one of the world's great centres of learning.[16]

To the north-west of Syracuse lies the large harbour of Augusta. This was captured through a raid mounted by the SAS.[17] The seizure of the two ports enabled the Eighth Army to receive not only supplies but also reinforcements of manpower, and on 20 July Montgomery decided to bring over a whole division, the 78th, from Sousse.[18] Horrocks's 10 Corps still remained in reserve in the Tripoli area.[19]

Sicily is a dry, rugged and largely mountainous island. The only flat area of any size on the Eighth Army's route through it is the Catania plain, which lies to the south of Mount Etna, and even this is no more than about twenty kilometres long and about twenty-five kilometres wide. The longest river on the island is the Simeto, which enters the sea a little south of Catania. It is reputed to have pieces of amber floating along it from time to time, though there is no record of any of this being picked up by Eighth Army troops.[20]

On 17 July a plan to attack Catania, which was strongly held by German forces, was abandoned. Instead Montgomery decided to advance to the Simeto and establish bridgeheads across it before attacking Paterno and Enna.[21] After that the Army would be confronted by the prospect of Mount Etna.

The Canadians, given the specific task of capturing Enna, were now heavily involved in the fighting. Of them Montgomery wrote to Brook: 'The Canadians are going great guns; they are very willing to learn and they learn very fast; they will be one of the best Divisions I have in due course.'

To Alexander he wrote shortly afterwards that it was 'definitely the wish of every officer and man in Canadian formations that they should be a part of 8 Army and known as such.' He had high praise for their commander, Guy Simonds, and quoted a Canadian officer as saying that because Canadians felt themselves so strongly to be part of the Eighth Army 'the glory of El Alamein and Mareth' was already their own.[22] All this did not prevent Montgomery from offending, indeed insulting, the Canadian Army Commander, General Andrew McNaughton, by not allowing him to visit his troops in Sicily. It was one of many examples of how he could let his military principles, which included an understandable dislike of battlefield visitors, override his political obligations.

A new affliciton from which the Eighth Army now began to suffer was malaria. This had begun to affect disturbingly large numbers, as had dysentery. In spite of this morale remained high.

Dress continued to be eccentric. On one occasion Montgomery came across a soldier driving an Army lorry and wearing a silk hat. With this the driver made a graceful sweep by way of saluting his Army Commander. Montgomery enjoyed the incident, and it prompted him to issue the only order on the subject of dress the Eighth Army ever received from him. It read: 'Top hats will not be worn in the Eighth Army.'[23]

Much of eastern Sicily is dominated by Mount Etna, the highest mountain in the island and the highest volcano in Europe. The Greeks believed it to have been either the mountain with which Zeus crushed the giant Typhon or the workshop of the Cyclopes. Its crater has long had a fascination for would-be suicides. The highest slopes of Etna are perpetually covered in snow. Sicily is therefore one of those scenically favoured Mediterranean regions in which it is possible to see snow and the flowering bougainvillaea at the same time. (No less memorably, I have myself observed in Sicily mimosa and poppies growing side by side and both in bloom.)

The volcanic lava of Etna has a fertilising effect. On the coastal strip to the east of the mountain the flourishing orchards of peaches and apricots contrast strongly with the rocky soil further south. On the slopes of the mountain itself the Etna violet peeps out from among the holy thorn.

The most disagreeable feature of Etna is the emission of sulphur fumes. In the heat of summer these, combined with the prevalent white dust, parched the throats of troops and even penetrated the handkerchiefs which they wore over their mouths.[24] The lava beds at times distorted the working of military compasses.[25]

Sicilian peasants do not normally live in the countryside, but gather together in small towns of more than a thousand inhabitants, a practice which is primarily a response to the long-standing dangers of banditry.[26] A number of these small towns lay in the path of the Eighth Army as it approached the Germans' defensive line based on the slopes of Mount Etna. They included Catenuova, Centùripe and Adrano.

Catenuova was captured by the Canadians on 30 July. Centùripe, which came to be known to Eighth Army troops as *Cherry Ripe*, is a natural fortress. Lawrence Durrell wrote of it: 'Centùripe with its jutting jaw and bronzed limestone – an immense calm necropolis where the rock for hundreds of yards was pitted like a lung with excavated tombs.'[27] There are indeed a number of caves near the road which links Catenuova and Centùripe. These were used by the Germans as defensive positions. It was extremely difficult to flush the Germans out, and after darkness they emerged to launch powerful counter-attacks, particularly against a battalion of the East Surrey Regiment.

The East Surreys were part of the 78th Division, which was now in action. Opposing it were German troops of the highest quality belonging to the Hermann Goering Division and the 3rd Parachute Regiment.

Centùripe is approached by a narrow, winding road along the side of a nearly vertical ridge. The road was everywhere visible from the hills above, where the Germans were installed. Around Centùripe itself the land is steeply terraced. At various points the road had been mined and breached, and ambushes had been prepared. The division had recently acquired mules for carrying equipment, but they were not yet properly trained.[28] The final approaches to Centùripe were too difficult even for mules, and troops had therefore to go in carrying everything they needed for close combat. Such was the effect of the sulphurous fumes from Etna that men needed to carry two full water-bottles each.[29]

The Divisional Commander, Major-General Evelegh, decided on a night attack. Centùripe was entered on the night of 1–2 August, but the Germans occupied the town in such strength that they forced an Allied withdrawal at first light.

In the initial attack the Irish Brigade of the 78th Division

A Polish soldier, British, Indian, Australian and a Czech soldier at Tobruk.

Men of the Long Range Desert Group, who operated far behind the enemy lines reporting enemy troop movements by radio.

New Zealand's Major General Bernard Freyberg, who was awarded the Victoria Cross in World War I, when he received twenty-seven wounds. In World War II he received three more — and further decorations.

Surrender of crew of knocked-out German tank to British infantry at Battle of Alamein.

Axis tanks in the desert showing how desert warfare sometimes resembled a naval battle.

Winston Churchill in Tripoli. The one occasion on which the Eighth Army appeared in impeccable parade-ground style.

Mussolini's Arco dei Fileni which marked the border of Tripolitania and Cyrenaica and was known to the Eighth Army as Marble Arch.

Graves of a Scottish soldier and an officer marked by tin hat and balmoral on their upturned rifles.

Sapper John Mckay of Sheffield (*above*) and two of his mates examining mines at Mareth.

Gurkhas brandishing their traditional knives, the Khurkis, at Medenine.

Kukris,

General Montgomery in a tank tunnel wearing his Tank Corps beret during the pursuit through North Africa.

had been held in reserve. It was now committed, and on 3 August the 6th Battalion of the Royal Inniskilling Fusiliers entered Centúripe and held it. Montgomery described its capture as 'a feat which will live in the annals of British arms', a comment treasured by the regimental historian alongside the Duke of Wellington's statement that at Waterloo it was the Inniskillings who saved the centre of his line.[30]

Adrano is another fortress town, with a castle built in the eleventh century by Roger I, the Norman ruler of Sicily. There was more prolonged fighting before it was captured on the night of 6–7 August. On 8 August Bronte too was captured. This small town gave its name to the dukedom which Ferdinand IV, King of Naples and Sicily, conferred on Nelson in gratitude for services rendered.

While determinedly defending the approaches to Etna the Germans decided to withdraw their forces from Catania, and on 5 August the town was captured without opposition.[31] This made another port available to Allied shipping.

Catania, Sicily's second largest city, grew up in the shadow of Mount Etna – almost, it might be said, in defiance of it. Etna was indeed at one time the city's name, and in 1669 an eruption from the volcano virtually filled its harbour.

TO THE STRAITS OF MESSINA

While the Eighth Army was advancing slowly north and north-east the US Seventh Army had the task of moving up the western side of the island. This it did with considerable speed assisted by excellent political intelligence, for an appreciable proportion of the American invading forces – possibly as high as 15 per cent – was of Sicilian origin.[1] This not only facilitated negotiations, often with representatives of the Mafia, for large-scale desertions from the Italian armed forces; it also helped to establish good personal relations between an invading army and the local population.

For the most part American troops were more popular in Sicily than those of the English Army. Many of them had direct family ties. Their general outlook and conduct seemed more easily comprehensible. Aldo Bonaventura, who as a young man worked for the Eighth Army in Taormina in a fairly general capacity, summed up certain differences when, speaking of British troops, he said to me: 'At first they seemed so stiff. They didn't even move their hands when they spoke.'

All Allied troops were nominally under the ban known as non-fraternisation with the enemy. In Italy this was manifestly unworkable, for no man with normal feelings could possibly avoid all contact with people who greeted him with wine and flowers, and whose dark-eyed and underfed children pleaded appealingly for chocolate.

At a high-level conference on the non-fraternisation policy Patton delivered himself of the judgement that 'fornication ain't fraternisation, not if you keep your hat on.'[2] There do not seem to have been any dissenting opinions.

The further moves of Patton's army towards and into Palermo were facilitated by the German decision, made known to the Allies through Ultra, to concentrate all forces in the north-east corner of Italy. Patton himself described the advance to Palermo as 'the fastest *Blitzkrieg* in history', but in reality there was some *Blitz* but very little *Krieg*.

Patton's fame and that of the man to whom he had handed over command of the US Second Corps in North Africa, Omar Bradley, rests rightly on their achievements in northern Europe. The advance to Palermo was little more than an exercise in political intelligence and logistics.

Montgomery, for his part, had come to the conclusion that the capture of Adrano was the key which would open the door to fairly rapid advance. 'When I get to that place,' he wrote to Harding, 'the Bosche will be in queer street.'[3] His judgement was proved right. By 14 August, a week after Adrano had been taken, the Germans had broken off all contact and begun their final retreat from Sicily. On 15 August troops of the 50th Division entered Taormina.

So enchanted was Montgomery with the sight of Taormina that he departed from his hitherto invariable practice of living in austere surroundings, and established himself in a luxurious villa with a spectacular outlook from the cliff-top over the Ionian Sea. He was by no means the first Englishman to be captivated by Taormina's charms. Nelson succumbed too. D.H. Lawrence occupied a villa in Taormina for some three years. Lawrence Durrell described it as 'anchored in mid-heaven'.[4]

Many of the fine gardens surrounding the villas perched on Taormina's cliffside were laid out by the British.[5] British residents had also contributed to giving Taormina the reputation of being uncommonly permissive in comparison with the rest of Sicily. Montgomery himself described it rather more sedately as being 'famous as a resort for honeymoon couples'.[6]

With its medieval streets, its splendid Greco-Roman theatre, the snow-covered summit of Etna visible nearly everywhere and, some hundreds of metres below, the sea and the sands where Naxos once stood, Taormina was a startling contrast with anything men of the Eighth Army had yet seen in Sicily. Moreover it was largely free from the rubble and devastation which had generally marked the Army's progress.

On 17 August advance patrols of the Eighth Army and of the US Seventh Army entered Messina almost simultaneously.

Messina, the setting of Shakespeare's *Much Ado About Nothing*, has a history of destruction and resurgence even more comprehensive than that of Catania. Time and again a fine city was destroyed by earthquake. The worst of these occurred on 28 December, 1908, when within thirty seconds some 60,000 people were killed. About 90 per cent of the buildings were wholly or partly destroyed. The people of Messina thereupon set about the work of reconstruction, using, as in Catania, such façades of churches and other outstanding buildings as had been spared. In World War II Messina was a destroyer and submarine base for the Axis powers. In consequence a new devastation was perpetrated, and when the Eighth Army entered the city it was largely rubble.

However depressing the sight of the city may have been, the view from the harbour remained spectacular. For the Eighth Army it was also daunting, with towering mountains, manifestly formidable obstacles, dominating the straits from the mainland.

On 17 August 1943 Hitler had created a new German Army, the Tenth, incorporating all the German forces in central and southern Italy. In command of this was Heinrich von Vietinghoff, who was directly responsible to Kesselring.[7]

The conquest of Sicily had been completed in thirty-eight days. After the initial airborne landings, in which the burden had been fairly evenly shared between the invading forces, the Eighth Army had had to do virtually all the severe fighting. Of its performance its commander wrote:

> The Eighth Army had been born, trained and grown to manhood in the North African deserts and it was a great source of satisfaction to me that it adapted itself so readily to the very different conditions prevailing in Sicily. This confirmed my view that once a fighting machine has been trained thoroughly in the basic principles of warfare, it will have no great difficulty in operating successfully in whatever conditions of climate and terrain it may have to face.[8]

Of the part played by one of the constituent parts of the Eighth Army, the 23rd Armoured Brigade, its historian, Captain M.A. Ash, wrote: 'Sicily was the hardest, the bloodiest and, above all, the most disillusioning campaign in which the brigade had served during the war.'[9]

For the Canadians too it had been a hard campaign. Out of an initial strength of 11,843 men, 2,310 – that is to say nearly one in five – were casualties.[10]

German casualties were also heavy, amounting to some 37,000 men. But once again the Germans carried out a retreat with skill and discipline. From the way in which they did so it became apparent that in Albert Kesselring, Luftwaffe General, who had earlier been given the principal airman's role in the attack on the Soviet Union, the Allies faced a supreme commander who was no less resourceful than Rommel.[11]

Kesselring was later to state that, in contrast with the British evacuation at Dunkirk, he had brought out over the Straits of Messina to the Italian mainland all serviceable material of value as well as complete German formations.[12] In the face of the Allies' superiority in the air this was a considerable achievement. It was made positive by a deplorable lack of coordination of the Allies' naval, air and military forces.

On 3 September 1943, not long after the fighting in Sicily had come to an end, a meeting took place in an olive grove near Syracuse which was to have an important influence on the future conduct of the war.

The government which King Victor Emmanuel had entrusted to Badoglio had begun encouragingly by dissolving the Fascist Party and abolishing the Fascist Grand Council. This strengthened Churchill in his belief that it was a government he could deal with and that it would be right to respond to the requests for an armistice which were secretly being conveyed. 'Disregarding etiquette,' as he explained to Roosevelt, he sent appropriate messages to the King through Switzerland.[13]

Negotiations were conducted mainly in Portugal, but they were hampered for a time by the lack of any direct means of communication between Badoglio and the Allied High Command. This difficulty was largely overcome as a result of a suggestion made by Commander Gerard Holdsworth, who was in charge of the Special Operations Executive's activities in Italy, and who later told me the full story.

A young wireless operator named Dick Mallaby, who was half British and half Italian, had been parachuted into northern Italy in order to make contact with resistance forces. He had landed in a lake and been captured, and Mussolini's government had planned to execute him with full publicity. Mallaby, whom I had known in Palestine, where he instructed agents in radio-telephony, had a pleasant, gentle, almost lackadaisical manner. I doubt whether he showed any emotion when learning that he had been condemned to death.

Mussolini's fall saved Mallaby, and Holdsworth suggested

he should now act as Badoglio's wireless operator, using the radio, ciphers and crystals he had taken with him. This was arranged; negotiations continued; and the Allies' armistice terms were fully accepted.

At the meeting in the olive grove near Syracuse, General Castellano, one of Badoglio's principal military supporters, signed the documents of the negotiated surrender. It was agreed that the terms should be kept secret until after Allied landings had taken place further north.

The date, 3 September 1943, was the fourth anniversary of the day on which Britain had entered World War II. At the end of four years one of her enemies had been defeated, largely by the Eighth Army.

PART FIVE:
THE ITALIAN MAINLAND

(September 1943–May 1945)

LANDINGS ON THE MAINLAND

The Straits of Messina, which divide Sicily from the mainland of Italy, are at their narrowest point only about three kilometres wide.

Although the setting is one of extraordinary beauty, the straits have long had a sinister reputation. On two of the rocks, one on each side of the channel, the sea monsters Scylla and Charybdis were thought to have dwelt. Charybdis, whose home was on the Sicilian side and who sucked in and spouted out water three times a day, snatched six men out of Ulysses's ship. Scylla, who dwelt on the mainland side, had six heads and yelped like a puppy. Travellers in more recent times have seen strange shapes, suggestive of palaces, rising out of the water.[1]

The Eighth Army was assigned the task of landing after crossing the straits, but the operation was regarded to some extent as a subsidiary thrust. Another assault, under American command, was to be made in the Bay of Salerno south of Naples, and this was given priority in the allocation of resources.

In normal conditions train ferries regularly cross between the port of Messina and the mainland terminals of Villa San Giovanni and Reggio di Calabria, a distance of some eight kilometres. In an appreciation prepared for the Eighth Army it was stated that if all these ferries could be put into operation they could transfer some two to three divisions a week.[2]

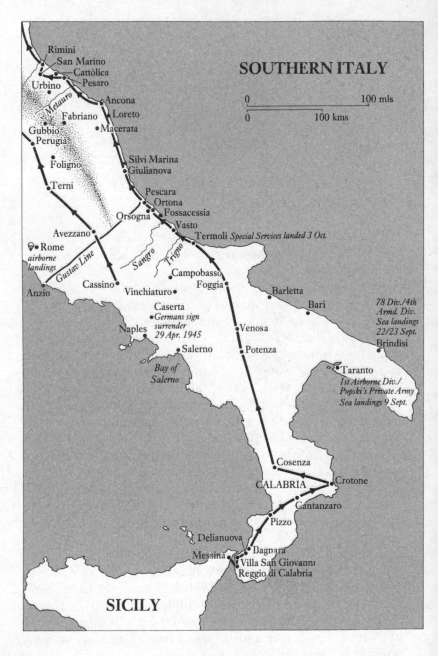

SOUTHERN ITALY

0   100 mls

0   100 kms

Rimini
San Marino
Cattòlica
Pesaro
Urbino
Metauro
Ancona
Fabriano
Loreto
Macerata
Gubbio
Perugia
Foligno
Silvi Marina
Giulianova
Terni
Pescara
Ortona
Orsogna
Fossacessia
Avezzano
Vasto
Rome
airborne
landings
Termoli *Special Services landed 3 Oct.*
Gustav Line
Sangro
Trigno
Cassino
Campobasso
Anzio
Vinchiaturo
Foggia
Barletta
Caserta
*Germans sign
surrender
29 Apr. 1945*
Bari
*78 Div./4th
Armd. Div.
Sea landings
22/23 Sept.*
Naples
Venosa
Brindisi
Salerno
Potenza
*Bay of
Salerno*
Taranto
*1st Airborne Div./
Popski's Private Army
Sea landings 9 Sept.*

Cosenza
Crotone
CALABRIA
Cantanzaro
Pizzo
Delianuova
Bagnara
Messina
Villa San Giovanni
Reggio di Calabria

SICILY

Because of the shortage of vessels and the time needed to bring the port of Messina into full operation it was estimated that the Eighth Army would be able to employ only two infantry divisions, which would be reinforced by one armoured brigade, one infantry brigade and some commando units. Montgomery considered this inadequate and made a strong protest. As a result the shipping resources allotted to him were slightly increased.[3]

Allied strategy in the Mediterranean theatre of war was at this time largely determined by the availability of shipping, particularly of vessels from which men and equipment could be landed. Not long after the landings on the Italian mainland Churchill was to telegraph General George C. Marshall, the United States Chief of Staff, on the subject of tank landing craft: 'How it is that the plans of two great empires like Britain and the United States should be so hamstrung and limited by a hundred or two of these particular vessels will never be understood by history.'[4]

The Eighth Army was now temporarily reduced to two corps, the 13th and 30th. The third, 10 Corps, had been placed under the command of the man who was to be in charge of the landings at Salerno, the American Lieutenant General Mark W. Clark, who had replaced Patton and whose command was now known as the United States Fifth Army. Clark's army and Montgomery's were to act largely independently of each other under the sometimes nominal control of Alexander, whose command came to be known variously as the Allied Armies in Italy and the 15th Army group.

Before the crossings were made the Eighth Army does not seem to have been as well informed as it usually was, through Ultra, of German intentions. Montgomery sent some reconnaissance parties across the straits, and they returned with the information that Italian soldiers were deserting and joining civilians who had taken to the hills to avoid the impending battle.[5] He was not altogether satisfied with this information and decided it would be prudent to

follow established practice and carry out a heavy bombardment of Reggio before any landings were attempted. Considerable damage was in consequence inflicted on the town.
In the course of the bombardment a number of animals
escaped from a zoo, including a puma and a monkey, both
of which later attacked Canadian soldiers.[6]

Landings took place near Reggio on 3 September, the day
of the signing of the armistice. The weather was fine, and
the sea was calm. Few of the assault troops landed at the
right time or on the right beaches, but as there was no
opposition this was of little account.[7] Reggio itself was taken
without difficulty, and the 3rd Canadian Brigade consoli-
dated its position.

The landings whereby the Eighth Army first reached the
continent of Europe were in fact among the easiest tasks
which it had had to perform. Nevertheless, as the troops
advanced, they quickly had foretastes of the natural obstacles which would confront them on the Italian mainland.

On this south-western extremity of the toe of Italy deep
gorges, whose sides are almost perpendicular, separate a
long succession of hills. There are after a time, I noticed, as
I drove along, rocky outcrops with little growing except
cactus and gorse. There is thickly wooded country providing
excellent cover for defending forces, and even where the
countryside becomes a little gentler it is still one of hills and
valleys. Then, as the road continues north, the hills become
even steeper, the few villages being barely distinguishable
from the hills on which they are perched, for both village
and hill are formed from the same stone.

There was already in 1943 plenty of evidence of the skills
with which latter-day Italians, following the tradition of the
ancient Romans, have constructed roads. Spanning gorges,
as they did, these roads clearly invited the attention of
enemy demolition units. Indeed, before long evidence began
to accumulate that German policy at this stage was to rely
on demolitions rather than rearguard actions to delay the
progress of the Eighth Army.

That demolition had been skilfully carried out was soon apparent. In an attempt to maintain contact with the enemy and ascertain his strength, a battalion of Princess Patricia's Canadian Light Infantry pressed forward towards Delia-nuova, some twenty-five kilometres north of Reggio. But although the brigade's transport had been safcly landed, demolitions prevented it from being brought up, and the troops advanced on foot until some enterprising men found an abandoned Italian quartermaster's store with a large number of bicycles. They then hauled these up the sides of ravines, and it was on requisitioned Italian bicycles that the first Canadian troops entered Delianuova.[8]

To speed up the advance, landings were made by Eighth Army units at Bagnara, a village which claims the remark-able distinction of possessing the authentic hat of the Virgin Mary, and at Pizzo, a little further to the north. At Pizzo a small but well-organised German rearguard resisted effec-tively for a time.

An early objective of the Eighth Army was the capture of Catanzaro, which is built on top of a precipitous cliff and dominates the narrowest neck of the land between the Ionian Sea and the western Mediterranean. This neck, which is a little over thirty kilometres wide, takes the form of a plain dividing two mountainous regions, one to the south and the other to the north. Catanzaro was found to be undefended, and it now became clear to Montgomery that the Germans had abandoned the extreme south of Italy. He therefore decided to press on and capture the port of Crotone and some airfields in the plain which could accommodate the Royal Air Force.[9]

Crotone, which was taken on 9 September, was once the Greek city of Croton, renowned for its medical school, its athletes and the beauty of its girls. Local models were said to have been used for a painting of Helen of Troy.[10]

Apart from the enthusiastic welcome they continued to receive, Eighth Army troops found little in the villages of Calabria to attract them. The traveller today may not

deviate greatly from this judgement, for the region is one
which impresses mostly because of its coastline and hills.
For centuries it was little known to the outside world.
Perhaps the best writer in English on Calabria was Norman
Douglas, the lustful former diplomat at the Court of St
Petersburg. His *Old Calabria* was first published in 1915. In
it he wrote: 'I have not yet encountered a single English
traveller, during my frequent wanderings over South
Italy. . . The adventurous type of Anglo-Saxon probably
thinks the country too tame; scholars, too trite; ordinary
tourists, too dirty.'

In the three-quarters of a century which followed changes
were much less than might have been expected, and it is one
of the stranger phenomena of the modern tourist industry
that the extreme south-west coast of the mainland of Italy
has still largely evaded its clutches.

The September weather in the Calabrian mountains was
a refreshing contrast with the July heat of Sicily. There were
Canadians who found it reminded them of eastern Canada
in late autumn, and in the evenings they also found that
their khaki drill shirts and shorts gave little protection
against the cold. Some thereupon showed how fully they
had accepted Eighth Army views on what constituted pro-
priety in dress by appearing in warmer, heavier black cotton
shirts. These had come from the same quartermaster's store
as the bicycles used for entering Delianuova, and had been
intended as uniform wear by members of the Italian Fascist
party.[11]

Progress continued for a time to be largely unopposed,
for the German commander von Vietinghoff was primarily
concerned with the threat presented by the landings at
Salerno. One consequence of this was that, for the first time
since it began to operate in conjunction with Allied formations, the Eighth Army had an easier passage than its allies.

The Salerno landings began six days after the crossing of
the Straits of Messina. The original plan had included an
airborne drop near Rome. The abandonment of this enabled

the Germans to confront the forces landed at Salerno in strength; for some time the outcome of the ensuing battle was in doubt, and plans for the evacuation of the Allied force were even drawn up a week after the landings.

But the bridgehead was held, and by the first week in October the Germans had come to the conclusion that they could not inflict a defeat. They therefore decided to make their next stand along a line south of Rome.[12]

Of the troops, numbering nearly 170,000 who took part in the Salerno landings, about 100,000 were British.[13] Nevertheless – and in spite of the participation of 10 Corps, for long an integral part of the Eighth Army – the landings and the battle which followed cannot properly be considered a part of the annals of the Eighth Army. Similarly neither Salerno nor Naples, to which Salerno was the gateway, can be regarded as having been on the Eighth Army's route. The involvement of the Eighth Army was only as a means of relieving pressure on those landed on the Salerno front.

ADVANCE INTO APULIA

Between the signing of the armistice near Syracuse and the landings at Salerno secret negotiations, of which General Eisenhower was in charge, had continued with the new Italian Government, and Eisenhower came to the conclusion that Badoglio was sincere in his desire to help the Allies, an opinion with which Churchill concurred.[1]

In spite of having been Governor-General of Libya and Commander-in-Chief of operations in Abyssinia Badoglio had shown some resistance to Mussolini. He had for instance resigned from his post as Chief of Staff following the disastrous Italian campaign in Greece, to which he had been opposed.

Eisenhower's opinion, which met with the approval of the American, British and Soviet governments, was that Italy should be given the status of co-belligerent or, as it might less tactfully be rendered, an ally which must do as it was told. In this way some useful additions could be made to the Allies' armed strength. In southern Italy there were three Italian divisions, admittedly rather ill-equipped, as well as naval and air forces.

The Allies' proposals, which included the requirement that Italy should declare war on Germany, were conveyed in detail to Badoglio on 27 September. Other conditions were that the Italian government should be anti-Fascist and that the Italian people should have the right to choose their

own form of government once the enemy had been driven
out of Italy. Meanwhile military and, to some extent,
political control would be exercised by the Allies' Supreme
Commander.

Badoglio accepted the terms, and on 29 September 1943
he and Eisenhower signed what was known as the 'comprehensive instrument of surrender' on board HMS *Nelson* in
Malta. An Italian military mission to Eisenhower's headquarters was brought into being, and on 13 October Italy
formally declared war on Germany. The Italian military
formations, now on the Allied side, were at first given the
task of guarding lines of communcations.

In the implementation of all these changes the position of
the King, insignificant though he was as an individual, was
of major importance. The Italian armed forces had taken an
oath of loyalty not to Mussolini but to the Crown, so they
were not in breach of that oath when they came out on the
side of the Allies. This was in clear contrast with what had
been happening in Vichy France where, since the government of Marshal Pétain had evident claims to legitimacy,
members of the French armed forces who turned against
him did so in defiance of an oath to which many of them
attached grave importance.

An indication of the willingness of members of the Italian
armed forces to break away from the alliance with Germany
is to be had from the figures of prisoners of war taken by
the Eighth Army. During the fortnight following the landings in the Reggio area on 3 September these amounted to
19,325, of whom eighty-five were German.[2]

The seat of the new Italian Government was for a time in
Brindisi, to which its members had been brought, first by
fishing boats from the small port of Ortona and then by
naval vessels.[3]

Brindisi and Taranto are both major ports, and largely as
a result of secret negotiations with the Italian authorities
both were secured without effective opposition. The 1st
Airborne Divison began landing at Taranto from naval

vessels on 9 September and thereupon came under Eighth Army command.[4]

Another unit which landed unopposed at Taranto was Popski's Private Army, whose reputation had been growing and which was now widely considered a desirable body to join. Peniakoff interviewed every volunteer personally and accepted about seven out of a hundred. He also introduced before long his own rules concerning the growing of beards. This, he decided, was to be a privilege only of men who had been in at least five actions.[5]

Taranto had been the scene of an important British naval victory early in the war, when on the night of 11–12 November 1940 aircraft of the Fleet Air Arm attacked a group of Italian ships there, damaging two battleships, two cruisers and two auxiliary vessels.

There was at one time a common disease among the people of Taranto, which was probably of hysterical origin and which became known as tarantism. One of its symptoms was a tendency to dance, and the belief grew up that the best means of working the disease out of the system was to dance as strenuously as possible. Hence the name of the *tarantella*, an exercise in which the dancers whirl around at high speed.[7] The people of Taranto have another considerable claim to distinction, for they are reputed to have imported the cat into Europe.

Bari is the third port which, together with Brindisi and Taranto, forms a triangle in the heel of Italy. Elements of the 78th Division and the 4th Armoured Brigade began landing there on the night of 22–23 September.

Meanwhile the Canadians' advance had continued north in the direction of Potenza, which stands at a height of nearly 1000 metres. On 20 September, as units of the Royal 22ème Régiment began to encircle the town, a troop of the Calgaries entered it, and German resistance soon collapsed.

Potenza, which had a population of about 30,000, was the second town, of any size after Reggio, which the Canadians had encountered on the mainland. After what they had seen in the villages many were surprised by its modern appearance – it had indeed been rebuilt after nearly total destruction by earthquake – and in particular by its possession of a sports stadium. Track events were quickly staged.[8]

In seventeen days from 3 September the Eighth Army advanced about 450 kilometres on the mainland of Italy. The Germans had not only destroyed bridges and viaducts and tunnels, in all of which the mountainous country abounds; they had also ploughed up railway sleepers and destroyed the rails one by one.[9] They had demolished sections of cliff faces along which roads had run, and in the villages they had reduced houses to rubble, which was then used to make roads impassable.[10]

They had to time the work of demolition so that their own troops could retreat in good order, and occasionally they left it too late. When approaching Potenza, for example, the Canadians came upon a party of German engineers who were preparing to destroy a bridge, and were able to drive them off just in time.[11] But in general the work of destruction was skilfully carried out.

To counter it the Eighth Army had one enormously valuable asset. This was the invention of a civil servant in the Ministry of Supply named Donald Bailey. During a journey by car to have a look at a rather unsatisfactory kind of military bridge Bailey, who was travelling with a senior officer in the Royal Engineers, drew on the back of an envelope a sketch of something he thought would be much more efficient. The principle was similar to that of a Meccano set. The Sapper officer was impressed; trials were undertaken; and production began in 1940 in factories which until then had been making greenhouses and bedsteads.

The Bailey bridge consisted of sections each about three metres in length and linked together by a steel pin which locked each joint securely. The number of sections required was dictated by the width of the river to be spanned. The bridge could be assembled on the remains of a demolished bridge or on pontoons. It could also be put together on the river bank on rollers and then pushed across. It was a piece of equipment far superior to anything comparable in the German Army. The bridges had of course often to be put into position under enemy fire, but the speed of their erection was remarkable.[12]

Within a few months of landing on the mainland of Italy Royal Engineers of the Eighth Army were to establish a Bailey bridge some 400 metres in length, or the equivalent of four football pitches. It spanned the River Sangro and was at the time the longest Bailey bridge in the world.

13

THE FOGGIA PLAIN

To the north of Potenza, in the area traversed by the Ofanto river, the countryside becomes flatter. This is the approach to the Foggia plain, and in 1943 the region was still manifestly a part of the poverty-stricken south. This impression of pervading poverty was accentuated by the sight of the civilian population on the move, women in black carrying bundles of what they had been able to salvage from their ruined homes, children, old men, donkeys, trudging patiently along the roads.

They had escaped from the Allied bombing or from villages commandeered or blown up by the Germans or from battlefields. Alternatively they might be going to friends or relations who lived in the country and would be willing to share with them such food as could be produced. The general impression was of a population of destitute gypsies.

I vividly recall a journey I made by jeep between Bari and Naples during the war. The evidence of poverty was deeply depressing. Then suddenly the main street began to fill with a procession to mark some saint's day. Now there was colour, life, pageantry, music, flowers, smiles, tangible ecclesiastical riches. Drabness was banished.

Another of my wartime memories is of a different kind of village procession. On this occasion the population had turned out to greet an American soldier, who was deemed to have come home. Grandmothers were weeping and children were skipping. The most significant feature of the event was that the soldier was at least a head taller and far more strongly built that any of those – a number of them clearly his blood-relations – who had stayed behind in Italy.

The airfields in the Foggia area had been regarded from the outset as one of the most important prizes that an invasion of the mainland of Italy could offer. From there bomber aircraft could reach such targets as the Romanian oilfields as well as factories in southern Germany and Austria, while avoiding the huge concentration of anti-aircraft guns and fighter planes which the Germans had assembled in the west.

Foggia itself, yet another town with a history of destruction by earthquake, was captured on 27 September, but before the airfields could be safeguarded further advances were necessary.[1]

On 3 October a Special Service Brigade of Army and Marine Commandos was landed at Termoli together with a raiding squadron of the SAS. Immediately it became clear that the point at which the Germans would offer determined resistance had been reached. Powerful counter-attacks were launched, and for four days there was intense fighting. Then the Germans withdrew. A German document which the SAS captured stated that Termoli was to be retaken at all costs and that the British were to be driven into the sea.[2] That this never occurred was an important victory for the landing party.

With the Eighth Army's line now secured from Termoli south-west through Campobasso to Vinchiaturo the airfields were, in Montgomery's judgement, secure.[3] Some pressure had also been taken off the Fifth Army, for as a result of the landings at Termoli a panzer division, which had been held in reserve in the Naples area, was rushed to the east coast.[4] Even so, with the knowledge that German resistance could now be expected everywhere, Montgomery decided to pause until he was satisfied that his supplies would support further advances and heavy fighting.

More formations could now be brought into action. These included the 8th Indian Division commanded by Major-General Russell, which had arrived in Italy on 24 September. Most of its battalions had seen service in the Western Desert and, earlier, in East Africa, but as a divisional formation it was new.

By 22 October Montgomery decided he had sufficient resources to attack across the river Trigno, the most formidable river obstacle the Eighth Army had yet encountered in Italy. For much of the year the water is about thirty to forty metres wide, but after autumn rains it can be as wide as a hundred metres, and it was now autumn. The escarpment is at some points thirty to forty metres high.

The battle of the River Trigno was fiercely contested. It began on the night of 22–23 October, when the Royal Irish Fusiliers sent two companies to try to form a bridgehead and discovered the bridge blown and a gap of some seventy metres in its place. It ended effectively with the capture of Vasto and Cupello by the 78th Division.[5] Of Cupello an official report stated: 'This small town, high above the battlefields, had been regarded as the keystone of the defence of this coastal region. Civilian casualties were high and it was a long time before the area could be cleared or regarded as hygienic.'[6]

While the battle was still taking place Montgomery expressed concern about the Eighth Army's lack of reinforcements in Italy, paricularly of infantry officers. 'My Army,' he wrote, 'was launched to the attack of the Trigno position last night with some battalions as low as 17 officers, and there is not one single infantry officer replacement on the mainland. Some drastic action would seem to be indicated.'[7]

This was not Montgomery's only cause for concern. The advantage which the terrain had given to the defenders, even when they were in full retreat, had been apparent, and it was not difficult to envisage how an enemy who had taken up a strong defensive position could benefit. There was also the prospect of winter in territory where mountains predominate and snow lies deeply. The campaign in which the Eighth Army had been engaged on the mainland had, up to this point, been unquestionably successful. Yet already its commander had begun to doubt whether he knew exactly what his army in Italy was expected to accomplish. These doubts were to be relevant to the whole future conduct of the Italian campaign.

14

THE LAST BATTLE UNDER MONTGOMERY

The Allies' campaign in Italy suffered continually from differences between American and British political and strategic thinking.

Soon after the United States had been brought into the war by the Japanese attack on Pearl Harbor in December 1941, Roosevelt decided that priority must be given to the campaign to defeat Germany. This the British welcomed as indicating both breadth of vision and generosity. It was in the interpretation of Roosevelt's policy that the differences arose. The United States Chief of Staff took it to mean that the invasion of northern France should be launched as soon as possible and that other campaigns in Europe were, at best, diversions. Churchill had other views.

'Great prizes,' he informed Alexander, 'lie in the Balkan direction.'[1] Some of these prizes were political gains for the future, in which neither Roosevelt nor the United States Chiefs of Staff showed much interest. But Churchill could also see major current military advantages emerging from an Italian campaign. In particular he placed great hopes in the Allied landings which were planned to take place at Anzio, to the south of Rome, in January 1944. These, he believed, could before long enable the Allies to deploy large forces in northern Italy and even oblige the Germans to withdraw beyond the Alps.

For this to happen, as Churchill appreciated, United States policy would have to be modified. In warning Alan Brooke of the dangers of weakening the Allied forces on the Italian front, he wrote: 'It is not right to pillage the Mediterranean by pulling out all the plums. We must not become more Yankee than the Americans.' Soon after writing this he had to resist an American proposal to establish a purely defensive front in Italy and transfer aircraft from there to China.[2]

In his strategic thinking Montgomery, who paid little attention to long-term political considerations, tended to agree with the Americans in his assessment of the importance of the Italian front. From the outset he regarded the landings in Sicily as a necessary rehearsal for the invasion of Normandy. After reaching the mainland he wrote to Brooke: 'It is a mistake to drive the German armies from Italy. I would keep them there, with a hostile population, and difficult communications which we bomb daily. But we must have as much of Italy as we want for our own purposes.'[3]

Churchill's policy and that of the military leaders were both defensible, and this led, perhaps inevitably, to compromise. This was to be reflected in nearly all the major Allied decisions affecting the Italian front during the next two years.

There were also differences between the prevailing American and British attitudes towards Italy's internal problems. Americans tended to believe that the primary British concern was to prop up a discredited monarchy. British observers countered this by stating that the American policy, at least in Sicily, served largely to reinstate and reinvigorate the Mafia. There was some truth in both charges. But in any case, neither policy was necessarily detrimental to the prosecution of the war, and in general, personal relations between American forces in Italy and the Eighth Army were extremely cordial. Having served with a number of American officers in Italy and been, for some time, a member of an American mess, I know this from first-hand experience.

But the political and military differences at the highest level were never satisfactorily resolved, and they were the cause, not only of some questionable strategic decisions, but also of not a little personal rancour.

As the winter of 1943–1944 approached the main concern of both Eisenhower and Alexander was to make sure that the gains which had been made in Italy were not lost through a German counter-offensive.

At the end of October 1943, the number of Allied divisions in Italy was fourteen. They were initially confronted by nine German divisions, but it was calculated that some fourteen more German divisions were by then in northern Italy, and with their comparatively short lines of supply the Germans could, it was felt, quickly bring numerically superior land forces into action. The Allies would still have control in the air, but Alexander did not rule out the possibility that the Germans would recapture Naples.[4]

Eisenhower too considered the German forces in Italy were more than were needed for merely defensive purposes and for the maintenance of internal order. The conclusion reached from this assessment was that the Allies must continually retain the initiative.[5] In the coming winter this belief was to make heavy demands on the fighting forces.

For the Eighth Army the main objective before winter set in fully was the crossing of the River Sangro, which flows from the Apennines in a north-easterly direction, reaching the sea approximately half-way between Vasto and Ortona. This is the region of the Abruzzi, mountainous territory with numerous rivers and valleys. It has no large towns, and in the thickly wooded areas, in addition to the wild boar, there were still some wolves and even bears. On the mountains snow already lay thickly.

The German defensive strategy was designed to take full advantage of the rivers which run for long stretches through deep ravines. It was based not on a single defensive line, but on a system of positions organised in depth so that any penetrations the Eighth Army made could be quickly sealed off.

The valley of the Sangro seems to the military eye to have been designed by nature for purposes of defence. In the lower reaches of the river the hills to the south fall steeply more than a hundred metres to a narrow plain. To the north, some four or five kilometres from the river, there are hills of similar height and steepness. These provide perfect observation points for artillery. Olive groves and farm buildings could serve as convenient screens.

Montgomery decided to launch his main attack in the coastal area, where he could have the support of naval bombardment. The attack was to be undertaken by 5 Corps under the command of Lieutenant-General Allfrey. Included in the Corps were the 78th Division, which had been almost continuously in action since the landings in Sicily, and the 8th Indian Division. The New Zealand Division, which had arrived in Italy fairly recently, was to operate on their left.[6]

Success, it seemed, might well depend on the continuation of fine weather. This would enable armoured units to operate on firm ground. In fact shortly before mid-November the weather broke. On the 15th rain fell continuously; the river began to rise; and vehicles were bogged down in the approaches. Some patrols succeeded in crossing the river, but were driven back, and then found they could not recross. Sappers who tried to prepare fords found that the approaches were so flooded that hard-core put down before the water had subsided was immediately washed away. As a result of all this, infantry had to spend several days in forward areas without the support of anti-tank guns.

From 20 to 23 November the weather was so bad that no attack of any kind was thought possible. After that there was an improvement, and Allfrey summarised his intentions by stating that he would have to use 'whatever clubs were in the bag'.[7]

The decisive attack began in fine weather at 9.30 on the evening of 28 November. Towards the end of the next day it was clear that the Eighth Army had broken through the enemy line successfully, and Montgomery gave instructions that 78 Division was to clear the coastal village of Fossacesia of Germans and advance north-west to San Vito Chietino. The battle was a hard and costly one. Montgomery was to write of it: 'The Battle of the Sangro was the first real warning given to us that in close and easily defended country we could expect a need for ammunition on a scale far higher than that to which we had been accustomed.'[8]

The River Sangro battle was the last which the Eighth Army was to fight under Montgomery's command. By then he had been chosen to lead another army, which was to land in Normandy in June 1944.

On 30 December Montgomery summoned all the officers and men serving at his headquarters, which was then at Vasto, as well as all corps and divisional commanders, to a meeting at which he took formal leave of them.[9] In a farewell message, which was read out to every unit of the Eighth Army, he stated: 'In all the battles we have fought together we have not had one single failure.' He added that those who formed it had made the Eighth Army 'a household word all over the world'.[10]

In response to the demands of the planners of the invasion of France the Eighth Army was to lose much more than its commander. Formations which had become famous through their part in the desert victories were among those transferred to northern Europe. They included the Desert Rats (the 7th Armoured Division) as well as the 50th (Northumbrian) and the 51st (Highland) Divisions. Of these last two Churchill, in a signal to General Marshall, stated: 'I feel in my marrow the withdrawal of our 50th and 51st divisions, our best. . . We are carrying out our contract, but I pray God it does not cost us dear.'[11]

What Churchill 'felt in his bones' gave rise within certain units of the Eighth Army to tensions, conflicts of loyalty and even mutiny. When men in the 50th and 51st Division learnt that they were to take part in the landings in northern France they received the news without illusions, but in good spirits. In the words of Ernest Kerans, who was one of them, 'five a.m. next morning saw a long, happy, singing, marching gang of men on their way to Tripoli docks, to be picked up by destroyers and anything else the Navy could find.'

At Tripoli disillusion came when certain units were informed they were to be sent to the Salerno front. This meant separation from their own divisions, from, as Kerans put it, 'the community to which they belonged, their familiar officers and comrades of their own units'.

The shock of this was such that there was a widespread refusal to obey orders. In consequence no fewer than 198 non-commissioned officers and men were tried by court martial in October and November 1943, convicted and sentenced to periods of penal servitude of between two and five years. More humiliating than the court martial sentences was the experience of some of the men, who, on being put into a prisoner-of-war camp, were jeered at by German prisoners.

The whole affair was kept secret from the general public and has remained largely unrecorded. It was an indication of the strength of the allegiance men felt towards their own fighting formations, an allegiance which only those who have endured hardships together and seen their companions killed beside them can ever know or even, perhaps, fully understand.

The military authorities had the good sense to suspend the sentences and despatch the men involved to serve as reinforcements to Eighth Army units. In this way Ernest Kerans joined the 5th Battalion of the Northamptonshire Regiment, which formed part of the 78th Division. Before long he and others who had shared some of his experiences

Bailey bridge over river Sangro. This was at the time the longest Bailey bridge in the world. The Bailey bridge was the invention of a British civil servant, Donald Bailey, and was based on the Meccano principle.

On board HMS *Nelson* in Malta. L to R Lord Gort, Air Chief Marshal Tedder, Marshal Badoglio, Lt. Gen. Mason-Macfarlane, Governor and C.-in-C. Gibraltar, General Eisenhower, and General Alexander.

The ruins of the Benedictine abbey on Monastery Hill, Cassino, shortly after capture by Polish troops of the Eighth Army.

Polish Carpathian Brigade near river Senio, one of seven rivers which had to be crossed during the advance on Bologna.

Eighth Army troops
advancing
through the rubble
of a Sicilian village.

Partisans in
Florence firing on
German and Italian
Fascist troops.

Two German officers are escorted back to their lines after negotiating the terms of surrender. They had slowed the British advance by destroying the roads behind them and did not negotiate a surrender until 7 May.

Above: British move into Vienna on 30 July 1945. Behind armoured cars is "Karls" Church.

Right: British get a warm welcome after moving into their Zone of Occupation in the southern sector of Vienna.

were commended by their commanding officer for 'services over and above the call of duty'. He was to take part in the battle of Cassino, was later heavily shelled between San Marino and Imola, and eventually, as he put it, 'sent back to Florence, "bomb-happy".' His was a war of considerable distinction.

Another distinguished formation which was transferred to northern Europe was that of the French forces commanded by General Leclerc. Their journey, which had begun in Chad, was eventually to bring them triumphantly into Paris.

If Montgomery had been given a free hand, he would have taken even more formations with him. He told Brooke that, in his opinion, the New Zealand Division, being highly trained in mobile battle, would be better employed in western Europe than in Italy. This suggestion was not adopted, nor was Montgomery allowed to take all the corps and divisional commanders whom he rated most highly with him. Horrocks did go. So did the Canadian Guy Simonds. But the corps commander for whom he had been unstinted in his praise, Oliver Leese, was not allowed to leave.

As his successor in command of the Eighth Army Montgomery proposed Richard O'Connor, the former commander of the Western Defence Force, who had escaped from a prisoner-of-war camp. Brooke did not agree. Instead it was Leese, the 'big, burly, efficient, solid Guardsman', as Macmillan had described him, who was given the task of succeeding perhaps the most inspiring commander the British Army had known since the days of the Duke of Wellington.

Montgomery was clearly glad to be leaving. In a letter to John Harding he wrote: 'I do not think we can conduct a winter campaign in this country. If I remember right Caesar used to go into winter quarters – a very sound thing to do!!'[12]

For the Eighth Army a new stage in its long journey was beginning, one in which it would gain new strength from experience, acquire new formations from different countries, face new political, administrative and humanitarian problems, achieve new military victories, and witness new manifestations of the best and the worst in the human spirit.

THE IMPACT OF WINTER

The Italian winter came as a shock to most of the Eighth Army. Bad weather had already hampered operations, but it had been in the form of heavy autumn rain. Winter brought new problems.

Cyril Ray, the admirable historian of the 78th Division, was to write: 'The men began to joke bitterly about "sunny Italy" as Moore's men, in their hideous retreat over the snow-clad mountains to Corunna, a century-and-a-half before, had jested about "sunny Spain".' He wondered how it was possible that Englishmen in the twentieth century should have known so little about the climate of another European country. The explanation, he decided, was that peacetime visitors to Italy knew only the big cities and the favoured resorts.[1]

It was soon apparent that the local inhabitants had no illusions about the severity of their winters as they brought out their fur caps and black woollen cloaks. Before long too the Eighth Army talent for improvisation and adaptablity in dress once again became apparent. Desert wear was replaced by flying boots, Syrian sheepskin coats, mufflers and long leather waistcoats.

Montgomery's view on the difficulties of winter campaigning were shared by others. A staff appreciation stated: 'The Adriatic winter is severe; seaborne operations would be uncertain; on land progress would become impossible off the main roads owing to snow and mud; mountain torrents subject to violent fluctuations would create great bridging difficulties and flying would be constantly restricted by low cloud and mist.'[2]

Nevertheless offensive operations continued during the winter. One of these was an assault on Ortona, which was carried out by the Canadians.

Ortona is perched on top of a steep hill with a perfect all-round field of fire. Apart from a winding mountain road, which was easily destroyed, the only approach is up the sheer rock-face. More than a hundred metres below the town is the deep water harbour from which the Italian Government was evacuated to Brindisi.

In the summer of 1988 a leading figure in Italian resistance to the Germans, Francesco Cicoria, took me on a conducted tour of the Ortona region. As we approached the town itself, I wondered, as Horrocks had wondered on seeing Takrouna, how infantrymen, burdened by arms and equipment, could possibly have scrambled up that rock face in such a way that they could join battle with a determined and well organised enemy.

The enemy was, as it happened, exceptionally well prepared and well organised, for the Allies had decided not to subject Ortona, which then had about 10,000 inhabitants, to the kind of preliminary bombardment which had virtually flattened Cupello. The decision was made in the mistaken belief that the Germans would not offer a prolonged defence, and in the hope that the town could serve as a maintenance area and a rest centre for troops during the winter. The port too, it was hoped, could be operated to the Eighth Army's advantage.[3]

In the face of determined German resistance the Canadians fought their way into the outskirts of the town on 20 December. A whole week of house-to-house fighting followed in narrow streets and in solid buildings with thick stone walls. An entire Canadian platoon was killed when a house which it had just occupied blew up.

Ortona, where Canadian troops celebrated Christmas 1943 a little belatedly and in the midst of ruins, is today the site of an impressive Canadian war cemetery. A pictorial war memorial in the centre of the reconstructed town shows civilian fugitives, civilian dead and a soldier of the Eighth Army in tin helmet fighting his way through rubble. Stone walls pock-marked by bullets continue to serve as other memorials.

Much is still remembered and much still spoken about World War II in Italy. But outside Ortona awareness of the major part played by Canadian forces in the Italian campaign seems to be negligible. If their achievements are remembered at all, folk-memory has usually attributed them to the forces of the United States.

A few kilometres inland from Ortona stands the similar hill-town of Orsogna. The New Zealanders forced their way into Orsogna with tanks as well as infantry. In the fighting both on the outskirts and in the town itself they suffered many more casualties than had been expected, and they were eventually forced to withdraw.

A month later, in January, Tuker, commanding an Indian division, sat in his caravan in the grounds of a villa in the Apennines studying 'with distaste', as he afterwards wrote, a plan for the recapture of Orsogna. This, he wrote, 'would entail our fully laden infantry trudging laboriously through thigh-deep snow and soft mud to reach their enemy'. He added: 'There was no feasible way of taking Orsogna till the snow went.'[4]

During the winter of 1943–44 men of the Eighth Army began to be aware of two new factors which would become of increasing military significance in the campaign. One was the presence at large in Italy of thousands of escaped Allied prisoners of war, many of whom had already served in the Eighth Army. The other was the emergence of small Italian partisan bands.

Various Eighth Army units when sending out patrols had good reason to be grateful for the information supplied by

Italian farmers and others about road conditions and German troop movements. From this it was clear that the enthusiastic welcome the Army had received on arrival was now being translated into active help. Further evidence of readiness to help was afforded by the presence of small, irregular units, such as the Maiella Partisan Brigade, which had begun to operate in the mountains to the south and west of Ortona and Orsogna.[5] Much more was to be learnt about both escaped prisoners of war and partisans, and about the interaction of the two, as the campaign progressed.

Among the escaped prisoners to reach Allied lines near the River Sangro was the artist John Verney. He found the Eighth Army had changed much in a year. The cap badges and vehicle signs were different and for a time he had the feeling of being among strangers. This was not surprising in the light of the changes in the formations which constituted the Eighth Army. Yet he also sensed a difference of spirit. 'What was lacking?' he asked. 'Style perhaps? A sort of debonair flourish to its way of life?'[6]

Essentially, nothing may have been lacking, but soldiers are moulded by experience, and battles in the Italian mountains ending in the capture of towns devastated by both Allied and enemy action, with ruined homes and streams of refugees, taught different lessons from those learnt during the advance through indestructible and sparsely inhabited desert.

In the course of the winter the Eighth Army received an addition to its strength which was to prove of the greatest importance. This was the advent of the Polish Second Corps, whose commander Lieutenant-General Wladyslaw Anders, reported to Leese at Vasto on 10 February 1944.

The route by which the Polish army came to southern Italy was extraordinary. After Soviet forces had invaded eastern Poland in 1939 hundreds of thousands of Poles were removed to the Soviet Union, and General Anders, who had been severely wounded when fighting against the Germans, was one of them. He spent some time in the NKVD's notorious Lubianka prison in Moscow. Then suddenly he received a personal visit from Beria, the head of the NKVD, who informed him he was free.[7]

The reason for this change was that General Sikorski, Prime Minister of the Polish Government in exile, had reached an agreement with Stalin that a Polish army should be formed in Russia to fight against the Germans, who were then advancing swiftly in the direction of Moscow.

Anders, a man of great natural dignity with an upright carriage, a closely cropped and nearly bald head and, for a Pole, a somewhat impassive face and manner, was recognised as the obvious General Officer Commanding the new Polish force. For his Chief of Staff he chose Colonel Leopold Okulicki, a splended, swashbuckling cavalry officer, whom I had the privilege to consider a personal friend. He was later to be parachuted into Poland, to command the underground army, and to die in a Soviet prison.

It was estimated that a million and a half Poles had been put into Soviet prisons and camps, but they were scattered over a vast area. Typhus had killed many, and 15,000 Polish officers were known to be missing. The corpses of 4,000 of these, murdered by the NKVD, were later found in a wood near Katyn. As a result only 17,000 Poles were present at the first parade taken by Anders and by the Soviet General Zhukov. They were all emaciated, and most of them had sores, but Zhukov, as well as Anders, was impressed by their soldierly bearing.

Steadily the number of Poles reporting for duty increased. Sikorski and Anders hoped to bring the strength of the army up to 100,000. Stalin did not want it to exceed 30,000, and Anders then put forward the suggestion that the army should be sent to the Middle East for training. For some reason which has never been satisfactorily explained Stalin agreed. As a result 115,000 Poles, including women and children, crossed the Soviet frontier into Iran. Never before had so many people emerged from the Soviet Union, all able to bear witness to the true nature of Soviet society under Stalin.

The newly formed Polish force did the bulk of its training in the area of Khanaqin in Iraq, near the frontier with Iran. It had much to learn, particularly about mechanised warfare, and it learnt assiduously. My most vivid memory from a visit I paid to them at Khanaqin is of young soldiers in tents lit by candles studying diagrams of the internal combustion engine deep into the night.

The Poles who succeeded in making their way out of Russia with Anders did so because they had considerable powers of endurance, or because they had been unusually lucky, or both. One of them, for example, Andrzej Grochowski – who had been condemned to fifteen years in a labour camp for so-called espionage – attributed his survival largely to his good fortune in being befriended by some Russian criminals, who stole boots, a jacket and a hat to keep him warm.[8]

In Iraq the Poles who had come out of Russia were joined by the Polish Carpathian Brigade, which had fought at Tobruk. By the time it reached Italy early in 1944 the Polish Second Corps was a body of exceptionally high morale and extremely well disciplined and trained.

There was also a deep seriousness in its attitude to war, derived largely from a knowledge of what the Germans were doing in their country. Harold Macmillan wrote of the Polish Second Corps: 'It was more than a military formation. It was a crusade.'[9]

THE BATTLE OF CASSINO

The landings at Anzio, which began in the early hours of 22 January, succeeded to the extent that a bridgehead not far from Rome was gained and held. The main purpose of the landings, which was to draw off so many German troops that the enemy would no longer be able to hold his existing defensive position, was not achieved.

The German position was known as the Gustav Line and extended south-westwards from the vicinity of Pescara. A full German retreat or the capture of large number of German forces, or even both, could be expected once the main body of the Fifth Army came together with the forces landed at Anzio. The German staff work which helped to prevent this in the winter of 1943–44 was described by Churchill as 'brilliantly flexible'. He also wondered how, if the German armies were fighting as well in Russia as they were in Italy, the Russians were now defeating them.[1]

An important feature of the German defensive position was the hill known as Monte Cassino. Here St Benedict established a monastery in the sixth century, which was rebuilt some 400 years later. After the dissolution of the monasteries, which took place in Italy in the nineteenth century, the abbey was designated as a national memorial. The Benedictine monks were recognised as its custodians.

Below the monastery hill lies the town of Cassino, the site of the former Casinum, a social centre of some importance

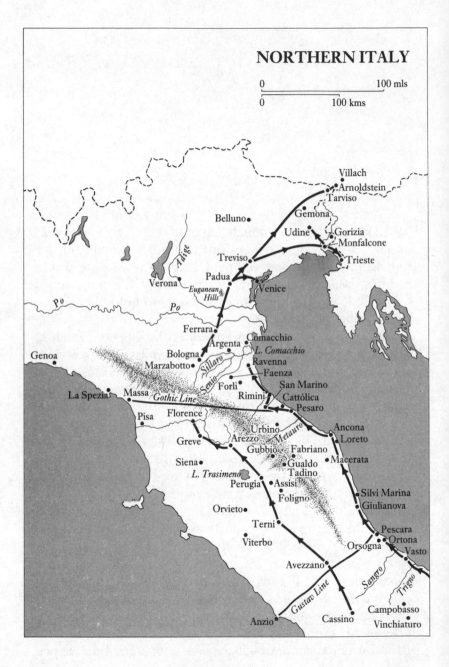

NORTHERN ITALY

0   100 mls

0   100 kms

under the Roman Empire. In a villa just outside the town Mark Antony engaged from time to time in orgies.

A frontal assault on Cassino was made by Fifth Army troops, some American, others from French Morocco and Algeria, over a period of a month beginning on 10 January. It achieved little.

The French commander, General Juin, considered the whole operation strategically unsound, but told his subordinate commander, General Joseph de Monsabert, that he must carry out orders as a matter of honour. Tuker shared Juin's opinion of the general strategy and later wrote: 'I could never understand why the US Fifth Army decided to batter its head again and again against this powerful position.'

Another assault was made in February, this time by the New Zealand Division, which had been placed temporarily under Fifth Army command. As the abbey was thought to be a central feature of the German defensive position, the Allied High Command decided that it must be bombed. This was done to devastating effect. Nevertheless the New Zealanders' attack was no more successful than those which had preceded it. Freyberg said later that Cassino reminded him of Passchendaele in World War I.[2] A further attack by the 7th Indian Brigade also failed.

On 20 March Alexander instructed the two Army commanders, Clark and Leese, to meet him the next day to decide future policy. He wanted Freyberg to be present too to give a first-hand account of the recent Cassino operations. In opening the meeting, Alexander stated that there were two options open. These were: '(a) to continue with the Cassino operation in the hope of capturing the monastery during the next three or four days, or (b) to call the operation off.'[3]

The decision taken was that another attack must be made on Monastery Hill and that this would now be the responsibility of the Eighth Army.

On 24 March 1944 Leese, whose early relationship with

the Polish Army commander was not without friction, informed General Anders of his plans for the next battle of Cassino.[4] These called for the capture of Monastery Hill by the Polish Second Corps. He gave Anders ten minutes in which to accept or reject his proposals. Anders accepted.[5]

The town of Cassino, or what remained of it, was already in Allied hands, with the 1st Guards Brigade, recently transferred from the Fifth to the Eighth Army, in occupation. The extent of the rubble was such that no tanks could make their way through it. A number of immobilised New Zealand tanks remained and now served as armoured pill-boxes. Unburied bodies were decaying, and sanitary arrangements were worse than primitive.[6]

In these conditions an officer in the Scots Guards received a letter from his mother telling him, if he happened to be in the neighbourhood, not to miss the opportunity of seeing the Benedictine monastery.[7] Another Guards officer, Henry Green, described the crypt of a church, which served as a battalion command post, as smelling of fried spam, disinfectant and human bodies.[8]

Having studied the results of the earlier battles, Anders decided to by-pass the town of Cassino and to attack from the north-west. An order of the day which he issued stated: 'Shoulder to shoulder with us will fight British, American, Canadian and New Zealand divisions, together with French, Italian and Indian troops. The task assigned to us will cover with glory the name of the Polish soldier all over the world.'[9]

There were also two Cypriot mule companies, which had been allotted to the Polish Corps. In 1941, as a response to the Italian invasion of Greece, there was a rush of volunteers for service in the Cyprus Regiment. A number of these volunteers were to see service as mule-drivers in Syria and Eritrea, as well as on the Greek mainland and Crete. Now they found themselves in Italy.[10] In their semi-combatant role they impressed Polish soldiers with their gallantry under heavy fire at Cassino and elsewhere.[11]

For thirty-six hours the men of the Polish Kresowa

Division were continuously in action without either food or water. Finally Monastery Hill was stormed. In the absence of a Polish flag the regimental pennant of the Podolski Lancers was raised over what remained of the monastery building. A trumpeter then played the *hejnal*, the traditional air familiar to the people of Cracow, which had once served to summon Poles to fight against invaders.[12]

The capture of the monastery was to some extent facilitated also by a successful advance made by French forces on the Polish left. In the monastery a cracked church bell was found alongside an unexploded shell. There were fragments of books and oil paintings, frescoes and sculpture.[13]

After the war the abbey was painstakingly rebuilt by the Benedictine monks, but a part of the town was deliberately left in ruins as a permanent reminder of what had occurred. An even more impressive reminder is the largest British and Commonwealth war cemetery in Italy.

In the Cassino battle the Polish Corps lost over 9 per cent of its total strength, nearly 4,000 officers and men in all.[14] It also gained the lasting esteem of the men of other nations serving in the Eighth Army. A Polish officer who served in Italy, Jerzy Juszczyk, later expressed to me the opinion that Polish soldiers were more 'ambitious' than the British. When Poles took over a section of a line, he recalled, greater activity followed: in particular more patrols were sent out.

Denis Hills, a colourful and talented adventurer and writer, who served as a British liaison officer with the Polish Second Corps, confirmed this judgement. 'The British,' he said, 'had been tramping along since 1940, and the Poles had to prove themselves.' They were 'less eager to get behind stones or dig a hole' and in consequence, in Hills's judgement, sustained more casualties.

In the summer of 1944 Hills's commanding officer told me that in his opinion the Polish Second Corps would have been the finest fighting formation then in Italy but for one shortcoming. This was lack of punctuality.[15]

After the battle of Cassino Leese sent Anders a warm message of congratulation, and their relations thereafter steadily improved. Perhaps it was of advantage to the proper utilisation of the Polish Second Corps that Montgomery no longer commanded the Eighth Army. He tended to be scathing about the military merits of allies other than those drawn from the Commonwealth, and when visiting Polish troops in Scotland he was reputed to have asked their commanding officer which language he spoke at home, German or Russian. Leese was increasingly respected by Poles as the campaign went on.

Among the other messages of congratulation which Anders received was one from Mark Clark, the commander of the Fifth Army. This he described as 'grudging'.[16]

Von Viethinghoff now came to the conclusion that the Gustav Line was no longer tenable, and decided on a general withdrawal. That this withdrawal was largely unimpeded by the Allies was a direct consequence of a decision taken by Clark, which delayed the pursuit of the enemy in order to capture Rome. It was a decision for which he has been witheringly condemned by military historians.

Almost the first to voice his dismay at the decision was Churchill. On 25 May he informed Alexander that 'the glory of the battle will be measured, not by the capture of Rome, but by the number of German divisions cut off.'[17] Judged by this standard the glory was negligible. It is difficult to find any convincing explanation of Clark's decision other than personal vanity and a misplaced patriotism. Rome was a great prize, and Clark was determined that no troops other than Americans should take part in the formal entry.

A statment Clark later made to an American journalist, that he had told Alexander if the Eighth Army tried to advance on Rome he would order his troops to open fire, can almost certainly be dismissed as bravado.[18] That he should have refused British participation was understandable in the light of the disparity up to that time between the public acclaim of the Eighth Army and that of its allies in the Mediterranean theatre of war. But what still seems inexcusable is his treatment of the Poles.

The Poles had captured Monastery Hill. The faith of the overwhelming majority in the Polish Army was Roman Catholic. Even the words of the Polish national anthem refer to the exploit of the Polish Legion commanded by General Dabrowski in capturing Rome in 1798. In the light of all this Alexander made a request, when he could have issued an order, that a detachment of Poles should take part in the entry into Rome. Clark refused.[19]

In May 1944 the Eighth Army consisted of four corps. Two of these were the British 10th and 13th Corps commanded respectively by Lieutenant-Generals Richard McCreery and Sidney Kirkman. The others were the 1st Canadian Corps commanded by Lieutenant-General E.L.M. Burns and Anders's Second Polish Corps. The 2nd New Zealand Division and units of the Italian Army were part of 10 Corps, and the 8th Indian Division a part of 13 Corps. The Polish Corps now included a South African Armoured Division.[20]

The South Africans had landed at Taranto late in 1944. Their Prime Minister, Field-Marshal Jan Christiaan Smuts, wanted the division to serve in Italy, but met some opposition from senior South African Army officers. Just as the South African infantry had been misplaced in the desert, so now it was argued that an armoured division was not needed in Italy, where in many places a mule was of more value than a tank. There was even a suggestion that the South Africans might be employed to keep the peace in Palestine. This proposal, which offered intriguing polititcal consequences, was not adopted, and Smuts eventually had his way.[21]

Leese believed that for campaigning in Italian mountain territory armoured divisions should be strengthened by the addition of an infantry brigade. Consequently the 1st Battalion of the Scots Guards was now made a part of the South

African Division. This began what the historian of the Scots Guard, David Erskine, called the battalion's 'happiest association of the campaign – if not of the whole war'.

He added: 'Never before had the Battalion worked in such close cooperation with armour, and the resource and agility of the South Africans in getting their tanks on to hills which would have seemed inaccessible to mere mechanics, gave the infantry confidence and won their unstinted admiration.'[22] Before long the South African Division, with its Guards component, was transferred from the Polish to the Canadian Corps.

As the Eighth Army continued its advance in the early summer of 1944 Leese was told to prepare for two alternative strategies. The Chiefs of Staff might, he learnt, expect the Eighth Army to move eventually into France, in which case his next main objective was to be Florence. Alternatively the Army's ultimate goal might be Austria and his next immediate objective Ancona.[23] It was perhaps indicative of the shifts in strategic thinking that, in the event, the Eighth Army advanced towards Florence and Ancona almost simultaneously.

The line of advance toward Ancona was for the most part along a coastal road running north-westwards from Pescara. A seaside town and minor port, with a pre-war population of some 30,000, Pescara was largely destroyed by the combined efforts of the opposing forces. One Allied air raid alone caused some 2,000 casualties, and the town was also bombarded from the sea.

The Germans then set about wholesale destruction. When they were about to leave they ordered the entire civilian population out of the town and largely demolished it, leaving mines and booby traps for the Eighth Army to deal with. It has been estimated that 80 per cent of Pescara was totally destroyed.[24] Today an almost entirely new and substantially larger town has been created.

Further along the coastal road there was less destruction. At first the hills to the west of this road came almost down to the sea with space only for little towns such as Silvi Marina and Pineto to be fitted in. After a time the mountains recede somewhat, and there is a well-wooded, but still narrow coastal plain from Giulianova to Ponto d'Ascoli. Then the mountains again came down to the sea, their sides in early summer ablaze with gorse and broom. In contrast with the landscape the towns along this stretch of the Adriatic coast are for the most part undistinguished.

The Polish Second Corps was instructed to pursue the enemy along the road at the highest possible speed and capture the port of Ancona. The hill-top town of Loreto, a natural fortress, was taken only after some hard fighting. Then on 18 July the Carpathian Lancers entered Ancona, a harbour town dominated by hills, after an advance of some 120 kilometres.[25]

The route towards Florence followed by the Canadians, the South Africans and the 1st Guards Brigade, passes through splendid, green Apennine scenery, taking in the cities of Viterbo and Orvieto, and leading on to the Chianti country.

Viterbo was a former papal residence with impressive medieval walls. In 1271 a new Pope had to be elected, and the Captain of the People of Viterbo, whose name was Rainero Gatti, finding the cardinals could not agree on their choice, locked them in the palace. Supplies of food and water were reduced, yet it still required thirty-three months of conclave before Pope Gregory X was finally elected.[26]

Orvieto is set on a rocky plateau dominating the valley of the River Paglia and has a splendid thirteenth-century cathedral, whose exterior is largely black and white marble. I can still recall with pleasure a glass of white wine I drank in a square in Orvieto in July 1944, which was in delightful contrast to the wines mostly on offer in southern Italy in wartime. These were rough and sour, and the roughest and sourest of all seemed to be sold to British and American officers' messes.

In general, drinking with safety and satisfaction in the

Mediterranean theatre of war called for a blend of discretion and initiative. One of the most striking examples of initiative was that of units of the Polish Carpathian Brigade which, during the siege of Tobruk, fermented some of their potato rations for the subsequent distillation of vodka at a time when other units had no access to alcohol of any kind.[27]

By contrast with all this my glass of white wine in Orvieto seemed strangely agreeable. I was at that time, like many other soldiers, too ignorant to know that Orvieto is the centre of some of the best wine-producing country in Italy.

To the north of Orvieto, near the border of Umbria and Tuscany, lies Lake Trasimene, on whose northern shore Hannibal destroyed a Roman army of 30,000 men in 217 BC after ambushing them under cover of mist. Near the lake the Eighth Army established a temporary headquarters in the summer of 1943, and here for a time its caravans came to rest.

Of the headquarters staff at this period Peniakoff wrote: 'A happy mixture of regular and wartime officers gave them breadth of outlook, freedom from prejudice, and a kind of universal competence.' He noted that the operational and intelligence staffs were formed largely by Oxford graduates and regretted that his own university, Cambridge, had not produced ' a similar body of men of general excellence'.[28]

Alexander meanwhile had set up a headquarters in the superb baroque palace at Caserta, rather more than thirty kilometres north-east of Naples. In the grounds of the palace a tented village soon grew up. Spending a night in one of the tents I was, for the first and last time in my life, prevented from sleeping by the singing of nightingales.

Nightingales were indeed a feature of the war in Italy in spring and summer. Raleigh Trevelyan in his *A Diary of Anzio and After* wrote: 'Those nightingales. . . It seemed that the worse things were the more they wanted to sing.' Nightingales were heard too at Cassino at the height of the battle.

ADVANCE TOWARDS FLORENCE

Optimism was widespread among planning staff and troops in the Eighth Army in the early summer of 1944. There was a general belief that at the very least there would soon be a rapid advance through the Po valley and the Lombardy plain.[1] Canadians even sang to the tune of *Lily Marlene*: 'We will debouch into the valley of the Po.'[2] In England the British Joint Planning Staff favoured an amphibious assault by four or five divisions on Trieste, followed by an advance into the Ljubljana area of Yugoslavia.[3]

The optimism was understandably fuelled by events taking place elsewhere. On 6 June the long-expected invasion of northern France by Allied troops, known by the code-name Overlord, began, and by the end of July the Germans were in full retreat. On the eastern front Soviet armies were already well inside Poland, and there was an immediate threat to Hungary. In the event these happenings elsewhere had the effect, not of expediting, but of seriously retarding the advance of the Allied armies in Italy.

In comparison with events on the Russian front since the summer of 1941 the campaigns both in North Africa and in Italy had been small-scale affairs. Nevertheless the Mediterranean theatre of war had for a long time been the only one in which the armies of the western Allies had achieved any success, but now it was regarded as of secondary importance and in the allocation of resources was treated accordingly.

With the object of increasing the strength of the Allied armies attacking Germany from the west it was decided to launch a sea-borne invasion of southern France in mid-August. The forces for this, nearly all American, were drawn largely from the United States Fifth Army in Italy. As a result Alexander lost nearly a quarter of the troops under his command.[4] To compensate for these losses a Brazilian division was added to the Fifth Army in Italy and a Greek brigade to the Eighth Army. Neither had battle experience comparable with that of the formations sent to France.

Churchill saw no need for the landings in the south of France and described the whole operation to Roosevelt as 'the first major strategic and political error for which we two have to be responsible.'[5]

Whether his judgement was right is still debatable, but there can be no doubt about the damage the operation did to the Allied campaign in Italy. Nor can there be much doubt that Roosevelt was motivated primarily by political considerations. With engaging candour he told Churchill that he would 'never survive even a light setback for "Overlord" if it were known that large forces had been diverted to the Balkans.'[6]

But there was one reserve of trained manpower in Italy of which full use had not yet been made. This was the Italian Army, and in the summer of 1944 steps were taken to bring it more into action.

The total strength of the Italian Army fighting with the Allies was the equivalent of about four divisions. Hitherto Italian troops had been used to guard communications, particularly the railways, to clear minefields and to provide mule companies and other forms of transport. It was not until the spring of 1944 that the body known as the Italian Corps of Liberation saw action as a part of the Eighth Army on the Sangro front.

One of the tasks of Italian liaison officers was to convince the commanders of other formations in the Eighth Army that, in spite of the disastrous record which the Italian armed forces had had in World War II, the Italian Army now had real fighting potential. The task was made more difficult by the poor quality of much of its equipment.

A number of these liaison officers were young men who spoke excellent English, a skill they owed largely to English nannies. For the most part they were to become men of considerable standing in post-war Italy. They played a small but significant role in fostering a new respect for Italian military prowess among Eighth Army commanders.

Italians fighting against Germans with the Eighth Army faced particular hazards, since feelings between the two former allies were such that no Italian wanted to be taken prisoner. Italian officers going out on patrol were even advised to discard their insignia and pretend to be British private soldiers.[7]

Long before the Italians were engaged in combat duties on the Allies' side large numbers of British officers and men had good reason to feel grateful for Italian acts of courage and Italian feelings towards Germans. These were the escaped Allied prisoners of war.

In the negotiations for the armistice with Italy conducted in the late summer of 1943 Churchill had insisted that everything possible should be done to prevent the Germans from removing British prisoners held in Italian camps and taking them to Germany.

After the armistice the gates of many Italian camps were indeed thrown open and the inmates encouraged to leave. Elsewhere, although the Germans succeeded in removing the prisoners, a number escaped by jumping from trains,[8] and at one stage 11,000 Allied ex-prisoners were thought to be at large in parts of German-occupied Italy.[9]

Many of these were taken into the homes of Italian families, who readily accepted both the risks and the expense involved. One ex-prisoner, Eric Newby, was later to describe how a number of Italians, after deciding it was too risky to continue to shelter him in their own houses, chose instead to build him a new one, which was completely hidden by trees. Having installed him there, they regularly brought him food, much of which had to be bought on the black market.[10]

Many of the rural families who sheltered escaped prisoners also had to accommodate friends and relations from the towns. That it was possible to provide food for all was largely due to the survival of traditional forms of husbandry in Italy. Today it is possible to travel, as I have done, many hundred of miles in Italy without seeing a cow or a pig. But when World War II broke out most Italian farmers still had a few animals in addition to the crops they cultivated.

Often escaped prisoners came across partisan bands in the course of their wanderings. Some joined the bands, and a few assumed command of them. One of these, Major Gordon Lett, an officer in the East Surrey Regiment, became in time a kind of unofficial provincial governor, being called upon to settle disputes and even on one occasion asked to grant a divorce.[11] It was almost as if the roles of the *condottieri*, the medieval soldiers of fortune, some of whom were Englishmen, were being reenacted.[12]

Militarily the importance of the partisan bands was steadily increasing. Their numbers grew as young men took to the hills to avoid being deported to Germany for forced labour. Their equipment improved too as the Special Operations Executive, operating in Italy under the name of No. 1 Special Force, organised parachute drops. But in the summer of 1944 the bands were not yet under the Eighth Army's direct command, and the most valuable contribution of the Italian resistance was probably still being made in the cities rather than by guerrilla units operating in the countryside.

To the east of Lake Trasimene lies the city of Perugia, which is built on a group of hills. From its highest point there are spectacular views over the valley of the Tiber some 300 to 400 metres below.

Perugia has long been an important centre of communications. Nevertheless, although there was fighting in the mountains separating Perugia from Lake Trasimene, in which the Rifle Brigade was heavily involved, the Germans decided not to defend the city itself.[13] As a result the Guards Brigade had the happy experience of entering Perugia and finding it almost undamaged.[14]

Harold Macmillan later recorded a conversation in which Alexander told him of his pride in having saved a number of cities 'from any except minor damage and that wantonly inflicted by the enemy'. Seven cities were specifically mentioned. They were Rome, Florence, Pisa, Siena, Assisi, Perugia and Urbino.[15] Of these Perugia was the first to be captured by the Eighth Army: a masterpiece of Italian urban construction which had remained intact and as such a new experience for many.

Perugia has achieved near perfection by the inspired use through the ages of pink brick. Its period of pre-eminence was from the mid-thirteenth century, and its greatest glory is certainly the Piazza del Duomo. Here the Gothic cathedral faces the Palazzo Communale. On the outside walls of both there are pulpits, from which at one time the people of Perugia were exhorted or harangued.

In a well-intentioned phrase a guide-book written for English speakers, which I came across in Perugia, described the Piazza del Duomo as 'one of the most suggestive squares in Italy'.

In the late fourteenth century Perugia was the scene of a spectacular kidnapping by Sir John Hawkwood, the most famous of the English condottieri. Being owed money by the Pope for services rendered, Hawkwood seized a newly appointed cardinal and held him hostage as a means of extracting payment. To safeguard himself against a charge of mere pilfering he had an inventory made of the contents of the cardinal's baggage. This included a number of

women's dresses. In the end the Pope granted Hawkwood
two valuable estates in the Romagna, and he thereby
became the first foreign *condottiere* landowner in Italy.[16]

By the time Perugia was captured it was already clear to the
Eighth Army Command where the Germans would make
their next major stand. In June 1944 the Allies had gained
possession of a document which showed exactly where the
next German defensive line lay and how it had been
constructed. The document had been left behind when a
former headquarters of Kesselring's at Monte Soratte had
been abandoned. It confirmed in detail what had already
been surmised from aerial photography.[17]

The new defensive position, which had been built largely
by the forced labour of people whose countries had been
overrun by the Germans, was known as the Gotenstellung
or Gothic Line. Its eastern anchor was the town of Pesaro.
This was well chosen. To the north of Pesaro, almost as far
as Cattòlica, cliffs come down to the sea, and the Eighth
Army had therefore little chance of landing sea-borne forces
in the rear of the German line. The western anchor was
Massa, which lies between Pisa and La Spezia.

The Germans withdrew in good order to the Gothic Line,
fighting rearguard actions as they did so. As a result, lines
were fluid for some weeks, and the Eighth Army occasionally had difficulty in locating German formations. This was
made clear to me by a curious incident which occurred in
July when I had to travel, with a driver, by jeep from Rome
in order to report to General Anders, whose headquarters
was at that time outside Ancona. Our route took us through
Viterbo, Orvieto and Perugia.

As we left Perugia I saw on my map that there were two
roads running more or less parallel in the Ancona direction.
I therefore enquired at a Royal Army Service Corps post
which road had suffered less from demolitions. I was told
that the northern road was in much the better state of the
two, but that there might still be a few Germans in the area

through which it ran. The rivers across the southern route were fordable at that time of year by jeep, but driving through them was a slow process, and as I did not want to be late in reporting to General Anders, I told my driver to take the northern road. This brought us to Gubbio, which, as I have since discovered, is a fine city. In brilliant July afternoon sunshine it struck me only as peaceful and sleepy. At the bottom of the hill on which Gubbio is built there is a Franciscan monastery. A monk happened to be standing outside, and I had a short chat with him, mainly about road conditions. Then we drove on.

Two days later I had to report to General Harding at the Eighth Army's headquarters near Lake Trasimene. While I was waiting to be shown into his caravan a young officer on the intelligence staff announced with delight: 'We've just captured Gubbio.' My information that I myself had been there a couple of days earlier without discomfort was not, I noticed, received with much enthusiasm.

A few days after this encounter I read in the *Eighth Army News* that the German commander in Gubbio had threatened to turn the town into a second Cassino. The headquarters of this putative commander was said to be the Franciscan monastery.

The most striking modern feature of Gubbio is a memorial building surrounded by cypresses and flower-beds. Its exterior appearance is that of a chapel. Inside, it contains nothing but tablets on the walls, which state simply the names of forty citizens of Gubbio and the dates of their births and deaths. They were all executed as a reprisal for the killing of two Germans. Their ages ranged from seventeen to sixty-one. Guide-books produced in Gubbio today do not mention this memorial, presumably in order to avoid giving offence to German tourists.

Before any approach to the Gothic Line could be made the Eighth Army had to break through other defensive positions which the Germans had prepared. One of these was known as the Arezzo Line. In front of it the Army paused for more than a week and regrouped: then the main attack was launched by the 6th British Armoured Division and the New Zealanders.[18]

Arezzo was entered on 16 July, two days before the Poles captured Ancona and one day before, on the left of the Allied front, the United States 4th Corps crossed the River Arno east of Pisa.[19]

The Germans were now withdrawing all along their front, and beyond Arezzo the Eighth Army advanced towards Florence through the Chianti country. But here they met with severe opposition. Harry Klein, who served in the Imperial Light Horse/Kimberley Regiment, wrote that at this stage his unit experienced 'some of the deadliest fighting encountered in Italy'.

He added: 'Through minefields, and skirting demolitions, the advance was maintained through the steep green hills towards the highest ridges of that lovely but difficult country flanking the valley of the Arno.'[20]

When the South Africans entered the town of Greve in Chianti they found it almost deserted. Out of 3,000 of the original inhabitants only fifty remained, most of them old and infirm. The rest had made their way into the country-side, to join partisan bands or simply to find food.[21]

The town is dominated by the statue of Giovanni da Verrazano, the navigator and explorer who is said to have been the first European to land upon the future site of New York. A future Professor of War Studies and Regius Professor of Modern History at Oxford University, Michael Howard, has left an account of Greve as he saw it during the advance:

The place was in that state of messy untidiness which is inseparable from war, and is far more typical of it than any amount of horror:. . .the debris of a civilian house. . .dusty and looted; and superimposed on it the debris of the army – weapons and ammunition, piles of

web equipment, washing and writing materials hanging
out of packs, maps and mess tins and tins of rations;
mattresses dragged from beds. . .windows barricaded
with washstands; men sleeping on the floor under mos-
quito nets. . .flies, flies, flies. That is war in comfort,
indoors, in summer.[22]

Robert Frost of the Royal Natal Carabiniers recorded a
happier impression of the Greve countryside in his diary:
'Good news of German disorder. Wind reveals lashings of
vino stacked round the boles of trees in the orchard by
blowing away sheaves of wheat.'

In contrast with this was the sight recorded in the diary of
another South African soldier, who wrote: 'There were five
Germans there, buried after their throats had been cut by
enraged members of this simple country community.'[23] This
was a scene which no longer occasioned great surprise, for
members of the Eighth Army had become increasingly
aware in the summer of 1944 of the hatred felt by Italians
for the Germans now occupying their country. They were
beginning too to hear of some of the measures taken by the
Germans which served to fan that hatred.

Nor was the anger of millions of Italians directed only
against Germans. In the areas under German control remnants of the former Fascist administration continued to
serve the occupying power, in some cases perpetrating
cruelties which rivalled those of the Germans.

In its approach to Florence the Eighth Army received
active help from the Italian partisans and, in particular,
from a British SOE officer attached to them named Charles
Macintosh. Born in Uruguay of New Zealand parents,
Macintosh had been recruited in Venzuela, where he had
been working for the Shell Company. A quiet-spoken man
who immediately inspired confidence, he later committed
his experiences in Florence to print, with self-deprecating
modesty.

Macintosh secretly entered Florence while it was still

under German occupation, with five other men in an American scout car. Before long he made contact with a partisan, who assured him that he knew of a secret passage built by the Medici, which connected the Palazzo Vecchio to the Palazzo Pitti on the other side of the River Arno.

As the Palazzo Vecchio was the German SS headquarters, this information was potentially of considerable importance. Macintosh had first to decide whether to believe the partisan. Secret agents who succeed in wartime are forced sooner or later to rely on instinct, and Macintosh felt he could trust the man, improbable though the story of the secret passage must have seemed. In fact, as Macintosh soon learnt, the passage did exist. It was more than three kilometres in length, and the Germans clearly had no knowledge of it.

With the help of partisans who had been infiltrated into the SS headquarters a clandestine telephone was installed in the Palazzo Vecchio, with a line laid down through the whole length of the secret passage.[24] Information received by this telephone link was conveyed by the driver of the scout car to a point in the city where a radio transmitter could be operated. In this way detailed intelligence was brought to the Eighth Army for six days running about German troop locations and planned movements.

One of the most important pieces of information conveyed in this way was sent on 11 August, when it was learnt in the Palazzo Vecchio that the Germans were beginning to withdraw from some of their positions along the River Arno.[25]

The first Eighth Army unit to enter Florence was a patrol of the Imperial Light Horse/Kimberley Regiment, consisting of half-a-dozen men. They came in through the Porta Romana, and as they did so they heard the thunderous sound of explosions coming from within the city. The Germans, they later discovered, were demolishing bridges across the River Arno.[26]

Shortly before the demolition began, a German order had been issued to the people of Florence stating that the

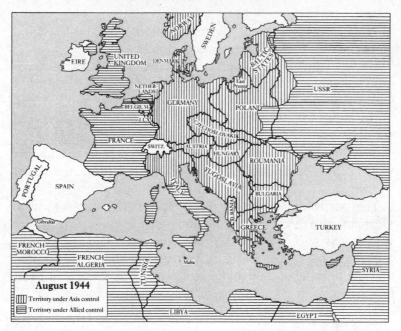

August 1944
Territory under Axis control
Territory under Allied control

German Command had treated Florence as an open city, i.e. one which would be spared destruction by both sides. It went on to state that as the attitude of the Allies was uncertain all the occupants of buildings in the immediate vicinity of the Arno must vacate them by noon on 30 July.[27] The bridges across the Arno were then blown up, with one exception. This was the famous Ponte Vecchio. Its preservation may be regarded as an admirable act, although Italians point out that the Ponte Vecchio was of limited military use, as it was too fragile to support the passage of tanks.

Harry Klein was among the first South Africans to enter the city. Later he came to the Palazzo Vecchio, where the Germans had occupied the magnificent council chamber known as the Salone dei Cinquecento, which was once the meeting place for 500 representatives of the people, and where Michelangelo's Genius of Victory still stands. Here, he wrote, 'people went hysterical at the sight of us and embarrassed us by even kissing our feet.'

He went on: 'What struck me immediately was the large number of wounded lying around being tended by nuns. I learnt that most of them had been wounded when Jerry had blown the bridges.'

Other Eighth Army formations followed the South Africans. Macintosh recalled seeing Gurkha troops advancing with perfect discipline in the manner prescribed for street fighting.

The partisans also came out in force. They engaged the Germans north of the Arno and settled numerous scores with Fascists who had served the Germans. But the part of the city which lies to the south of the Arno was taken without fighting and virtually intact, and it is there that most of Florence's architectural glories are to be found.

REFRESHMENT FOR THE SPIRIT

In the letters, diaries and reminiscences of members of the Eighth Army the word 'sightseeing' begins to appear with greater frequency in the summer of 1944. This is not surprising. For more than a year and a half during its journey from El Alamein the Eighth Army had grown familiar with poverty-stricken villages and with towns which consisted largely of rubble. Now, from Perugia onwards, large cities of antiquity and distinction were being captured with most of their buildings intact. In some of these cities headquarters could be established. Others, as soon as military requirements permitted, could serve as rest centres and, as such, provide refreshment for the spirit, the mind and the body.

Florence in particular became a magnet for those who could escape for a time from the battle-front. One man who expressed on paper his appreciation of what the city and its surrounding countryside meant to him was Lieutenant-Colonel H.B. Hudson, a British officer in the Indian Army, who arrived in Italy in 1944 to take command of the 3rd Battalion of the Mahratta Light Infantry.

Hudson was able to visit Florence more than once. 'I had,' he wrote in a typescript which was later deposited in the India Office Library in London, 'to get the filthy smell of dead bodies, smoke screen and explosives out of my nostrils. I had been away from Europe for nine years. So the brilliance of the picture quite dazzled me, and as I walked through the vineyards beneath the Servite monastery or along the streets of Florence I became intoxicated.'[1]

As I came once more to Florence I tried to imagine the impact it had made on men of the various nationalities which composed the Eighth Army. People making their first visit to Florence are well advised to prepare themselves culturally for the wealth and strangeness of what they are about to see. In the Eighth Army opportunities for such preparation were limited, and suddenly men found themselves with a Renaissance city laid out before them which in the fifteenth century had been more populous than Rome.[2]

Matteo Palmieri, a Florentine chemist, who lived in the fifteenth century, declared that every intelligent man ought to give thanks to God for being born in an age which had seen a flowering of genius such as had not been known for the past thousand years.[3]

This was the city to which men came after years of fighting. Here they visited the squares most frequented by tourists today, in particular the Piazza della Signoria, where the Palazzo Vecchio, lately occupied by the SS, stands. Some, guided by Florentines who showed them their city with pride, may have tried to picture the square as it was on the last day of carnival in 1497, when the citizens of Florence, goaded by the masterful monk Girolamo Savonarola, piled up their possessions of scent and false hair, dice and cards, which were then solemnly burnt.

Another square which the soldiery visited was the Piazza del Duomo. One of them indeed told me that the black and white marble strips on the exterior of the church buildings put him in mind of football jerseys. Others may have seen in them a unique method of bringing light to grandeur.

Of the grandeur none could surely have had any doubt. The size of the cathedral was determined by the requirement that the whole population of Florence should be able to enter it to celebrate Easter and other great festivals. As a result it can hold some 30,000 people.

The great art galleries of Florence, which some of the discerning visited, had remained open during the German occupation and had been well cared for, though there is today a permanent exhibition of art treasures removed by the Germans from Italy and since returned. It reveals a fairly catholic taste in the looters, although there was a strong tendency to favour fleshy nudes.

The Eighth Army commandeered as a headquarters in Florence the Savoy Hotel, situated in a fashionable square, and for the people of Florence life returned to something approaching normal fairly soon after liberation. Lieutenant-Colonel Hudson noted: 'In the *piazza* men sat at tables outside the cafés; the women walked about to show off their dresses. Italian young women always seemed to be well dressed, even after years of war.' This, he was told by an escaped British prisoner named Tony Oldham, who had commanded a partisan battalion, was because 'the material had been the best curtains before the war and every Italian woman was an expert seamstress.'

In Fiesoli, which is an older settlement than Florence but which, because of its proximity, has come to be regarded almost as an extension of the city, fighting continued for about a week after Florence had been liberated.

Fiesoli is a hilltop and hillside town with villas and gardens, stone walls and terraces, Etruscan ruins and a fourteenth-century cathedral. It also had during World War II a building where Italian Fascists tortured their prisoners, and an establishment which housed a number of British subjects. These were nuns belonging to the Little Company of Mary, an order founded in Nottingham by a woman named Mary Potter. In 1882 she received permission from Pope Leo XIII for the order to perform its so-called apostolate of the dying in Italy.[4]

The order's convent in Fiesoli is a fifteenth-century building, fronted by gardens from which there is a spectacular view over the city of Florence. Here the homeless were taken in during the war, and for a time Germans troops were billeted.

During all this time the nuns maintained the practice of the living rosary, which meant twenty-four hours of continuous prayer. But they were also sufficiently worldly-wise to run up the Irish flag whenever the German commander in Fiesoli became threatening, and to know just where to find black market supplies to feed all those who had thrown themselves on the nuns' mercy.

On my journey through Italy in the summer of 1988 I spent several evenings in the company of the nuns and their guests. The nuns taught me much about humanity, and I taught them how to sing *Green Grow the Rushes O*.

Once Florence had been liberated Leese decided that the main attack of the Eighth Army must be switched to the east coast. This called for the involvement of 5 Corps, which was commanded by Lieutenant-General Charles Keightley and which for some time had been held as an Army Group reserve, available to support either the Eighth Army or the United States Fifth Army if and when either succeeded in breaking out into the Lombardy plain. The Fifth Corps and the Canadian First Corps were to concentrate in the area of Foligno, which lies east and a little south of Perugia and almost directly south of Gubbio. From there they were to be moved to the Adriatic coast.[5]

To enable this manoeuvre to be carried out thousands of vehicles would have to cross the Apennines. Only two roads could be used for heavy traffic, one north-eastwards from Foligno to Macerata, and the other northwards from Foligno through Gualdo Tadino to Fabriano. Neither road was of good quality and sixteen Bailey bridges had to be laid down. It was also necessary to keep the passage of vehicles as secret as possible, so when movement finally began on 15 August, much of it took place at night without the use of headlights but with specially placed verge lights to help at difficult bends. By day vehicles were halted in hollows away from towns and villages, and contact with civilians was forbidden. Ten days and nights were needed for the movement to be completed, and although German reconnaissance aircraft flew over the area, there was no evident enemy reaction and no significant redeployment of German forces.[6]

The late summer offensive was launched as soon as the movement had been completed. Its first main objective was the capture of Rimini. After that, it was hoped, there would be a break-out into the Po valley.

PESARO, SAN MARINO AND RIMINI

As it advanced in the direction of Pesaro in September 1944, the Polish Second Corps had under its command the Italian Corps of Liberation, which included mountain troops of the 4th Bersaglieri Regiment. On 25 September the Polish Carpathian Lancers, after crossing the River Moro, entered Pesaro, but they were forced to withdraw in the face of strong German counter-attacks.[1]

A further attack was launched, now by the Canadians, on 29 September, and as they advanced north and east the German commander in Pesaro decided to pull out in order to avoid being encircled. The city was liberated on 2 October. The Germans had destroyed houses and woods on the outskirts in order to give themselves a better field of fire, but the city itself was little damaged.[2]

Pesaro, which is dominated by two hills, one to the north and the other to the south, is a seaside town planned and built on generous lines. Broad avenues of holm-oaks, limes and beeches are lined with solidly prosperous villas. Rossini was born in Pesaro, and the making of musical instruments has long been a tradition in the city. Discovering this, a bandmaster of the Queen's Bays took the opportunity to replace instruments which had been slowly wearing out since 1939. As a consequence the band found itself in good enough heart and good enough shape to venture to perform in the Rossini Theatre.[3]

After abandoning Pesaro the Germans established a new defensive positon south-east of a line running from Rimini to San Marino. As a result the beautiful Renaissance city of Urbino, perched on two steep hills up which beeches and conifers climb, was spared any damage.

Urbino was the birthplace of Raphael. In 1631 it was annexed to the Papal State, and for more than two centuries, like other cities which shared this fate, it suffered a steady cultural decline. Hence its preservation – indeed, for a time, fossilisation – as a nearly perfect expression of the Renaissance spirit.

A strong infantry attack was made on the Rimini – San Marino line in September. The Cameronians entered the village of Borgo Maggiore on 20 September, and while fighting was still going on there San Marino also fell. Only small parties of Germans remained in the town, and they were quickly rounded up.[4]

Soon after San Marino had been captured Harold Macmillan paid it a visit. At that time he held the curiously named post of Minister Resident in the Mediterranean, a role which, he was later to say, could be performed satisfactorily only by a porpoise.[5] The post had been created because Churchill had wisely decided, after the Allied landings in North Africa, that somebody with ministerial rank should be attached to Eisenhower's headquarters to deal with the numerous political problems which must arise.

Macmillan was much intrigued by San Marino, an independent republic which had been governed by consuls, or captains-regent, since 1244. It claimed, and still does claim, to be 'the only example in the world of a microscopic republic maintained free, democratic and independent from the times of the Roman Empire to the present day'. In World War II about 100,000 people took refuge in San Marino, most of them from Rimini.[6]

Macmillan was accompanied on his visit by General Leese. 'We were received,' he recorded in his diary, 'by one of the co-regents – who wore white gloves and a very long swallow-tail coat (like a *maître d'hôtel*) – and by the cabinet.' The setting was the city hall, which is nineteenth-century Gothic and reminded Macmillan of Balliol College, Oxford.

After some wine-drinking and speeches the co-regent raised with Macmillan the question of compensation for damage caused to San Marino by bombing. But as he did so the noise of bagpipes being played in the square outside grew so loud that Macmillan was saved from having to answer.

Today San Marino obtains its revenue largely from tourism and the sale of postage stamps. Its rulers have also had the good sense to appoint as their Honorary Consul in London a man of exceptional generosity in the distinguished hotelier, Lord Forte. At an earlier date, Macmillan claimed, the sale of titles was one of the republic's chief exports. In particular he cited the example of an American benefactress who supplied San Marino with piped water and became known as the Duchessa d'Acqua-Viva.[7]

During the tour of the battlefront areas which he made at this time, Macmillan was much impressed by the respect which Leese, as commander of the Eighth Army, evidently enjoyed. 'Everywhere,' he noted in his diary, 'the general is received with smiles and greetings. He is indeed a very popular figure, and I told him he conducts the whole affair like an election campaign.'

Macmillan went on to point out the contrast with World War I, when 'a general was a remote Blimpish figure in white moustache, faultlessly tailored tunics, polished boots and spurs, emerging occasionally from a luxurious chateau.' An army commander was now 'a youngish man, in shorts and open shirt, driving his own jeep, and waving and shouting his greetings to the troops as he edges his way past guns, tanks, trucks, truck-carriers etc. on the crowded muddy roads, which the enemy may actually be shelling as he drives along.'

While the offensive in the Rimini area was still under way Macmillan learnt, to his regret, that Leese was to leave Italy to take up an appointment in the Far East. His successor was Lieutenant-General Richard McCreery, who was being promoted from the command of 10 Corps.

McCreery was to be the last commander of the Eighth Army. Of him Macmillan wrote: 'Dick McCreery is the most charming man – and a very clever one in addition. He has always struck me as one of the ablest of the military officers whom I have seen out here.'

Not the least of the many qualities which enabled Macmillan to succeed in the unusual role for which Churchill had cast him was the respect he felt for soldiers.

There were eleven German divisions engaged in the battle for Rimini.[8] Nevertheless the Canadian Corps, which bore the brunt of the fighting against them, succeeded in advancing from the River Metauro, which enters the sea a little to the south-east of Pesaro, to the River Marecchia, which flows through Rimini, a distance of nearly fifty kilometres, in twenty-six days.[9]

Leese had earlier decided that the 3rd Greek Mountain Brigade should be assigned to the Canadian Corps in order to gain battle experience. On the night of 14–15 September the Greeks, with a New Zealand motor battalion in support, captured the village of San Lorenzo in Strada. A week later, on the night of 20–21 September, they had the considerable distinction of entering and occupying Rimini slightly ahead of the New Zealanders. The Greek flag was flown from the town hall, and the Greek commander, Colonel Tsakalotos, then asked for a Canadian flag to be flown beside it.

In reply to a letter containing congratulations from the Canadian divisional commander, General Vokes, Tsakalotos wrote: 'We are happy because they come from glorious warriors. We knew this and now the satisfaction is greater when our small contribution is recognised.' He ended his letter: 'Long live Canada.'[10]

The Germans were driven out of Rimini only after heavy fighting, and they continued to counter-attack and to shell the city. As a result it suffered considerable damage. Now, by advancing far enough to liberate both Florence and Rimini, the Eighth Army had breached the Gothic Line, but the German defence was in depth, and in 1944 there was to be no break-through to Bologna and beyond.

In October the Army was held up by heavy and persistent rain. The terrain too was found to be little more suitable for advance by motorised forces than the mountains through which the Eighth Army had fought for so long. The countryside to the north-west of Rimini contrasts strikingly with that to which the Eighth Army had grown accustomed. With the last range of the Apennines still visible in the distance on the left, the landscape becomes flat, and fruit grows in abundance. Much of the land is reclaimed marsh, and there are numerous streams and canals with high protective dykes. The waterways nearly all run from west to east and are natural tank obstacles. The October rains transformed much of the land into sticky mud.

These physical difficulties, considerable though they were, could no doubt have been overcome had the Eighth Army remained as strong as it had been in the summer. In fact it suffered further depradations. Formations continued to be transferred to France, and others were now required for yet another operational zone: Greece.

The Germans, who had been in occupation of Greece since 1941, decided to limit their commitments and withdraw, and there were threats of both a communist take-over and a civil war. To prevent either, and to maintain order until elections could be held, the British government despatched a military force to Greece in October 1944. Among the formations chosen for despatch to Greece from Italy was the 4th Indian Division.

Fighting continued in Italy in the final months of 1944, but it was already clear that another winter would have to be endured before a large-scale offensive could be undertaken. The Eighth Army did during this period cross the Rubicon, the river which flows into the sea to the north-west of Rimini and which once divided Italy from Cisalpine Gaul. But it did not advance a great deal further.

'Give me a sandstorm any day.'

WINTER STALEMATE

The Eighth Army's advance up the east coast was successful enough for an attack on Ravenna to be planned to take place in December 1944. The preparations for this brought about a new relationship between the Eighth Army and the Italian partisans.

In October the partisans in the Ravenna area received appreciable supplies of arms, some being dropped from the air and some landed by boat on a beach between Porto Corsini and Casal Borsetti. The partisans were also in contact with Popski's Private Army, with whom they established a good *rapport*, and plans for joint action were discussed. The most effective partisan leader in the Ravenna area was a former Italian Army officer named Arrigo Boldrini, who had adopted the pseudonym of Major Bulow.

After talks with other partisan leaders and with Peniakoff, Boldrini decided to make direct contact with the Eighth Army command, and on the night of 18–19 November he set off in a rowing-boat from the beach where arms had been landed, down the coast to Allied-occupied territory. It was perhaps indicative of the suspicious attitude towards the Allied High Command adopted by the more politically-minded partisan leaders that, before going on his mission, Boldrini asked for a guarantee of safe return within forty-eight hours. Accompanying him were four oarsmen, a radio-operator, a delegate from another partisan group and two non-commissioned officers in the Royal Air Force, who were escaped prisoners of war. They took with them a large flagon of wine.

Boldrini was well received at the headquarters of the Canadian Corps in the coastal village of Viserba. He then spoke to two British intelligence officers, Major Archibald Colquhoun and Captain John Rendall, who, in discussing plans for an attack on Ravenna, stressed the importance of minimising damage to the town. Boldrini was particularly impressed by Rendall's knowledge of the history of Ravenna and of its buildings.

Boldrini came back accompanied by an Italian-speaking Canadian officer, Major Denis Healy, and soon after his return he learnt that in the attack on Ravenna the partisan forces were to operate as an integral part of the Canadian Corps. This they were to do in conjunction with an assault group which included the 27th Lancers and Popski's Private Army.[1]

From the outset it was accepted that the saving of as much of Ravenna's heritage as possible must be a prime consideration. This, the Eighth Army Command decided, could best be done by rapid action on more than one front. The Canadian Corps had the task of advancing to the right of the main Ravenna defences, with the British Fifth Corps in the centre and the Poles on the left. The assault group which included Popski's Private Army and the partisans was to advance on the extreme right along the Rimini – Ravenna coast road.

The first attack was launched on 28 November, but it was not until the evening of 4 December that the Canadians finally succeeded in liberating Ravenna.[2] Success was achieved largely through an encircling movement carried out by Princess Louise Dragoon Guards, but the contribution made by the partisans was important, in particular the preservation of one of the churches of which Colquhoun and Rendall had spoken, Sant' Apollinare in Classe, which is situated a few miles outside Ravenna.

The Germans had used the tenth-century bell-tower, which dominates the flat and undistinguished countryside, as an observation post and had surrounded the church with anti-aircraft batteries. Peniakoff believed that a sudden surprise attack with the help of partisans might save the church, and he persuaded the Canadians to allow him to try. Cooperation with the partisans was in the event perfect. A mixed detachment occupied the bell-tower, disarmed the look-outs, and took a number of other German prisoners.[3]

In this way a church of extraordinary distinction was saved. Sant' Apollinare in Classe has three naves, which were consecrated in the year 549, and which are divided by two rows of columns of veined Greek marble. In the apse there is a mosaic in green and white and gold depicting the transfiguration of Christ on Mount Tabor.

The whole church is an example of how skilfully the shape of the Roman basilica was adapted to meet the needs of early Christian churches, and although there are, it may be thought, even finer examples of the art of mosaic in Ravenna itself, there can be few churches anywhere more startling to the passer-by who is unprepared for what he is going to see.

The coast along which Popski's Private Army and the partisans advanced is fringed with pinewoods. Byron described it as 'the silent shores which bounds Ravenna's immemorial wood'.

When they entered the town itself those who were unfamiliar with it and, in particular, with its extraordinary wealth of sixth-century churches and mosaics may well have thought the main square, the Piazza del Popolo, to be its outstanding feature. The buildings date largely from the fifteenth century, are of gentle proportions, pink and gold in colour, and were clearly designed under Venetian influence.

On 8 December a meeting took place in a British brigade headquarters at which representatives of the Italian partisans put forward proposals for their future employment. One of these was that they should be part of a regular formation. Another was that they should be armed accordingly and not have to depend on weapons suitable for guerilla warfare.

The Eighth Army officers present were faced with a dilemma. The Bonomi government had already formally agreed that once particular areas had been liberated the partisan units involved should hand in their weapons and be disbanded. This was a reasonable precaution designed to prevent the proliferation of private armies where there was no enemy to fight. On the other hand, officers who had seen the partisans in action around Ravenna, including Peniakoff, Colquhoun and, most importantly, a Canadian General, Charles Foulkes, argued in favour of their retention as a fighting force, and eventually this judgement was accepted.

The outcome was that on 14 January 1945 when the Cremona group of the Italian Army took over a section of the front from two Canadian divisions, it incorporated the 28th Garibaldi Partisan Brigade. These partisans had now become a part of the Eighth Army.[4]

The Allied High Command had at one time envisaged a major winter offensive in Italy in 1944–45. That the offensive did not occur was due not only to the weather and the depletion of the forces on the Italian front: the troops who remained were for the most part tired, and in the Eighth Army in particular there was a serious shortage of ammunition. In spite of careful hoarding in November it was estimated that heavy firing could be sustained for only seven days.[5]

There were continual engagements between patrols. Shortly before Christmas the Canadians came across an order issued by General Heidrich, commanding the German 1st Parachute Corps, which stated: 'In static battle conditions such as the present fighting should never cease. The "leave me alone and I will leave you alone" attitude must be entirely absent.'[6] In fulfilment of this policy the Germans began during the winter to use a new type of large rocket projectile, and German patrols showed considerable enterprise in attempts to penetrate the Allies' lines.[7]

On the Eighth Army side fairly large-scale attacks were launched in December by both the 2nd New Zealand and the 10th Indian Divisions. Casualties in the Indian Division were heavy. But on 10 January orders were issued suspending offensive operations indefinitely.

Before this decision was made changes had occurred in the structure of the higher command. On 12 December 1944 Alexander had succeeded General Sir Henry Maitland Wilson in the semi-political post of Supreme Commander at Caserta, and Mark Clark had taken on Alexander's role as Commander of Fifteenth Army Group. McCreery remained in command of the Eighth Army, and Lieutenant-General Lucian K. Truscott was brought over from France to take command of the US Fifth Army. With Clark's assumption of Alexander's role the Eighth Army, for the first time since it was formed, found itself part of an army group under American command.

Some of the Eighth Army troops who had endured the winter of 1943–44 in Italy began to wonder how often the cycle of spring offensive and winter stalemate would be repeated.[8] A system of reliefs was organised in order to give formations as much rest as possible.[9] Some troops were able to visit cities which had been liberated in the summer and autumn offensives. For others different forms of distraction were devised.

In Forlì the Irish Brigade celebrated St Patrick's Day by staging a massive football match in the main square, in which the Royal Inniskilling Fusiliers energetically joined. In many of the leisure activities of the Irish Brigade an ecumenical spirit prevailed. When the Pope, for instance, had granted a special audience earlier in the year to the brigade, a number of Protestant Orange Lodges had been represented.[10]

Individuals as always, created their own diversions. A

New Zealand battalion order was obliged to state that all ranks must refrain from killing fish in rivers by hand grenades. (Another order, issued at the same time, stated that they must refrain from wearing civilian head-dress.)[11] But in January snow fell heavily, and the tedium of static warfare intensified.

The stalemate applied too to some extent to the partisans. Alexander issued an instruction that they should prepare themselves for helping the spring offensive, and meanwhile confine themselves during the winter to obtaining information and carrying out sabotage and surprise attacks. This was not well received within the partisan movement. Bands had been steadily growing in strength; they did not wish to lose their momentum, and discipline in idleness comes less easily to guerrilla forces than it does to uniformed troops.

There was also the problem of how to employ the deserters from the enemy who in growing numbers had begun to join the partisans. The 36th Garibaldi Brigade, for instance, included Russians, Poles, Czechs, Yugoslavs and Frenchmen who had been conscripted into the German forces, as well as at least one German, a man who had learnt that his family had been arrested by the SS.[12]

Some of the partisan leaders believed Alexander's call for restraint was a political act, since a directive was also issued discouraging 'the indiscriminate expansion of the partisan movement'. But it was also true that in the prevailing circumstances large-scale guerrilla attacks could be militarily effective only in support of a planned army offensive. Quiet and sustained sabotage by those engaged in building or repairing German defensive positions could well be more useful.

Then, in January 1945, a new body was added to the strength of the Eighth Army. This was the Jewish Brigade. Its origins were various. Under the British mandate a Palestine Regiment had been formed, consisting of three battalions, two Jewish and one Arab. But with the growing antagonism between Arabs and Jews, which the prospect of the ending of the mandate served to encourage, this was clearly a fragile structure. Nevertheless, Jewish proposals to create an independent body to fight against the Germans had been received with limited enthusiasm by British officials committed to the nearly impossible task of maintaining strict impartiality between Jews and Arabs. It was not therefore until August 1944 that the British War Office, after four years of discussion, had withdrawn all objections to the establishment of a Jewish Brigade.

Churchill himself was strongly in favour of the creation of such a body, and he wrote to Roosevelt: 'This will give great satisfaction to the Jews. . . and surely they of all people have the right to strike at the Germans as a recognisable body. They wish to have their own flag which is the Star of David on a white background with two light blue bars. I cannot see why this should not be done.'[13]

The Palestine Regiment was the main source of recruitment for the Jewish Brigade. Another was the Polish Army which included many Polish citizens who were not ethnic Poles, in particular Ukrainians, Byelorussians and Jews. As trained soldiers these former members of the Polish Army were welcome recruits to the Jewish Brigade, and the distinguished soldier Moshe Dayan was later to describe Anders affectionately as 'the father of the Israeli army'.[14]

The first commander of the Jewish Brigade was Brigadier Ernest Frank Benjamin, a regular British Army officer of Canadian origin. There were other British officers too, some of whom had already had long service with the Eighth Army. One of these was Major Edmund L. de Rothschild, who had been commissioned in the Royal Bucks Yeomanry and had fought at Cassino. He recalled later encountering British, French, Russian, Hungarian, Czech, Polish, Italian and Yemeni Jews in the Brigade, but, perhaps surprisingly, no Americans.[15] Within the ranks a wide variety of languages was spoken, but all orders were given in English. The shoulder-flashes bore the words 'Jewish Infantry Brigade Group' in both English and Hebrew.

With remarkable speed the Jewish Brigade began to command the respect of other formations in the Eighth Army. Arnold Graves, an officer in the Royal Engineers, described it as 'the most efficient outfit' he had ever encountered. When taking over a section of the line from British or American troops, he said, he would simply be told the direction in which the minefields lay and their general extent. The Jewish Brigade gave him precise angles and measurements.[16]

For the Polish Corps in Italy the winter of 1944–45 was a period of considerable distress caused by events in the Soviet Union. In February Roosevelt and Churchill met Stalin at Yalta and acquiesced in Stalin's decision to extend Soviet territory substantially at the expense of Poland. A high proportion of those serving in the Polish forces in Italy, Byelorussians and Ukrainians as well as Poles, came from the areas which were to be annexed. They had no desire to return to territory under Soviet occupation and were sceptical of the prospects for a Poland ruled by the kind of government which Stalin was now installing.

Increasingly, members of the Polish Corps began to ask what purpose their efforts could now serve. There were even some suggestions that they might lay down their arms, and McCreery took reports of these seriously enough to discuss them with Anders, emphasising at the same time that it would be impossible to withdraw the Polish Corps as there were no other units which could replace it. Anders replied that he had no intention of putting the Eighth Army in a difficult position and that the Polish Corps would fight on.[17] This it was to do with new distinction when the Eighth Army launched its final offensive in the spring of 1945.

BOLOGNA AND FERRARA

The Allied offensive in the spring of 1945 was timed to begin on 9 April, when the Eighth Army was to attack across the River Senio. It would then advance in the direction of Argenta along a front stretching from Faenza north-eastwards towards the shores of Lake Commachio.

The Eighth Army was now a very different body from that which had fought some of the earlier campaigns. The Canadians, who had played so important a role since the landings in Sicily, were no longer present, having been transferred to north-west Europe. Over 92,000 Canadians had served in Italy. Their casualties numbered more than 26,000.[1]

There were now four corps in the Army. On the right in the spring offensive was 5 Corps, consisting of the 56th and 78th British Infantry Divisions, the 2nd New Zealand Division, the 8th Indian Infantry Division, the 6th South African Armoured Division and an Italian Combat Group. The Polish Corps was assigned to the sector between Faenza and Ravenna. On its left 10 Corps now consisted only of the Jewish Brigade and the Italian Friuli Combat Group.

Further west was 13 Corps, which John Harding now commanded. It was made up of the 10th Indian Infantry Division, the Italian Folgore Combat Group and what was called an 'ad hoc' formation of six battalions. In reserve were the 6th British Armoured Division and the 2nd Parachute Brigade.[2]

In a speech which he made shortly before the offensive began, the Eighth Army's Commander, Sir Richard McCreery, likened the Army to 'an old steeplechaser, full of running, but rather careful'. The occasion was a race meeting which McCreery had organised at Cesena as a boost to morale.

McCreery was himself a skilled steeplechase rider. John Strawson, who at that time was commanding a squadron of the 4th Hussars and who later became a major-general, historian of the SAS and one of the most illuminating analysts of the campaign in Italy, described McCreery as 'the greatest cavalry soldier of his generation'. He added that he was 'that rare coalition of a brilliant staff officer and higher commander'.[3]

Before the battle began McCreery surveyed the terrain from an Auster aircraft and saw how the Germans had added to the natural difficulties by extensive flooding. The only firm ground seemed to be the road from Ravenna to Ferrara. Argenta lay almost in the middle of this, and its capture would therefore be of major importance.

After intensive bombardments the Senio and the Santerno were crossed, and on the sixth day of the attack the New Zealanders reached the River Sillaro. Here they were faced with a formidable bridging problem, for the distance between the banks was some 70 metres, but they succeeded in crossing without heavy casualties.[4]

Some formations, including Commando units in 5 Corps, were now equipped with amphibious tanks, but they were not easy to manage, and assault boats, which were much more vulnerable to enemy fire, often had to be used instead. At the approach to Lake Commachio, with the sea on the right and the lake ahead on the left, the advance had to be made along a narrow spit of land covered in scrub the height of a man's shoulders, and then through sand dunes which were thickly sown with mines.[5]

Clearly the Germans were still fighting determinedly.

Kesselring was no longer in command. He had been seriously hurt in a car accident in November 1944 and was later appointed Commander-in-Chief in the West. Von Viethinghoff had succeeded him in the supreme command on the Italian front, and although by April 1945 the plight of German armies elsewhere was virtually hopeless, he still planned an orderly retreat towards the Po, and skilful delaying actions were still conducted.

One man who took part in the fighting on Lake Commachio was a Dane named Anders Lassen. When war broke out in 1939 he was serving as a seaman in a tanker. Learning that the master had had instructions to make for a German port, he led a mutiny and had the ship diverted to Bahrein, where a British crew were taken on board.

From England in the early years of the war he took part in a number of irregular small boat operations. He then moved to the Mediterranean theatre, where he acquired a considerable reputation. A tall, blond young man with strikingly good looks, a general appearance suggestive of a Viking and a taste for eccentricity in dress which was exceptional even by Eighth Army standards, he became a member of the Special Boat Service and was awarded the Military Cross with two bars.

Nevertheless he periodically expressed a wish to become involved in what he called the 'big war', and with this object he joined the Commandos. He now held the rank of major in the British Army, and he was given the task of leading a diversionary attack across Lake Commachio while the main assault was made along the lake's western shore. He had sixty men with him, and he was instructed to cause as many casualties and create as much confusion as possible in order to give the impression that a major landing was taking place on one of the islands in the lake.

The crossing of the lake, which is extremely shallow, was made silently in thirty canoes, which carried weapons, ammunition and radio equipment. After paddling through the night Lassen's party reached an island. Here they had to remain throughout the day in total silence with their canoes and themselves covered by bracken.

The next night they came to another island. Here their presence was discovered by the enemy, who subjected them to nine hours of continuous bombardment. Lassen then sent a signal asking for Commando troops to be sent to hold this island. This would allow him to leave it and attack the strong German positions in the town of Commachio.

The road to Commachio lies along a small dam with water on both sides. Lassen led a party of seventeen men along it. The first enemy position they reached held four Germans and two machine-guns. Lassen successfully eliminated it by throwing in hand-grenades. In the face of heavy fire from several directions he then raced forward and silenced a second enemy position. At the third post the Germans appeared to surrender. Lassen was preparing to accept the surrender when a burst of fire came from a Spandau gun. Lassen was hit more than once and fell to the ground.

Then, in the words of the official citation, 'Major Lassen refused to be evacuated as he said it would impede the withdrawal and endanger further lives.' He died and was posthumously awarded the Victoria Cross.[6]

The line of advance of the Polish Corps meanwhile continued in the direction of Bologna. Before it lay a succession of rivers, the Senio, the Santerno, the Sellustra, the Sillaro, the Gaiano, the Idice and the Savona. All had high dykes of solidly packed earth on both sides, and all were copiously mined. Marek Swiecicki, a war correspondent with the Polish Corps, was appropriately to entitle his chronicle of the campaign *Seven Rivers to Bologna*.

In his book he describes how a preliminary bombardment by American aircraft caused a number of casualties among Polish troops, inducing Anders to point out to Mark Clark that soldiers did not like dying before the action had begun. He describes how tanks with flame-throwers caused grey earth, green grass and bronze trees all to flame in crimson light. He tells too of a second-lieutenant who had lost a hand at Cassino, had been posted to a training school, had applied for leave, and then rejoined his old unit in time to take part in the offensive.

The Indians on the right of the Poles seem to have responded cheerfully to the coming of spring. 'I remembered,' Swiecicki writes, 'their miserable, huddled forms during the winter days on the Italian front. Now they looked almost happy.'[7]

The Indian troops, of whom Swiecicki wrote, in fact came from territories with widely differing climates. Lieutenant-Colonel Hudson, on being posted to his battalion of the Mahratta Light Infantry, recorded that he had been conditioned to believe that all the best Indian Army soldiers came from the northern part of what then constituted India, or from Nepal: Jats, Jat Singhs, Punjabi Muslims, Gurkhas, Gurkhalis and such Pathans as could be enlisted. Now he found himself in command of predominantly southern Indian troops and was surprised by their high quality.

'All the Indian officers,' he wrote, 'were good. Amongst the British officers there were one or two rather weak youngsters – the war had been going on a long time and good material was getting scarce. I liked them all, even the rather grim businessman from Madras who, I thought, regarded the war as an infuriating interruption of his cricket.'[8]

As the Poles and the Indians advanced, civilians crowded the roads. Swiecicki observed that clearly the Germans did not have enough aircraft to attack them. He had noticed that in Solarola the Germans had blown up a school and a shelter where children were taking refuge, and in Faenza they had given the same treatment to a hospital where there were wounded prisoners. Of Italian feelings towards Germans he wrote: 'The strongest impression left on one was the people's hatred, absolutely sincere, boundless and bottomless.'

The offensive lasted a little more than a week. On 17 April tanks of the Carpathian Lancers, the regiment which had been the first to enter Ancona, began driving into the streets of Bologna. Soon afterwards the Polish flag flew from the Palazzo Communale, and Anders took over the government in the name of the Eighth Army. Over 26,000 prisoners were taken.

With the liberation of Bologna, troops of the Eighth Army entered a region of Italy greatly different in appearance, and different too in traditions. In the first months of the campaign on the mainland they had known the impoverished and largely mountainous south. In the summer of 1944 they had advanced through the green hills and splendid Renaissance cities of Tuscany and Umbria, but now they had reached the north and found at first a vast plain without a hill in sight. There were differences too in the cities, differences which were apparent but not immediately explicable. There was also evidence of a bitter hatred towards the German occupying power which exceeded anything the troops had yet encountered.

Bologna was, like Florence, a city in which partisans had been active while the Germans were still in occupation. It has good communications and for this reason served some time as the hub of a large area through which German reserve troops were moved. As such it was an important centre for the gathering of intelligence.[9]

Some nine months had passed between the liberation of Florence and that of Bologna, and during that time the efforts of the SS to eliminate the partisan movement, and indeed all forms of Italian resistance, were steadily intensified. In the autumn of 1944, 1,830 people were massacred in the village of Marzabotto. They were nearly all women, children and very old men, as the able-bodied had already taken to the mountains. In another village, Sant' Anna di Stazzema, 560 people were killed on one day in September 1944. These are only two items in the lengthy record.[10]

My time in Bologna was largely spent in the company of

former partisans. There is today in Italy a nationwide, well-organised and well-funded body known as the Associazione Nazionale Partigiani d'Italia, which serves to keep the memory of Italian resistance alive. In Bologna the organisation is particularly strong, and it records with pride examples of extraordinary courage shown by Partisans, both men and women.[11]

Some 15–20 per cent of the partisans in the Bologna area were women, and of these nearly one-third bore arms. The others served as nurses, runners and orderlies. A Bologna girl named Irma Bandiera, who was a liaison officer between Partisan groups, was betrayed, captured and tortured. She had her eyes put out, but refused to speak. She was finally killed in front of her own home.

In one family there were seven brothers, all of whom had knowledge of partisan activities, and all of whom refused to divulge what they knew. They were killed one by one in the presence of their mother, who shortly afterwards died of a heart attack.

Bologna must surely be more richly provided with arcades than any other in Europe. Their total length is nearly 40 kilometres, and the pedestrian can, in consequence, traverse the city largely under cover. This is fortunate, for the climate of Bologna, which lies only a little above sea level, is, by Italian standards, rather disagreeable.

Like all major Italian cities Bologna is plentifully endowed with fine churches, yet the secular buildings are no less impressive. One of these is the Palazzo Communale, from which after the liberation of Bologna the Polish flag flew for a time. The building was for long the residence of Papal Legates, who were the most powerful men in Bologna. Access to the first floor was up a ramp suitable for horses. I tried to picture messengers arriving with despatches, and important visitors in flamboyant clothes, riding up to seek audience of the bejewelled Legate, until at the end of the day the ramp leading to all the splendour reeked of manure.

To many of the Eighth Army troops who passed through it the name of Bologna was associated with a fallacy. Bologna is a city in which food is taken seriously, and its citizens indignantly repudiate any claim to the dish known as *spaghetti bolognese*. When one considers what is offered world-wide under that name, the indignation is understandable. Evidence of past concern for the quality of food can be found in an early law, which prescribed that any fish which remained unsold at the end of a day must have its tail cut off so that it could be distinguished the next day from freshly caught fish.[12]

The Allied capture of Bologna opened up the road to Ferrara, a road which leads across flat, largely featureless, market-garden country. After World War II a resistance museum was set up in Ferrara in a part of the city rich in Renaissance palaces. The museum does, as might be expected, record activities of partisans in the Ferrara area betwen 1943 and 1945. Rather more questionable is the attention paid to the activities of Che Guevara and the Palestine Liberation Organisation.

With the capture of Argenta and Commachio and the advance of the British 6th Armoured division into Ferrara the first part of the Eighth Army's spring offensive was successfully completed. The enemy's next defensive line could be expected at the River Po.

ONWARD TO VENICE

The April offensive of the Fifth and Eighth Armies succeeded as fully as had been hoped and perhaps more than
had been expected. Von Viethinghoff felt obliged to convey
to Hitler a situation report which he knew would be thor-
oughly unwelcome. Further retreat, he considered, was the
only means of preventing the Allied Fifth and Eighth
Armies from crushing the German front. To this desperate
prognosis he added the fact that he now had no mobile
reserves.

McCreery shortly afterwards summarised what had happened on his front by stating that the Eighth Army had
gained a decisive victory after hard and bitter fighting in
spite of the fact that the enemy had had 'great advantages
of ground, strong defences on a series of river obstacles,
extensive flooding and deep minefields'. The decisive factors
had, as always, been 'the magnificent fighting qualities of
our soldiers and good junior leadership'.[1]

The advance which followed was extraordinarily rapid. In
contrast with the narrow rivers set in deep ravines encountered earlier, the Po has a width and dignity as it approaches
the sea. Yet it was crossed without difficulty. Nor did the
Adige, another wide river, prove a serious obstacle.

Then came the Euganean Hills, a region of spas and
splendid villas. In the lines which he composed in these hills
Shelley wrote:

> Beneath is spread like a green sea
> The waveless plain of Lombardy,
> Bounded by the vaporous air,
> Islanded by cities fair.[2]

One tank crew of the 10th Royal Hussars encountered an unusual obstacle. This was a treacle factory. It had been bombed some time earlier, and several craters which the bombs had formed had become filled with treacle. It was barely visible, and the tank crew, in the course of a patrol, drove their tank into one of the craters. The spectacle of the crew escaping from the treacle was enjoyed by numerous Italian onlookers. The ultimate fate of the tank has not been revealed.[3]

One of the 'cities fair' of which Shelley wrote while in the Euganean Hills was Padua. Units of the Rifle Brigade passed through Padua by night, almost without pausing, as they made their way north-eastwards towards Treviso.[4] Other units which came later and had more leisure to observe were more fortunate.

Of Padua's many churches, one in particular must surely have impressed soldiers towards the end of a long campaign. This is the basilica dedicated to St Anthony. It would be difficult to believe, without seeing it, that a church of such immensity could be decorated quite so lavishly. Every surface and corner seems to have been filled with fresco or statuary, most of it the work of exceptionally skilled craftsmen. In startling contrast with all the colour is Donatello's crucifix over the main altar, dark, stark and simple.

The United States Fifth Army captured Verona and Milan and then swept westwards through Genoa, eventually making contact with French forces. The Eighth Army's ultimate objective was now Austria. As it advanced there were some skirmishes, but little evidence of organised delaying action. German resistance, in short, seemed at last to be collapsing.

The Rifle Brigade, after passing through Treviso, continued north and north-east. Some units made for Belluno, where a large force of German paratroops surrendered. Others advanced to Udine, to find it already in the hands of partisans. Near Udine there was a skirmish with Russian troops, who had been conscripted by the Germans and who were described as Cossacks. They refused to surrender and withdrew into the nearby hills.[5]

That, at a time when some of the best German fighting troops were ready to surrender, these Russian conscripts were determined to keep their force intact, and, if necessary, even to operate where the rule of law did not prevail was an interesting revelation, the full significance of which was not yet apparent to most of the Eighth Army troops. Meanwhile other Eighth Army forces drove eastwards from Padua with the object of capturing Venice. These were New Zealanders and Popski's Private Army.

Like Tripoli earlier in the campaign, Venice was pictured by many in the Eighth Army as the journey's end, the city they had long been approaching. Peniakoff, for one, had long declared that his sole war aim was to drive a jeep round St Mark's Square. Freyberg had known Venice in the 1920s and 1930s and had taken an understandable liking to the Hotel Danieli. This, he decided, was to be the New Zealand Club.

An advance force of New Zealanders under Colonel J.I. Thodey reached Venice about 4 p.m. on 29 April.[6] The Germans had at one time prepared a defensive position, of which the mud flats of Venice's lagoon would have served as the left flank, but now they resisted only briefly, withdrawing troops by barge along the waterways.[7]

New Zealand tanks were parked near Venice's railway station, which lies outside the town. Some officers, guided by partisans, then reconnoitred the city. The now familiar welcome with wine and kisses followed while the partisans scoured Venice for enemy troops. They found nearly 3,000 and delivered them to a large garage. The next day a New

Zealand officer went by boat to the Lido, and then to the islands of Murano and Burano, to demand the surrender of the German garrisons there.[8]

Napoleon Bonaparte had once had the hitherto unique distinction of being able to report the capture of Venice. Freyberg had now emulated him.

Popski's Private Army reached Venice shortly after the New Zealanders. Not only did Peniakoff achieve what he wanted for himself: he led a procession of jeeps, all of which went round St Mark's Square seven times.[9]

That formations which had fought in the desert long before the battle of Alamein should have been the first to reach Venice was altogether appropriate, for Venice was the last city of importance to be captured before the German resistance in Italy finally collapsed.

Approaches, with a view to surrender, were first made to the Americans and the British in Switzerland on the initiative of SS General Wolff. These had to be reported to the Soviet Government under the terms of an agreement, for just as the Western Allies had at one time feared that the Soviet Union would conclude a separate peace with Germany, so now the Soviet government was deeply suspicious of the intentions of the United States and of Britain.

The negotiations continued, and on 29 April two German officers from the Army in Italy signed an instrument of surrender at Caserta. Winston Churchill expressed his delight in the achievements of both the Eighth Army and the Fifth Army in a message in which he stated: 'Never, I suppose, have so many nations advanced and manoeuvred in one line victoriously.'[10]

Because of the need to keep allied governments fully informed, the public announcement of the outcome of the meeting at Caserta was delayed until 2 May. Then Alexander announced the unconditional surrender of General von Viethinghoff and the German South-West Army group numbering one million men. The day before the announcement was made Hitler committed suicide in a bunker in Berlin.

THE FATE OF TRIESTE

Freyberg did not pause in Venice for long. His next objective was Trieste, where the presence of Eighth Army troops was considered imperative for political reasons. Indeed the beginning of the advance on Trieste may be considered the point at which the Eighth Army's role ceased to be almost exclusively military and became largely political.

The country in which guerrilla forces resisted the Germans most effectively in World War II was Yugoslavia, and as the war came to an end Marshal Tito's partisans emerged as a formidable fighting force. In Yugoslavia's northernmost province, Slovenia, there were nine divisions under the command of the Yugoslav Army, and Yugoslav forces had made it clear that they did not intend to remain within the country's pre-war frontiers. Indeed, in the Italian province of Venezia Giulia it was estimated that there were about 70,000 Yugoslav troops, well equipped with infantry weapons, as well as possessing about eighty tanks and more than thirty aircraft.[1]

In February 1945 Alexander had visited Tito in Belgrade, when he had received an assurance that the Allied Military Government would be able to operate in Trieste once the city had been liberated, and that Yugoslav local administration would be functioning in liberated areas. Future frontiers remained undefined. All this offered plenty of scope for misunderstanding.[2]

There was a sizeable Slovene population in pre-war Italy. Under Fascist rule it had been an oppressed minority, a ban even being imposed on Slovenes' use of their native language. Many Slovenes understandably sought revenge, and there was furthermore a general tendency among them to regard the River Isonzo, which runs slightly to the west of Gorizia, as the natural frontier between Italy and Yugoslavia. This belief took little account of the fact that, whereas there were many Slovenes in the surrounding countryside, the great majority of the inhabitants of Trieste itself were Italians.

Freyberg's New Zealanders and certain British formations, including the 12th Lancers and the 1st Battalion of the Scots Guards, which were all instructed to make for Trieste, were therefore engaged in a kind of race with the Yugoslav partisans – a race for which the prizes might be considerable.

In 1382 the city of Trieste had chosen to be placed under the protection of the Habsburg Empire rather than that of the Republic of Venice. The city, as it stands today, is largely a creation of the nineteenth century, but the effects of the decision taken in 1382 are still apparent. Nowhere are they more evident than in the great square which, in spite of its name, Piazza Unità d'Italia, is unmistakably a product of the Austro-Hungarian Empire, with its neo-classical structures such as the Governor's Palace, the Town Hall and the Lloyd-Triestino building with nudes on its facade as comfortably curved as any in the Folies Bergère. The Habsburg Empire influence is also evident elsewhere in the city in coffee-houses, which look as if they had been transported directly from Vienna.

Trieste became a great port when it was part of the Austro-Hungarian Empire. It was ceded to Italy by a secret treaty signed in London in 1915 and was thereby cut off from its natural hinterland. In 1945, therefore, although there were Trieste citizens who looked forward to the creation of a free port, independent of Italy and of every other country, the great majority of the city's inhabitants wanted Trieste to be part of Italy.

As soon as the New Zealanders approaching the city crossed the River Isonzo they noticed a change in attitudes and in atmosphere. Yugoslav partisans could be seen marching in columns. Portraits of Tito and posters announcing that this was Yugoslav territory lined the roads. The only concession to Italians seemed to be a few flags showing the Italian colours with a red star in the middle.[3]

At Monfalcone the Yugoslav partisans appeared surprised by the sudden arrival of Eighth Army troops. Freyberg met the partisan commander, General Drapsin, and pointed out that the force he was leading was only an advance formation, and added, to obviate any possibility of misunderstanding, that the main body of 30,000 would follow shortly with 150 tanks.[4]

The race for Trieste was narrowly won by the Yugoslav partisans, who began to enter the city on 1 May. Within Trieste it was generally known that three blasts on sirens would be the signal that liberating forces had arrived. No such signal was given, for the Italians did not consider the Yugoslavs to be liberators.[5] Indeed to this day unhappy memories of the Yugoslav presence are still vivid. One picture which seems to have implanted itself firmly in folk-memory is that of partisan women soldiers openly relieving themselves in the streets.

The next day Eighth Army units entered Trieste. German forces were by now largely confined to the harbour area, and they could be seen crowding on board boats, to await the arrival of the British and New Zealanders, in order to avoid having to surrender to the Yugoslavs. On the afternoon of 2 May Freyberg formally accepted the German surrender, and the Eighth Army forces occupied the port.

Once again men of the Eighth Army found themselves being treated as liberators, not from the Germans this time, but from men who had fought the Germans with courage and distinction. It was a role which called for tact. Impartiality was less easy to show, and before long there could be little doubt about where the sympathies of most members of the Eighth Army lay.

The prevailing attitude of mind among the British troops was ably described in a letter from an unnamed officer in the Grenadier Guards, which found its way into a Foreign Office file and later to the Public Record Office.

We are right up in the north-east corner of Italy at Gorizia near Trieste, in the district which Tito intends to annex and in effect has already annexed. Our instructions are to keep open the lines of communications into Austria and at all costs, for obvious reasons of *haute politique*, to avoid a clash with the partisans; which means that we sit with our hands tied and are unable to interfere with what is going on.

And what is going on is not very nice. The Yugoslavs are in complete control, and are maintaining something in the nature of a reign of terror. Any Italian is liable to be denounced as a Fascist and be dragged off to a concentration camp; and at night bands of partisans go round with proscription lists, getting their victims out of bed and taking them off . . .

This we watch rather gloomily; and can do nothing even when, as happened last night, partisans force their way into an officer's billet and carry off his landlord . . . We are besieged by Italians every day. I, *l'ufficio inglese*, am stopped in the street by wretched little men with wives and children hanging behind them – crowds cluster despondently round the barrack doors – wanting protection, or a passage back into Italy properly; neither of which we can give them.

The officer summed up his own situation and that of his men by writing: 'It is not fun at all. We have to carry weapons, as the partisans do as well, and the guardsmen are not allowed to walk out. All shops, cafés, cinemas are closed, by order of the Yugoslav "Committee of Liberation". So our victory celebrations lack any real enthusiasm.'[6]

Men of the Eighth Army, as soldiers everywhere will, had pictured the war's end in a variety of gay and glittering lights. This was an end which none of them could have foreseen.

The principal problem for Eighth Army occupying forces was clearly going to be that of relations with the Yugoslavs, and at various levels efforts were made to bring about better mutual understanding. An early meeting between Harding and the Yugoslav General Drapsin led to a decision to arrange a British-Yugoslav football match.[7] Not long afterwards Maoris staged a concert and dance in a village, which led to a regular exchange of invitations to other similar functions between partisans and Maoris.[8]

Helpful though such efforts were, they would have achieved little had it not been for the political guidance which began to trickle down from the top. Tito, a Moscow-trained Communist, still looked to Stalin for guidance, and Stalin had come to the conclusion that the establishment of frontiers between Yugoslavia and Italy, and the use of the port of Trieste, were not issues which merited a serious disagreement with the governments of the United States and Britain. Yugoslav partisan conduct in consequence became noticeably less hostile.

The United States and British governments for their part worked in unison. Churchill informed Alexander that supporting Italy on the Trieste issue would probably serve to weaken the Italian communists, as he believed Italians cared more about Trieste and the surrounding country than they did about communism. Shortly afterwards he told him: 'In order to avoid leading Tito or the Yugoslav Commanders into any temptation, it would be wise to have a solid mass of troops in this area and with a great superiority of modern weapons and frequent demonstrations of the Air Force.'[9]

As an expression of Anglo-American unity an American

division was for the first time put under the command of the
Eighth Army. This happened early in May 1945 in the
Trieste area.[10]

If Tito and those who served him did feel any temptations
of the kind contemplated by Churchill, they did not succumb
to them. The American-British occupation of Trieste continued. The city was made part of a free territory by a peace
treaty signed in 1947, and it was then placed under the
protection of the United Nations. Frontiers acceptable to
both Italy and Yugoslavia were finally agreed in 1954. Only
with the signing of this agreement, which provided that
Trieste should be part of Italy, did American and British
troops finally leave.

This brief, but far from negligible, threat of conflict between
erstwhile allies had been a direct consequence of the new
division of Europe which was already becoming apparent, a
division between east and west, between Marxist one-party
states and nations which continued to try to conduct their
affairs in accordance with liberal and Christian traditions.
An early victim of this new division was the Polish Second
Corps, whose last battle on Italian territory ended with the
liberation of Bologna.

Numerically, in spite of the heavy losses suffered at
Cassino and elsewhere, the Corps was at the end of the war
considerably stronger than it had been when originally
formed. Then it had numbered about 56,000. Eventually
the figure was nearer 120,000, because of the influx of Poles
who had earlier been conscripted by the Germans to serve
in Italy as soldiers or as members of the Todt organisation
of forced labour.[11]

The title Anders gave to his book about the Polish Second
Corps was *An Army in Exile*. As such, the Corps had
developed the characteristics of a self-contained community,
and not simply a fighting force. It had for example a well
organised educational establishment, in which young soldiers were instructed by reserve officers in matriculation

subjects. Women too had a more active service role than in other formations of the Eighth Army, girl drivers being employed to bring ammunition up to the guns. This community was clearly going to remain in exile once the war was over. Indeed, when given the choice of where they wanted to live, only 310 of those who came out of the Soviet Union with Anders opted for repatriation to Poland.[12]

A considerable number came to Britain, where a Polish Resettlement Corps was set up to enable Poles to adjust to British life and employment. On the whole this worked well, in spite of determined opposition by the National Union of Mineworkers to Poles who wanted to work in the coal-mines.

At least the solutions found to the problems of the future welfare of members of the Polish Second Corps had been defensible. Far more complex was the situation of the huge number of people whose homelands were either the Soviet Union or Yugoslavia, who did not wish to return to those homelands, and who found themselves in areas controlled by the Eighth Army, either in prisoner-of-war camps or in partisan bands. The way in which the great majority of these people were disposed of seems likely to remain a subject of controversy long after personal memories of the terrible happenings which occurred have been lost.

Of the conduct of the men he commanded Peniakoff later wrote:

> We preserved the decencies through the violence and the licence of war: raped no women, tortured no one, looted in moderation and only from those who could well afford to lose, drank decorously (by soldierly standards) and refrained from bullying, went wenching only with the best and, when we could, we looked after the girls we got into

trouble . . . Our behaviour was modelled on that Victorian ideal of a gentleman.

Popski's Private Army was an elite formation, and it would be absurd to claim that all members of the Eighth Army at all times behaved as decorously as those whom he described. No large conquering army in history ever has done so. What does emerge, however, after the passage of more than forty years, is the excellent reputation which members of the Eighth Army enjoy today among those Italians old enough to remember them. Of this I had, in the course of my journey, abundant evidence.

THE PRISONERS

In May 1945 there were, in addition to the Italian population, the Eighth Army and the Yugoslav partisans, about
one million people in the area controlled by the Fifth Corps
of the Eighth Army.[1] The great bulk of this million were
prisoners of war. The rest were members of independent
partisan bands, refugees and other displaced persons. All
needed food, and the majority had to be fed from Eighth
Army resources.

The huge administrative problems which the Corps faced
in consequence were complicated by political factors. Many
of the prisoners of war were Soviet citizens, some of whom
had volunteered to serve the Germans, but most of whom
had been forcibly conscripted. There was a sizeable force of
Yugoslav Četniks, followers of General Mihailovič, who
had been the first to offer resistance to the German occupiers. These men were bitterly opposed to Tito's partisans.
There were also, as was discovered later, an appreciable
number of Russians who had fought on the German side
and who were not Soviet citizens.

The British military had clear instructions about what was
to be done with the Soviet citizens who were prisoners of
war. They were to be returned to the Soviet Union in
accordance with an agreement reached between Anthony
Eden and Molotov on 16 October 1944 and confirmed the
next day by Churchill when he met Stalin.[2] Further details

of how the agreement was to be implemented had been worked out at Yalta by representatives of the Soviet, American and British governments early in 1945.

The agreement, considered superficially, was not unreasonable. The men in question had given help to the enemy of one kind or another. At the end of the war it was the established practice for prisoners to be returned to their country of origin. There was also the practical consideration that at the time of the Yalta meeting the Soviet armies had overrun German prison camps in which some 50,000 British and Commonwealth prisoners were held.[3] For this last reason alone the British government did not want any dispute with Stalin and Molotov about the return of prisoners.

Unfortunately the agreement did not specify the fate of prisoners who had no desire to return to the Soviet Union. Stalin did not want to admit the possibility that such people might exist in appreciable numbers, and the Western Allies chose not to press him on this point. Nor was account taken of the difficulty of distinguishing between those who had willingly assisted the enemy and those who had simply been conscripted by the Germans to do forced labour.

A number of Soviet prisoners were returned without difficulty. Some 8,000 Turcomans, for example, were captured near Ravenna. They were moved to a camp near Taranto, where they came under the control of a Soviet military mission. The camp was virtually unguarded, but no reports of escapes seem to have reached the British. From Taranto the prisoners were transported by ship to Odessa early in 1945. Denis Hills, who accompanied them, observed that as the voyage went on more and more seemed to regret their decision to return. After arrival they were sent to labour camps, and the general belief was that they would serve twenty-year sentences.[4]

Other Soviet prisoners were less docile, and increasingly force had to be used to return them. Nor did those members of the Eighth Army involved suffer from any illusions about what would happen to such men. Some enterprising British officers did quietly disobey orders. Colonel Charles Finlay, an officer in the Royal Artillery, managed to arrange for 800 Soviet Muslims to be put on board a ship bound for Egypt and consigned them to the care of King Farouk.[5] In a camp for Ukrainians near Rome Denis Hills, after coming to an agreement with the town major, allowed about half-a-dozen men a day to escape. Their subsequent movements were organised by a Ukrainian priest.

These, however, were exceptions. Elsewhere the task of handing over men, few of whom could fairly be classified as war criminals, in the knowledge that they would all face death or long imprisonment, was carried out reluctantly but in accordance with instructions. The British government needed the help of the Soviet Union in restraining the Yugoslavs and, later, in effecting an entry into Vienna, and these considerations were paramount.

The forcible repatriations were a distressing and, it could be said, ignoble end to a long campaign. Worse was to follow when the Eighth Army entered Austria.

PART SIX: AUSTRIA

(May–July 1945)

OVER THE MOUNTAINS
INTO CARINTHIA

The country known as Austria which emerged at the end of
World War I was a comparatively small part of the old
Austro-Hungarian Empire. Many of its inhabitants believed
its future must lie in *Anschluss*, or union, with Germany, a
country whose language and, to a considerable extent,
culture it shared. Many others disagreed, but, in any event,
Austrians had little choice, for the treaty imposed by the
victorious powers in 1919 specifically forbade *Anschluss*
without the consent of the League of Nations.

Anschluss was in fact effected by unilateral action when
Hitler ordered German troops to march into Austria in
1936. It was his intention, at one stage, to establish an
independent Austrian Nazi government, but he quickly
abandoned the idea and decided that Austria must be
regarded simply as a part of Germany. As such it was
administered throughout World War II.

The foreign ministers of Britain, the United States and
the USSR, agreed by contrast at a meeting in Moscow in
November 1943 that at the end of the war a free and
independent Austria should be established. A temporary
division of the country into zones of occupation by the
Allied powers was also agreed without great difficulty.

The conquest of Austria was effected by Soviet forces. By
13 April 1945, before the Eighth Army had even crossed

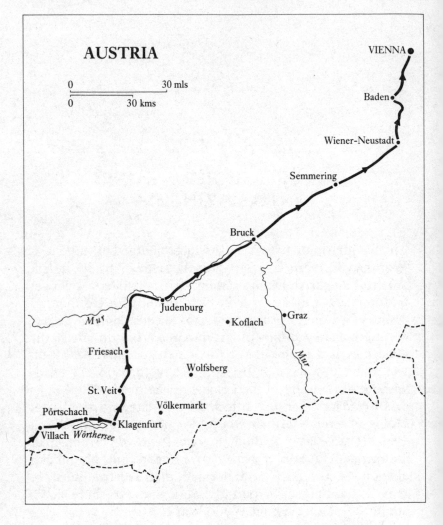

the River Po, the Red Army was in occupation of Vienna. The Allied governments had agreed that, like Berlin, Vienna would be under the joint control of Soviet, American, British and French forces, but the actual entry of western forces into the city still had to be negotiated with Soviet commanders, who were already well established.

The agreed British zone of occupation, in addition to a small enclave in Vienna, consisted of the provinces of Carinthia and Styria. With the collapse of German resistance United Kingdom units of the Eighth Army therefore began to move from Italy into Carinthia without delay.

The route they followed from Udine to the Austrian frontier is varied and spectacular. There is at first much arable land, which presents a notable contrast with the vines and olives further south. The mountain country begins near Tarcento and is immediately suggestive of central Europe, with tidy villages in valleys, little rococo churches, and houses with steeply sloping roofs, all strikingly different from the dominant medieval hill-towns and castles of the Apennines.

After Gemona the road continues north-eastwards through a deep, narrow and abundantly green valley. The mountains are now so formidable that at times the sky is almost shut out. Waterfalls pour down their sides. When the leading Eighth Army units passed through, freed from the burdens of war and with opportunities to admire the scenery, chestnuts were in blossom and snow lay on the peaks. Shortly before the frontier town of Tarvisio is reached the valley broadens out, and in May the fields were awash with buttercups. The border is crossed through the Würzen Pass, in which lies the Austrian frontier town of Arnoldstein.

Almost immediately after the frontier the landscape becomes gentler. At the approach to the Wörthersee the scenery is of a kind to be found in all countries fortunate enough to possess a portion of the Alps. The grass is lush; lilac and copper-beech flourish, and conifers provide the backdrop. The principal sounds are bird-songs, and the works of man seem clean.

Lieutenant-Colonel Peter Wilkinson, an officer of SOE who had spent some time in Yugoslavia, led one of the advance columns into Austria. 'It was an extraordinary sight,' he wrote. 'The train puffing up from Arnoldstein as though it was any day of the week; surprised German soldiers hurrying out from breakfast to see the column pass, and not infrequently to cheer; one lieutenant and a platoon of soldiers goose-stepping (of all things) down the road to meet us.'

At Klagenfurt he found a newly established local government official, who was happy to surrender the city. From the public there was an enthusiastic welcome which Wilkinson attributed more to 'terror of Tito and the Russians than any love of us'.[1]

The principal problems confronting the Eighth Army as it moved into Austria were, in order of priority, how to restrain the Yugoslav partisans; how to establish a suitable and effective local government structure; and how to dispose of well-armed groups of Cossacks and others who had made their way across the mountains from Italy.

British troops reached Klagenfurt, the first important Austrian city which they occupied, on 9 May. During the next three days there was a steady build-up of Yugoslav forces in the area. Among the posters with which they plastered the walls of Klagenfurt was one which read in translation:

The Yugoslav Army has entered Carinthia in order to cleanse the land of Nazi criminals and bring liberty and democracy to Slovene Austrians. Complete victory over the Germans has now been attained by the Yugoslav Partisans alone . . . We hereby make known that throughout the whole of liberated Carinthia the military authority of the Yugoslav Army has been established . . . The population and all branches of our administration are to extend every help to our Army and to obey unconditionally all published decrees.[2]

Arrests of Austrians and looting followed. Wilkinson described what he witnessed as

a shocking sight for a regular soldier like myself. Ditches piled high with every sort of war material – the partisans themselves gorged with loot beyond the dreams of avarice, each courier with at least six personal weapons and so strung with field-glasses, torches etc. that they were often unable to mount their newly acquired (and often thoroughbred) chargers. The scene that night, during which the pillage went on unabated, lit by the eerie light of burning vehicles, is quite unforgettable.[3]

Harold Macmillan, as Minister Resident, was officially informed that the Eighth Army in Austria was not yet strong enough to deal effectively with any hostile action on the part of the Yugoslavs.[4] Once again, as in Trieste, there were days of acute tension, and once again, for no reason immediately evident to outsiders, the Yugoslavs changed their policy. They now began a general withdrawal from the Klagenfurt area.

Two weeks later Marshal Tito announced: 'Only a few days after our troops were forced to leave Carinthia cries of distress and appeal are already reaching us from our brothers in Carinthia.' He added: 'I firmly reject the accusation that we have any intention to conquer by force.'[5] As no physical force was exercised against the Yugoslav partisans by the British or by anyone else, the conclusion seems irresistible that the order to Tito to renounce any claims he had on Carinthia came from the Soviet Union.

*   *   *

Arrangements had to be made, meanwhile, for the future government of the whole country. There were many refugees from Austria, a high proportion of them Jews, who had spent World War II in Britain and who were determinedly anti-Nazi. But they had little social cohesion, and they had not formed even the nucleus of an Austrian government-in-exile.

Nor was there an effective Austrian resistance movement with which the Allies could make contact. In a recent exhibition which I saw in the Rathaus in Vienna it was stated that 2,700 Austrians were condemned to death for resistance. They must have been brave people, for to resist tyranny actively as an individual, or as part of a small isolated group, requires far more courage than to act as one of a large body of insurgents.

The Special Operations Executive, which was generally so successful in establishing contact with and promoting resistance in countries under German occupation, had made little headway in Austria. A few agents, including Sigmund Freud's grandson, Walter, were parachuted in during the final stages of the war, but their impact was slight. In 1813 British agents had helped to promote a rising against Napoleon in the Tyrol.[6] Their successors in World War II, some of whom were very gifted people, could not achieve anything comparable, for there was no climate of revolt in which they could operate.

In the absence of any recognised pro-Allied body in Austria or in exile, other arrangements had to be made for the country's immediate government. A controlling body, the Allied Military Government, was drawn from the Eighth Army and supplemented by professional administrators who had recently donned Army uniform.

The principal administrative problem, it was clear from the outset, was going to be that of finding enough food. Even in the countryside people were living largely on pea-soup.[7] In the cities the shortages were much graver.

Lieutenant-Colonel Wilkinson was not favourably

impressed by early administrative efforts in Carinthia. A number of the officers seemed to him too young and inexperienced. As they settled into their tasks, probably the most effective were certain ex-professionals, such as policemen, who, although wearing a new kind of uniform, had to carry out tasks with which they were already familiar.

The recruitment of Austrians to serve the Military Government proceeded fairly smoothly. Towards the end of the war the Combined Services Detailed Interrogation Centre had set up a camp near Rome, where Austrian prisoners with experience of central or local government engaged in seminars and prepared themselves in other ways to take part in the immediate post-war administration of Austria.[8]

In Austria itself there was no shortage of volunteers. In one Carinthian town the difficult problem of selection was solved only after a Field Security section had found a list of local Freemasons which had been prepared by the Gestapo. This was passed to a senior British officer who, himself a Freemason, had no doubt about where to look for the administrators he needed.[9]

At a meeting held in London of a sub-committee of the War Cabinet it had been decided that 'fraternisation was forbidden, not only with German and Austrian military personnel remaining in Austria, but with any other nationals – whether military or civilian – who might be found there.' In explanation it was stated that 'a very mixed bag of people might be found in Austria, including Quisling Serbs, Croats, Slovenes, Hungarians etc., and that it was possible that the Germans or Austrians might encourage such Quislings to get on good terms with the occupying forces.'[10]

As the policy of non-fraternisation trickled down from the top it became steadily amended by reality. Soon after the 78th Division had moved into Austria its commander, Major-General R. K. Arbuthnott, issued an order stating: 'Troops will not make the running in any friendly relations. They will not consort with civilians more than necessary.

Apart from this, a correct and friendly attitude will be adopted.'[11]

Austria is one of the most seductive countries in the world, and the welcome which the British occupying forces received took many forms. In Linz, for example, they were greeted by a choir dressed in the uniform of the *Hitler Jugend*, who sang *God Save the King*, the words and music of which they had recently and hurriedly learnt.[12] But it was a welcome expressed with charm and for the most part, although for a variety of reasons, with sincerity.

In consequence a policy of non-fraternisation was no more feasible in Austria than it had been in Italy. Non-commissioned officers and men, observing how rapidly their superior officers acquired secretaries, were among the first to resent it.[13] Attachments were formed, some of which in time led to marriage, and living in Austria today there are Englishmen who have enjoyed more than forty years of successful marriage to Austrian women of exceptional charm, not a few of whom were at one time convinced supporters of Adolf Hitler.

'She says she IS Lili Marlene.'

ROUND-UP OF THE COSSACKS

As the Eighth Army initially made its way through Carinthia there had been confused scenes of migration and retreat. A report included in an official document produced by the Allied Military Government stated:

The road from Klagenfurt through Völkermarkt and Wolfsberg to Köflach was an unforgettable spectacle. Remnants of German units, Cossacks on horseback, Hungarians in horse-drawn transport with their wives and families, processions of horses stretching mile after mile, were heading west from the avenger, stretching over hills and valleys as far as the eye could see; most of the men and women on horses seemed exhausted and the German soldiers, in particular, had a hopeless look of complete disillusion and defeat. Tito forces were everywhere.[1]

The 'avenger' referred to was of course the army of the Yugoslav partisans, and when this withdrew some order could be imposed. But the Cossacks remained in place as an intractable problem and, at the same time, an extraordinary example of mid-twentieth-century folk migration.

When German armies reached the northern Caucasus in 1942 they received an enthusiastic welcome, and thousands of Cossacks took advantage of their arrival to leave their homes and move westwards. Taking their possessions with them in horse-drawn carts, these migrants, including old men, women and children, made their way slowly across Poland and Germany until they reached northern Italy, where they were settled first near Friuli, and later near Tolmezzo, which lies to the north of Udine. The able-bodied men served as valuable recruits to the German armed forces, and the colony was joined by a considerable number of Cossacks from western Europe who had emi-grated there after the Bolshevik revolution.

As the experience of the Rifle Brigade in the closing days of the war had shown, the Cossacks became a well-disci-plined force, and they retreated over the mountains from Italy to Austria in good order.

Nor were they the only people emanating from the Soviet Union who appeared in large numbers in Austria as the war came to an end. Another, even more substantial force of ex-Soviet citizens had been fighting in Yugoslavia under the German General Helmut von Pannwitz and had acquired a deplorable reputation for committing atrocities against the civilian population.

Both groups surrendered their arms to the British, who were now faced with the problem of how and where to dispose of them. Harold Macmillan paid a visit to Klagenfurt on 13 May and afterwards noted in his diary: 'Among the surrendered Germans are about 40,000 Cossacks and "White" Russians, with their wives and children. To hand them over to the Russians is condemning them to slavery, torture and probably death. To refuse, is deeply to offend the Russians, and incidentally break the Yalta agreement. We have decided to hand them over.'[3]

This is a clear summary of British government policy, of the moral predicament, and of the decision taken. The tragic task of implementing the decision fell to Lieutenant-General Charles Keightley, who commanded 5 Corps, and, lower down the line, to the Argyll and Sutherland Highland-ers and the Royal Inniskilling Fusiliers. Deception and force were both used. Nearly 1,500 Cossack officers were invited to what they believed would be a meeting with Alexander. The purpose of this manoeuvre was to separate them from their troops. They were then informed that they were to be handed over to the Soviet authorities.[4]

The hand-over, first of the officers and then of the other ranks, had to be conducted by force if it was to take place at all. The number of Cossacks who killed their families and then committed suicide rather than accept repatriation is not known for certain, but the suicides are believed to have exceeded a hundred.[5]

Shortly after Macmillan's visit to Klagenfurt, Alexander sent a signal to London stating: 'Handover of respective nationals to Russians and Yugoslavs agreed.'[6] Among the Yugoslavs were a considerable number of Croat Ustaši, who had sided with the Germans. But there were also bands of Serbian Četniks, whose loyalties were more equivocal.

Under Mihailovič and other local leaders the Četniks had in places resisted the Germans and had been prepared to act in cooperation with any British or American force which might have landed in Yugoslavia. Mihailovič unwisely decided to attack the partisans, whose policies he opposed, and in consequence the Četniks were driven more and more into collaboration with other Serbian forces, who were effectively pro-German.

The Četnik bands which escaped first to Italy and then to Austria may well have become demoralised. When the 9th Queen's Lancers took over a barracks which 4,000 Četniks had just abandoned they were astounded by the squalor they found, the lack of sanitary arrangements and the leaking roofs.[7] But demoralised or not, the Četniks were no more – and arguably much less – deserving of the treatment accorded to them than the Cossacks. Nor was their fate after they had been handed over to the authorities now controlling their country any more enviable.

Soviet goodwill, which the British government so assiduously sought, was not much apparent in the early negotiations concerning the occupation and control of Vienna.

Early in May Churchill appointed McCreery Commander of the British Military Commission for Austria, but the announcement of the appointment had to be delayed because of disagreement with the Soviet Government over the formation of the Allied Control Commission.[8]

An exploratory British mission headed by Major-General Winterton was permitted to visit Vienna, but its first meeting with the Soviet Commandant, Lieutenant-General Blago-datov, on 4 June 1945 was described as 'somewhat chilly'. Marshal Tolbukhin, Blagodatov's superior was, by contrast, cordial, but he told Winterton his mission's task must be completed as soon as possible. Winterton replied that his instructions were to remain until ordered by his superiors to return. This was accepted, but the mission was prevented from going beyond the city limits or reconnoitring airfields.

On 9 June Alexander telegraphed Churchill: 'Here is the capital of Austria which by agreement is to be divided, like the city itself, into four zones; but no one has any power there except the Russians and not even ordinary diplomatic visits are allowed. If we gave way in this matter we must regard Austria as in the Sovietised half of Europe.' He went on to suggest that Western Allied withdrawals to agreed zones in Germany should be postponed until satisfactory arrangements for the occupation of Austria had been made.[9]

Negotiations continued. For a long time the British had had to take most of the initiative in dealing with the Soviet government over Austrian affairs. Indeed, as late as January 1945 the American Ambassador in London, John G. Winant, had told the Foreign Office he could not yet say whether the United States government would or would not take over the zone in Austria allotted to it.[10] But now the British, the Americans and the French were acting in concert.

They agreed that the centre of Vienna, known as Bezirk 1, should be controlled equally by the four powers. The rest of the city, they considered, should be subdivided in a manner which took account of the geographical location of the zones of occupation of Austria as a whole. In other words, the Soviet zone should be to the east, the American and French to the west, and the British to the south. The British zone would include Schönbrunn Palace and, as it happened, much of the best residential accommodation in Vienna.[11]

By the end of June general agreement had been reached more or less on the lines the Western allies had advocated. The Soviet authorities then accepted that limited British, American and French military forces should be permitted to make their way to Vienna.

JOURNEY'S END

The road from Klagenfurt to Vienna became in time familiar to most of the British occupation troops. McCreery's policy was to limit the numbers in Vienna to a reasonable minimum, largely because of food shortages, and to call on regiments stationed in Carinthia to provide the Vienna garrison in rotation.[1]

The country to the north of the Wörthersee, to which Klagenfurt is linked by canal, is exceptionally beautiful. There is at first a blend of woodland, pasture and arable, with mountains continually in sight, but never dominating. Along the valleys of the Gurk and the Metnitz the road runs through St Viet and Friesach to the border between the provinces of Carinthia and Styria.

In Styria the landscape opens out again until a new barrier, that of the Seetaleralpen, appears, rugged yet sumptuously green. A number of the churches have onion-shaped tops, recalling Turkish influence, which was still powerful in the late seventeenth century,

Through the deep valley of the Mur the road continues to Judenburg, which acquired its name from a large Jewish settlement in the Middle Ages. Here the advancing British and Soviet armies had met in May 1945. There had seemed for a time to be the threat of an awkward confrontation, but then the two commanding officers lunched together and agreed to accept the River Mur as a temporary barrier between them.[2] Judenberg thus became the scene of the main handover of Cossacks and of the first shootings of those handed over.

Peter Wilkinson, who was appointed political adviser to McCreery, and who was later to return to Austria as British Ambassador, was a member of the mission under General Winterton which made a preliminary visit to Vienna in June 1945. In a telegram sent on 9 June, recording his immediate impressions, he described the population as being in a state of 'high nervous tension'. Lack of normal forms of communication had, he suspected, bred exaggerated reports of Russian behaviour. Nevertheless 'removal of capital goods is still being carried out, likewise seizure of such objects as wireless sets, cars, clothes, linen, furniture and watches.'

The British, he reported, had been greeted from the outset with 'embarrassing warmth'. War damage to the city was severe, and the bread ration was not only small, but varied according to the kind of work done.[3]

During the war the German government had made extraordinary efforts to increase food production. In Vienna even the famous Heldenplatz in front of the Hofburg Palace was ploughed up for the growing of potatoes.[4] Distribution too was well organised, and it was after the war, not during it, that the population of Vienna as a whole first was hungry.

John Reid, a police inspector, who arrived with the first column motoring up from Klagenfurt, was astonished to learn that the daily average calorie intake in Vienna was no more than 900. Households had gas by rota for only three hours in the day, and neighbours would therefore come in to share it.[5]

Most of the destruction in the inner city had been caused by the fighting in April 1945, when the German Waffen SS continued to resist the Soviet forces street by street. But there had also been consistent bombing of Austrian cities, beginning in 1944, after the Germans had moved important war industries into Austria, including factories making optical instruments, U-boats and parts for the V2.[6]

Among the casualties from the street fighting was the splendid late Gothic church of St Stephen, which was later to be largely rebuilt, although a number of choir-stalls were irreparably lost.

At their first meetings relations between British and Soviet soldiers tended to be correct but distant. A number of Russians were puzzled by what they considered the unsoldierly appearance of British troops in shorts and open-necked shirts.[7] Later they were to exhibit signs of envy when, on the occasion of the Allied parade, the Argyll and Sutherland Highlanders, as they had done in other cities before, clearly captivated the onlookers.[8]

Schönbrunn in the British zone offered a more immediately attractive prospect than the ravaged centre of Vienna. British staff officers – and there were a number of them – who had served in the Allied headquarters in Caserta and later found themselves in Schönbrunn, had a privileged insight into the glories of the baroque. (War did provide such unforeseen benefits. As a very junior officer I worked for some weeks in the Van Dyck room in Wilton House. If my memory is correct, one of the portraits was concealed by a large map, but otherwise the pleasure was uninterrupted.)

Schönbrunn was intended by the Habsburgs to be larger than Versailles. In fact it is not, but in its defence Austrians point out that its grounds are larger than the principality of Monaco. It had, when it was a royal residence, 150 kitchens. Its colour is the yellow chosen for the Habsburgs' summer residence, for which purpose it was built, but the Empress Maria Theresa became understandably so addicted to this splendid palace that she sometimes decided, to the dismay of her courtiers who preferred the city of Vienna, that summer began as early as the first week in May.

Long before the British arrived in 1945 Schönbrunn had witnessed dignity in defeat. In the gardens beyond the

fountains the huge memorial known as the Gloriette com-
memorates a war the Austrians lost. At the end of World
War I the last Habsburg Emperor Charles signed a document in Schönbrunn renouncing all further participation in
affairs of state. He then decorated one of the ministers who
had brought him the document of renunciation with the
Grand Cross of the Order of St Stephen. Other ministers
received lesser awards.[9]

In the inner city the British chose well by establishing a
senior officers' club in the Hotel Sacher. The fame of this
hotel still rests largely on the cake known as the Sachertorte,
whose origin is said to have been in the year 1832, when a
sixteen-year-old apprentice named Franz Sacher produced a
concoction which satisfied the requirements of Metternich.

The hotel itself is of later date. In 1869 a new Opera
House was opened. The interest aroused by this event, the
criticisms of the design and the controversy which raged
were such that one of the architects committed suicide.
Seven years later the Sacher Hotel came into being opposite
the Opera House. To meet the discreet needs of the Opera
House's patrons it specialised in the provision of dining-
rooms for two known as *séparées*. More than a hundred
years later I found that the Sacher's atmosphere was still
unmistakably one of opulent privacy.

That the British were made so welcome in Vienna was
partly, as in Trieste, because they were found preferable to
some other so-called liberators. But there was also a strong
tradition of anglophilia in the city. Commenting on the years
shortly before World War I, the painter Oskar Kokoshka
said: 'The whole of my Vienna was in love with England.'[10]

Vienna, until the end of World War I, had been the
capital of an empire rather than of a national state. As such
it was cosmopolitan in spirit, in culture and in language,
with a tradition of making foreigners welcome. An important reason why Vienna was chosen as the site of the congress
which decided the future of Europe at the end of the

Napoleonic wars was that nowhere else outside France could the educated classes be relied on to speak French, which was then the language of diplomacy.[11]

Vienna also had a tradition of accepting conquerors or, at least, of giving them, on arrival, the benefit of the doubt. Napoleon Bonaparte expressed surprise at the warmth of the welcome he received in Vienna in 1805, when people turned out in large numbers to watch the march-past of troops who were to some extent regarded as liberators. But when he appeared before Vienna again four years later the citizens were wiser: he was bitterly opposed, and this time his conquering troops marched through empty streets with closed shops.

So too, with even more disastrous results, had the Viennese welcomed Hitler, who, on returning to the city where he had once known a life of poverty and failure, had the intoxicating experience of addressing a huge and cheering crowd from a balcony of the ancient Hofburg Palace of the Habsburgs.

When I came to Vienna at the end of my journey I found Austrians still trying to come to terms with some of the appalling consequences of their ready acceptance of Hitler. In an exhibition in the Rathaus entitled '1938' I saw displays calling attention to the fact that 100,000 Jews and other Austrians died in the concentration camp in Mauthausen. Later a thoughtful, sensitive Austrian, who had lived through the war and occupation, said to me: 'We deserved all we got.' It was an admission which could only command respect.

The Allied occupation of Vienna lasted for ten years. There are Austrians who today say they could endure another war more easily than they could endure another occupation. But they concede that the arrangement, whereby each of the four occupying powers took turns to exercise at least nominal control over the centre of Vienna for a month, worked surprisingly well.

No one power was able to gain a dominant position, nor did the Soviet authorities make any serious attempt to create the kind of puppet government which they had installed in other countries of eastern and central Europe. When a general election was held in Austria in November 1945, out of 165 candidates returned only four were Communists.

The withdrawal of all four occupying powers was absolute, and with it the freedom and independence which Austria had been promised became reality. The last soldier to leave was, as it happened, British.

The Eighth Army had advanced from El Alamein to Vienna in order to prevent a single power from gaining dominion over Europe and many other parts of the world. For similar reasons the armies of the Duke of Wellington had advanced across the Iberian peninsula into France. Yet there were differences.

The principal enemy the Eighth Army fought was more than simply an expanding European power. It was a highly trained and effective army, working in conjunction with a secret police force, both of which were there to do the bidding of a dictator of almost limitless evil. One of this dictator's beliefs, which he loudly proclaimed, was that the people he ruled were a *Herrenvolk*, a master race.

Not the least of the Eighth Army's achievements was to show that there is no master race. The excellently commanded, disciplined and equipped German armies were continually and, in the end, decisively defeated by an army comprising Poles and Greeks, Moroccans and Jews, Maoris and Gurkhas – men whose outstanding fighting qualities the campaign indisputably proved.

For the British it can be a source of abiding pride that this army was under British command and that the great majority of its soldiers at all stages in the campaigns came from the United Kingdom of Great Britain and Northern Ireland.

The Duke of Wellington once observed that it was 'a damned long way from Torres Vedras to Waterloo'. He was right, but it was a much longer way from El Alamein to Vienna.

ADVICE TO TRAVELLERS

Those who wish to go where the Eighth Army once went –
and I can strongly recommend any who are interested to do
so – will have to make certain decisions affecting their route.

Armies often advance on broad fronts, and no one can
hope to go over all the ground which the Eighth Army
covered. For much of the route, however, the line of
advance is a clear one. In Egypt, Libya and Tunisia it
follows the main coastal road with, in Tunisia, diversions to
take in Kairouan and, perhaps, Gafsa. In Sicily too there is
a clear line of advance up the east coast from Syracuse to
Catania, skirting Mount Etna to the west, and then up the
east coast again from Taormina to Messina.

Through Southern Italy it may be best to follow the line
of the Canadians from Reggio through Catanzaro and
Potenza to Foggia, though there is an alternative route
including Taranto and Bari, which Eighth Army units took,
but along which there was little fighting.

It is after Cassino that the main problems of choice arise.
One reason for this is that when it was finally decided that
the Eighth Army must capture Monastery Hill the Fifth
Army, on its left, was confined to a relatively narrow coastal
strip, and the Eighth Army's front was correspondingly
widened.

There were then two main Eighth Army lines of advance,
one through Perugia and Arezzo to Florence, the other up

the east coast to Ancona and Pesaro. I myself followed both routes, but the traveller who has time to take only one may be well advised, because of both scenery and architecture, to take the central or Florence route. From this diversions to the east can be made, to ensure the inclusion of Pesaro, Rimini and Ravenna – all of importance in the campaign – as well, perhaps, as Assisi, Urbino and Gubbio.

From Florence the recommended route leads through Bologna, Ferrara, Padua and Venice to Trieste. The route into Carinthia, and then from Klagenfurt to Vienna, is fairly straightforward, as the maps indicate.

The quality of the hotels in which I stayed naturally varied. In Tunisia I happily used as my base for some time the Sheraton Hotel in Hammamet. The rooms here are set out in chalet style, and on the terrace of mine the wall was covered by bougainvillaea.

In Syracuse the Motel, conveniently situated near the ancient Greek theatre, is to be recommended. Outstanding among Sicily's hotels is the Monte Tauro in Taormina. I arrived there at 2 a.m. because of flight delays and was warmly greeted. The entrance hall and reception desk are in effect on the top floor, the restaurant and bedrooms being on various floors below, for the hotel runs down the side of the cliff face. An outdoor lift gives a magnificent view over the Ionian Sea – as indeed do the bedroom balconies – and eventually brings one down to the swimming pool. No less impressive, also in Taormina, is the San Domenico Palace Hotel.

In Perugia the Hotel La Rosetta has a delightful situation at the top of the town and is comfortable and reasonably priced. In Passigano in the small, unpretentious Hotel Trasimeno I was received with the warmest friendliness by the Pierini family, the daughter greeting me in the morning with a kiss on both cheeks because she had learnt that it was my birthday, and the father, on learning that my money and credit cards had been stolen shortly before in Florence, offering all kinds of help.

In Fiesoli I had the good fortune to stay in the convent in the Villa San Girolano, where some paying guests have the privilege of being accepted.

The Hotel Roma in Bologna, situated in the pleasantest part of the city, is of very high quality and not a very high price. In Ravenna I found the Hotel Centrale Byron moderately priced and good. In Pesaro I was made most comfortable at the Hotel Mediterraneo, probably the best of the many seaside hotels. Only in Trieste did I stay in a hotel of the de luxe category. This was the splendid Hotel Duche d'Aosta, which is situated in Trieste's most impressive square.

Of those hotels in Italy which fell a little, or more than a little, below the standard I expected I have preferred to write nothing.

Towards the end of my journey I had a few days' rest in the Hotel Werzer in Pörtschach. This was a delight. The hotel is on the shore of the Wörthersee, and the service was of the kind which, in London, I have experienced only in the Basil Street Hotel – in other words, flawless. The food too gave me continual pleasure. I have to admit that my enthusiasm for indigenous North African and most Italian cooking is limited. By contrast, in the Hotel Werzer I enjoyed breakfast, I enjoyed lunch, and I enjoyed dinner.

In Vienna I was comfortable and well looked after in the Hotel Rathauspark and much enjoyed my visits to the Hotel Sacher.

My final word of advice to would-be travellers is to equip themselves with a money-belt and to conceal it well. Unlike insurance policies, money-belts have no small print.

BIBLIOGRAPHY

Anders, Lieutenant-General W: *An Army in Exile* (Macmillan, 1949).

Arbizzani, Luigi: *Guerra, Nazifascismo Lotta di Liberazione nel Bolognese* (Ape, Bologna, 1973).

Arnold, Matthew: *Empedocles on Etna* (1852).

Barnett, Corelli: *The Desert Generals* (Allen & Unwin, 1960).

Beddington, Major-General W. R.: *A History of the Queen's Bays (The 2nd Dragoon Guards) 1929–1945* (Warren, 1954).

Bergonzini, Professor Luciano: Paper presented to Symposium No. 1 Special Force nella Resistenza Italiana, Bologna, 1987.

Bologna nella Resistenza (Mostra Storica, Museo Civico, Bologna 1977).

Bright, Joan (ed.): *The Ninth Queen's Royal Lancers 1936–1945* (Gale & Polden, 1951).

Brion, Marcel: *The Medici* (Elek, 1969).

Brook-Shepherd, Gordon: *The Last Habsburg* (Weidenfeld, 1968).

Burdon, R. M.: *24 Battalion. Official History of New Zealand in the Second World War 1939–45* (War History Branch, Department of Internal Affairs, Wellington (NZ), 1953)

Carver, Michael: *El Alamein* (Batsford, 1962).

Carver, Michael: *Harding of Petherton* (Weidenfeld & Nicolson, 1978).

Carver, Michael: *Dilemmas of the Desert War* (Batsford, 1986).

Chaplin, Lieutenant-Colonel H. D.: *The Queen's Own Royal West Kent Regiment 1920–1950* (Michael Joseph, 1958).

Chierichetti, Sandro: *Masterworks of Sicily* (Milan, 1980).

Clarke, Brigadier Dudley: *The Eleventh at War* (Michael Joseph, 1952).

Cody, J. M.: *28 (Maori) Battalion. Official History of New Zealand in the Second World War 1939–45* (War History Branch, Department of Internal Affairs, Wellington (NZ)).

Costa, Tiziano: *The Bologna Story* (Studio Costa, Bologna, 1985).

Crichton Stuart, Michael: *G Patrol* (Kimber, 1958).

Daly, Dorothy: *The Veneto* (Batsford, 1975).

Danuvar, Yves de: *De Londres à Tunisie* (Charles Lavanzelle, 1945).

Dearden, Seton: *A Nest of Corsairs* (Murray, 1976).

Dorning, Major W. A.: *A Concise History of the South African Defence Force* (South African Government, Department of Public Relations, Pretoria).

Douglas, Keith: *Alamein to Zem Zem* (Faber, 1946).

Douglas, Norman: *Fountains in the Sand* (Secker, 1912).

Douglas, Norman: *Old Calabria* (Secker & Warburg, 1915).

Durrell, Lawrence: *Sicilian Carousel* (Faber, 1977).

Ellenberger, Brigadier G. F.: *History of the King's Own Yorkshire Light Infantry*, Vol. VI (Gale & Polden, 1961).

Ellis, John: *Cassino. The Hollow Victory* (Deutsch, 1984).

Eperon, Arthur: *Travellers' Italy* (BBC, 1980).

Erskine, David: *The Scots Guards 1919–1955* (Clowes, 1956).

Fergusson, Bernard: *The Black Watch and the King's Enemies* (Collins, 1950).

Fielding, W. L.: *With the 6th Division. An Account of the*

6th South African Armoured Division in World War II (Shuter & Shooter, Pietermaritzburg, 1952).

Fleischer, Hagen: *The 'Anomalies' in the Greek Middle East Forces, 1941–1944* (Journal of the Hellenic Diaspora, Vol. V, No. 3, Fall 1978).

Fodor's North Africa (Hodder & Stoughton, 1986).

Foster, Major R. C. S.: *The Queen's Royal Regiment* (Gale & Polden, 1953).

Fox, Frank: *The Royal Inniskilling Fusiliers in the Second World War* (Gale & Polden, 1951).

Francesco, Carla di, and Borella, Marco: *Ferrara, the Estense City* (Ferrara)

Gilbert, Michael: *Road to Victory. Winston S. Churchill 1941–1945* (Heinemann, 1986).

Gissing, George: *By the Ionian Sea* (1901).

Graham, Lieutenant-Colonel F. C. C.: *History of the Argyll & Sutherland Highlanders 1st Battalion (Princess Louise's) 1939–1945* (Nelson, 1948).

Gunn, Peter: *The Companion Guide to Southern Italy* (Collins, 1969).

Hamilton, Nigel, *Monty. Master of the Battlefield* (Hamish Hamilton, 1983).

Hart, Captain B. H. Liddell: *The Tanks. The History of the Royal Tank Regiment and Its Predecessors*, Vol. 2, 1938–1945 (Cassell, 1959).

Hastings, Major R. H. W. S.: *The Rifle Brigade in the Second World War 1939–1945* (Gale and Polden, 1952).

Hibbert, Christopher: *Rome. The Biography of a City* (Viking, 1985).

Horrocks, Lieutenant-General Sir Brian: *A Full Life* (Cooper, 1974).

Howarth, T. E. B. (ed.): *Monty at Close Quarters* (Cooper, 1985).

Jerbi, Hamadi: *Tunisia* (J. P. S., Tunis, 1983).

Karner, Günther, and Weiss, Mario: *Der Wörthersee aus vergangenen Tagen* (Neumarkt, 1984).

Kearsey, Colonel A. and others: *The 10th Royal Hussars in the Second World War 1939–45* (Gale & Polden, 1948).

Keay, Robin: *Italy. Official History of New Zealand in the Second World War 1939–45* (Historical Publication Branch, Department of Internal Affairs, Wellington (NZ), 1967).

Keegan, John: Articles on Brimelow Committee Report, *Daily Telegraph*, 23 and 24 September 1988.

Keogh, Colonel E. G.: *Middle East 1939–1943* (Wilke, Melbourne, 1959).

Kippenberger, Major-General Sir Howard: *Infantry Brigadier* (Oxford University Press, 1949).

Klein, Harry: *Light Horse Cavalcade, 1899–1961* (S. Africa)

Knight, Colonel C. R. B.: *Historical Records of the Buffs* (Medici Society, 1951).

L'Armée française dans la guerre: Du Tchad au Rhin (GP, 1944).

Lassen, Suzanne: *Anders Lassen V.C.* (Muller, 1965).

Leitgeber, Captain Witold: *It Speaks for Itself* (Polish Forces Press Bureau).

Leonardi, Massimo di: Paper presented to Symposium No. 1 Special Force nella Resistenza Italiana, Bologna, 1987.

Lett, Gordon: *Rossano: An Adventure of the Italian Resistance* (Hodder & Stoughton, 1955).

Lewin, Ronald: *Rommel* (Batsford, 1968).

Lewis, Norman: *The Honoured Society* (Collins, 1964).

Lewis, Norman: *The Sicilian Specialist* (Collins, 1975).

Lloyd Owen, Major-General D. L.: *Providence Their Guide* (Harrap, 1980).

Macintosh, Charles: *From Cloak to Dagger* (Kimber, 1982).

Macksey, Kenneth: *Kesselring. The Making of the Luftwaffe* (Batsford, 1978).

Majdalany, Fred: *Cassino: Portrait of a Battle* (Longmans, 1957).

Mjadalany, Fred: *The Battle of El Alamein* (Weidenfeld & Nicolson, 1965)

Maughan, Barton: *Tobruk and El Alamein (Australia in the*

War of 1939–1945). Series 1. Vol. 3 (Australian War Memorial, Canberra, 1966).

Messenger, Charles: *The Tunisian Campaign* (Allan, 1982).

Miller, John: *Friends and Romans* (Fourth Estate, 1987).

Ministry of Information: *The Eighth Army* (HMSO)

Montagu, Ewen: *Beyond Top Secret U* (Davies, 1977).

Montemaggi, Amedeo: *L'Offensiva della Linea Gotica* (Giudicini & Rosa, Pesaro, 1980).

Montgomery of Alamein, Field-Marshal the Viscount: *El Alamein to the River Sangro* (Hutchinson, 1948).

Montgomery of Alamein, Field-Marshal the Viscount: *Memoirs* (Collins, 1958).

Moorehead, Alan: *The Desert War* (Hamish Hamilton, 1965).

Morris, James: *Venice* (Faber, 1960).

Morris, Jan: *The Venetian Empire* (Faber, 1980).

Musulin, Stella: *Vienna in the Age of Metternich* (Faber, 1975).

Nelson, Nina: *Tunisia* (Batsford, 1974).

Newby, Eric: *Love and War in the Apennines* (Hodder & Stoughton, 1971).

Nicholson, Lieutenant-Colonel G. W. L.: *The Canadians in Italy 1943–1945. Official History of the Canadian Army in the Second World War* (Cloutier, Ottawa, 1952).

Panayiotou, Nicos: *Cyprus Participation in the World War II* (Cyprus Popular Bank, 1985).

Paolucci, Antonio: *Ravenna* (Constable, 1978).

Peniakoff, Vladimir: *Private Army* (Cape, 1950).

Pereira, Anthony: *Sicily* (Batsford, 1972).

Pillement, Georges: *Unknown Italy* (Johnson, 1966).

Pillement, Georges: *Unknown Sicily* (Johnson, 1972).

Playfair, Major-General I. S. O., and others: *The Mediterranean and Middle East. History of the Second World War* (HMSO, 1954).

Portisch, Hugo, and Riff, Sepp: *Die Wiedergeburt unseres Staates* (Kremayr & Scheriau, Vienna, 1985).

Quilter, D. C. (ed.): *No Dishonourable Name* (Clowes, 1947).

Ray, Cyril: *Algiers to Austria. The History of 78 Division 1942–1946* (Eyre & Spottiswoode, 1952)

Richardson, General Sir Charles: *Send for Freddie* (Kimber, 1987).

Rocco-Bergera, Nina, and Rebeccha-Piperata: *Itinerary of Joyce and Svervo through Artistic Trieste* (Trieste).

Rossetti, Lucia: *The University of Padua* (Lint, Milan, 1972)

Rossi, Giuseppe: *The Republic of San Marino* (Government of San Marino).

Ruskin, John: *The Stones of Venice* (1853).

Selwyn, Victor, and others: *From Oasis into Italy. War Poems and Diaries from Africa and Italy 1940–1946* (Shepheard-Walwyn, 1983).

Shelley, P. B.: *Lines Written in the Euganean Hills*.

Simiot, Bernard: *La reconquête. De Bir Hakeim à Colmar* (Flammarion)

Slessor, Air Chief Marshal Sir John: *The Central Blue* (Cassell, 1956).

Smith, Denis Mack: *Cavour* (Weidenfeld & Nicolson, 1985).

Spiel, Hilde: *Vienna's Golden Autumn 1866–1938* (Weidenfeld & Nicolson, 1987).

Strawson, John: *A History of the S.A.S. Regiment* (Secker & Warburg, 1984).

Strawson, John: *The Italian Campaign* (Secker & Warburg, 1987).

Swiecicki, Marek: *Seven Rivers to Bologna* (Rolls, 1946).

Thucydides: *History of the Peloponnesian War*.

Tobler, Major Douglas H.: *Intelligence in the Desert* (Privately printed, 1978).

Tolstoy, Nikolai: *Victims of Yalta* (Hodder & Stoughton, 1977).

Trease, Geoffrey: *The Condottieri* (Thames and Hudson, 1970).

Vatikiotis, P. J.: *The Modern History of Egypt* (Weidenfeld & Nicolson, 1969).

Verney, Major-General G. L.: *The Desert Rats* (Hutchin-
son, 1954).
Verney, John: *Going to the Wars* (Collins, 1955).
Waley, Daniel: *The Italian City-Republics* (Longman, 1969).
Whiting, Charles: *The Long March on Rome* (Century,
1987).
Wright, John: *Libya. A Modern History* (Croom Helm)

NOTES

'PRO' indicates that the papers are to be found in the Public Record Office in Kew.

Part I

Chapter 1

1 Major-General G. L. Verney, *The Desert Rats*.
2 PRO FO 371/24624.
3 PRO FO 371/27428.
4 Major-General Sir Howard Kippenberger, *Infantry Brigadier*.
5 J. F. Cody, *25 (Maori) Battalion*.
6 Major-General I. S. O. Playfair, *The Mediterranean and Middle East*.
7 Michael Carver, *Dilemmas of the Desert War*.
8 Major W. A. Dorning, *A Concise History of the South African Defence Force*.
9 Major-General David Lloyd-Owen, *Providence Their Guide*.
10 Vladimir Peniakoff, *Private Army*.
11 Michael Crichton Stuart, *G Patrol*.
12 Peniakoff, op. cit.
13 Crichton Stuart, op. cit.
14 Ernest Kerans, Diary.

15 Brigadier Dudley Clarke, *The Eleventh at War*.
16 Ronald Lewin, *Rommel*.
17 PRO FO 371/31567.
18 PRO FO 371/31573.
19 Lloyd-Owen, op. cit.
20 Michael Gilbert, *Winston S. Churchill*, Vol. VII.
21 Lewin, op. cit.
22 Lieut-General Sir Francis Tuker, *Approach to Battle*.
23 PRO CAB 44/98.
24 Lieut-General Sir Brian Horrocks, *A Full Life*.
25 General Sir Charles Richardson, *Send for Freddie*.
26 Talk with Lieutenant-General Sir Thomas Pearson.
27 Bernard Fergusson, *The Black Watch and the King's Enemies*.
28 Barton Maughan, *Tobruk and El Alamein*.
29 Private letter from T. W. Japp.
30 Talk with Dr Anthony Clayton.
31 Gilbert, op. cit.

Chapter 2

1 Tuker, op. cit.
2 Kerans, Diary.
3 Maughan. op. cit
4 Captain B. H. Liddell Hart, *The Tanks. The History of the Royal Tank Regiment and its Predecessors*.
5 Lewin, op. cit.
6 Kerans, Diary.
7 Richardson, op. cit.
8 Tuker, op. cit.
9 Colonel C. R. Knight, *Historical Records of the Buffs*.
10 PRO CAB 44/98.
11 Harry Ramsbottom, Diary.
12 Keith Douglas, *Alamein to Zem Zem*.
13 Kippenberger, op. cit.
14 PRO CAB 44/101.
15 PRO CAB 44/100.

16 PRO CAB 44/101.
17 Maughan, op. cit.
18 Ramsbottom, Diary.
19 Horrocks, op. cit.
20 PRO CAB 44/102.
21 Richardson, op. cit.
22 PRO CAB 44/102.
23 Field-Marshal the Viscount Montgomery of Alamein, *Alamein to the River Sangro*.
24 Kerans, Diary.
25 PRO CAB 44/105.
26 Fred Majdalany, *The Battle of Alamein*.

Part 2

Chapter 3

1 John Verney, *Going to the Wars*.
2 PRO CAB 44/108.
3 PRO CAB 44/109.
4 John Wright, *Libya. A Modern History*.
5 *Encyclopaedia Britannica* (Senussi).
6 Wright, op. cit.
7 Peniakoff, op. cit.
8 Nigel Hamilton, *Monty. Master of the Battlefield 1942–1944*.
9 Horrocks, op. cit.
10 Keith Douglas, op. cit.
11 PRO CAB 44/108.
12 Dorning, op. cit.
13 PRO CAB 44/109.
14 PRO CAB 44/108l.
15 Richardson, op. cit.
16 Private letter from P. A. A. Thomas.
17 Tuker, op. cit.
18 Ramsbottom, Diary.
19 Ramsbottom, Diary.

20 Maughan, op. cit.
21 PRO CAB 44/105
22 Kippenberger, op. cit.
23 Major R. C. S. Foster, *The Queen's Royal Regiment.*
24 PRO CAB 44/109
25 Alan Moorehead, *The Desert War.*
26 PRO CAB 44/110
27 Foster, op. cit.
28 Keith Douglas, op. cit.
29 Ramsbottom, Diary
30 Major Douglas H. Tobler, *Intelligence in the Desert.*
31 Hamilton, op. cit.
32 PRO CAB 44/111
33 Hamilton, op. cit.
34 Harold Macmillan, *War Diaries.*
35 Horrocks, op. cit.
36 Hamilton, op. cit.
37 PRO CAB 44/111.
38 Montgomery, op. cit.
39 Kippenberger, op. cit.
40 Crichton Stuart, op. cit.
41 Michael Carver, *Harding of Petherton.*
42 Verney, op. cit.
43 PRO CAB 44/112.
44 Ramsbottom, Diary.
45 Kippenberger, op. cit.
46 Cody, op. cit.
47 Horrocks, op. cit.
48 *L'armée française dans la guerre; Du Chad au Rhin.*
49 Yves Danuvar, *De Londres à Tunisie.*
50 Hamilton, op. cit.
51 Tuker, op. cit.
52 Hamilton, op. cit.
53 PRO CAB 44/99.
54 Montgomery, op. cit.
55 Gilbert, op. cit.
56 Hamilton, op. cit.

57 Ramsbottom, Diary.
58 Wright, op. cit.

Part 3

Chapter 4

1 Charles Messenger, *The Tunisian Campaign.*
2 Messenger, op. cit.
3 Montgomery, op. cit.
4 Messenger, op. cit.
5 Hamilton, op. cit.
6 Ricky Hall, Diary
7 Gilbert, op. cit.
8 Knight, op. cit.
9 Montgomery, op. cit.
10 Messenger, op. cit.
11 Kerans, Diary
12 Hamilton, op. cit.
13 Horrocks, op. cit.
14 Hagen Fleischer, *The 'Anomalies' in the Greek Middle East Forces 1941–1944.*
15 Tuker, op. cit.
16 Private letter from James Whitton.

Chapter 5

1 Kippenberger, op. cit.
2 Peniakoff, op. cit.
3 Montgomery, op. cit.
4 Hamilton, op. cit.
5 Horrocks, op. cit.
6 Tuker, op. cit.
7 Joan Bright, *The Ninth Queen's Royal Lancers 1936–1945.*
8 Moorehead, op. cit.
9 Keith Douglas, op. cit.

10 Notebook kept by N. L. Mallins.
11 Victor Selwyn (ed.), *From Oasis into Italy*.
12 Selwyn, op. cit.
13 Peniakoff, op. cit.
14 Danuvar, op. cit.
15 Moorehead, op. cit.
16 PRO CAB 44/122.
17 PRO CAB 44/119.
18 Horrocks, op. cit.
19 PRO CAB 44/119.

Chapter 6

1 PRO CAB 44/122
2 Major-General W. A. Beddington, *A History of the Queen's Bays*.
3 PRO CAB 44/122.
4 Hall, Diary.
5 Hamilton, op. cit.
6 Gilbert, op. cit.
7 Hall, Diary.
8 Talk with Maurice Sarfati in Tunis.
9 D. C. Quilter (ed). *No Dishonourable Name*.

Part 4

Chapter 7

1 Hamilton, op. cit.
2 PRO CAB 44/122.
3 Hamilton, op. cit.
4 Lieut-Colonel G. W. L. Nicholson, *The Canadians in Italy 1943–1945*.
5 Hamilton, op. cit.
6 Kerans, Diary.
7 Hamilton, op. cit.
8 Nicholson, op. cit.

 9 Ewen Montagu, *Beyond Top Secret U.*
10 PRO CAB 44/127.
11 Hamilton, op. cit.
12 Gilbert, op. cit.

Chapter 8

 1 Quilter, op. cit.
 2 Richardson, op. cit.
 3 John Strawson, *A History of the S.A.S. Regiment.*
 4 PRO CAB 44/123.
 5 Nicholson, op. cit.
 6 PRO CAB 44/124.
 7 Fergusson, op. cit.
 8 Talk with Joseph Anderson.
 9 Selwyn, op. cit.
10 Kerans, Diary.

Chapter 9

 1 PRO CAB 44/124.
 2 Montgomery, op. cit.
 3 PRO CAB 44/127.
 4 PRO CAB 44/127.
 5 Charles Whiting, *The Long March on Rome.*
 6 PRO CAB 44/124.
 7 Kerans, Diary.
 8 PRO CAB 44/124.
 9 Norman Lewis, *The Honoured Society.*
10 Talk with Robert Perrin.
11 Hamilton, op, cit.
12 Kerans, Diary,
13 Carver, *Harding of Petherton.*
14 PRO CAB 44/123.
15 Anthony Pereira, *Sicily.*
16 Georges Pillement, *Unknown Sicily.*
17 Strawson, op. cit.

18 Montgomery, op. cit.
19 Carver, *Harding of Petherton*.
20 Lawrence Durrell, *Sicilian Carousel*.
21 PRO CAB 44/125.
22 Hamilton, op. cit.
23 Field-Marshal the Viscount Montgomery of Alamein, *Memoirs*.
24 Cyril Ray, *Algiers to Austria. The History of 78 Division*.
25 Lieutenant-Colonel H. D. Chaplin, *The Queen's Own Royal West Kent Regiment 1920–1950*.
26 Lewis, op. cit.
27 Durrell, op. cit.
28 Ray, op. cit.
29 Chaplin, op. cit.
30 Frank Fox, *The Royal Inniskilling Fusiliers in the Second World War*.
31 PRO CAB 44/126.

Chapter 10

1 Lewis, op. cit.
2 Hamilton, op. cit.
3 Carver, *Harding of Petherton*.
4 Durrell, op. cit.
5 Pillement, op. cit.
6 Hamilton, op. cit.
7 Mareksey
8 Montgomery, *Alamein to the River Sangro*.
9 Liddell Hart, op. cit.
10 Nicholson, op. cit.
11 Kenneth Macksey, *Kesselring*.
12 Nicholson, op. cit.
13 Gilbert, op. cit.

Part 5

Chapter 11

1 Norman Douglas, *Old Calabria.*
2 PRO CAB 44/128.
3 PRO CAB 44/128.
4 Gilbert, op. cit.
5 Montgomery, *Alamein to the River Sangro.*
6 Hamilton, op. cit.
7 PRO CAB 44/129.
8 Nicholson, op. cit.
9 Montgomery, *Alamein to the River Sangro.*
10 George Gissing, *By the Ionian Sea.*
11 Nicholson, op. cit.
12 PRO CAB 44/135.
13 Whiting, op. cit.

Chapter 12

1 PRO CAB 44/135.
2 PRO CAB 44/130.
3 Talk with Francesco Cicoria in Pescara.
4 Montgomery, *Alamein to the River Sangro.*
5 Peniakoff, op. cit.
6 *Encylopaedia Britannica* (Taranto).
7 Norman Douglas, op. cit.
8 Nicholson, op. cit.
9 Montgomery, *Alamein to the River Sangro.*
10 PRO CAB 44/136.
11 Nicholson, op. cit.
12 Talk with Arnold Graves near Lake Trasimene.

Chapter 13

1 Montgomery, *Alamein to the River Sangro.*
2 Strawson, op. cit.
3 Mongomery, *Alamein to the River Sangro.*

4 Strawson, op. cit.
5 PRO CAB 44/136.
6 PRO CAB 44/136.
7 PRO CAB 44/136.

Chapter 14

1 Gilbert, op. cit.
2 Gilbert, op. cit.
3 Hamilton, op. cit.
4 PRO CAB 44/136.
5 PRO CAB 44/135.
6 PRO CAB 44/135.
7 PRO CAB 44/136.
8 Montgomery, *Alamein to the River Sangro.*
9 Hamilton, op. cit.
10 Montgomery, *Alamein to the River Sangro.*
11 Gilbert, op. cit.
12 Carver, *Harding of Petherton.*

Chapter 15

1 Ray, op. cit.
2 PRO CAB 44/136.
3 PRO CAB 44/136.
4 Tuker, op. cit.
5 Talk with Francesco Cicoria in Pescara.
6 John Verney, op. cit.
7 Lieutenant-General W. Anders, *An Army in Exile.*
8 Correspondence with Andrew Grochowski.
9 Anders, op. cit.

Chapter 16

1 Gilbert, op. cit.
2 John Ellis, *Cassino.*
3 PRO CAB 44/135.

4 Anders, op. cit.
5 Ellis, op. cit.
6 Quilter, op. cit.
7 Ellis, op. cit.
8 Quilter, op. cit.
9 Anders, op. cit.
10 Nicol Panayiotu, *Cyprus Participation in World War II*.
11 Talk with Felicjan Pawlak.
12 Ellis, op. cit.
13 Anders, op. cit.
14 Papers in Sikorski Institute.
15 Talk with the late Brigadier Way.
16 Anders, op. cit.
17 Gilbert, op. cit.
18 Whiting, op. cit.
19 Whiting, op. cit.
20 PRO CAB 44/141.
21 Dorning, op. cit.
22 David Erskine, *The Scots Guards*.
23 PRO CAB 44/145.
24 Talk with Francesco Cicoria in Pescara.
25 Anders, op. cit.
26 Georges Pillement, *L'Italie inconnue*.
27 Talk with John Miller.
28 Peniakoff, op. cit.

Chapter 17

1 PRO CAB 44/145.
2 Nicholson, op. cit.
3 Gilbert, op. cit.
4 Nicholson, op. cit.
5 Gilbert, op. cit.
6 Gilbert, op. cit.
7 Talks with Dr Francesco Griccioli della Grigia and Brigadier Michael Hague in Florence and Rome.
8 John Miller, *Friends and Romans*.

9 Whiting, op. cit.
10 Eric Newby, *Love and War in the Apennines*.
11 Gordon Lett, Rossano: *An Adventure of the Italian Resistance*.
12 Geoffrey Trease, *The Condottieri*.
13 Major R. H. W. S. Hastings: *The Rifle Brigade in the Second World War 1939–1945.*
14 Quilter, op. cit.
15 Macmillan, *War Diaries*.
16 Trease, op. cit.
17 PRO CAB 44/145.
18 Erskine, op. cit.
19 Nicholson, op. cit.
20 Harry Klein, *Light Horse Cavalcade, 1899–1961*.
21 Talk with Carlo Baldini in Greve in Chianti.
22 Selwyn. op. cit.
23 W. L. Fielding, *With the 6th Division. An Account of the 6th South African Division in World War II*.
24 Charles Macintosh, *From Cloak to Dagger*.
25 Correspondence with the late Charles Macintosh.
26 Klein, op. cit.
27 Macintosh, op. cit.

Chapter 18

1 Typescript by Lieutenant-Colonel H. B. Hudson in the India Office Library.
2 Christopher Hibbert, *Rome. The Biography of a City*.
3 Marcel Brion, *The Medici*.
4 M. V. Caprani, *The Spirit and the Heritage. The Story of the Little Company of Mary in Italy*.
5 PRO CAB 44/145.
6 PRO CAB 44/145.

Chapter 19

1 PRO CAB 44/145.
2 Talk with Alessandro Servi in Pesaro.

3 Beddington, op. cit.
4 PRO CAB 44/145.
5 Speech to Annual Dinner of Special Forces Club.
6 Giuseppi Rossi, *The Republic of San Marino*.
7 Macmillan, *War Diaries*.
8 PRO CAB 44/145.
9 Nicholson, op. cit.
10 Nicholson, op. cit.

Chapter 20

1 Paper by Professor Luciano Bergonzini to Symposium No. 1 Special Force nella Resistenza Italiana, Bologna, 1987.
2 Nicholson, op. cit.
3 Paper by Professor Bergonzini, Bologna Symposium.
4 Paper by Professor Bergonzini, Bologna Symposium.
5 PRO CAB 44/147.
6 Nicholson, op. cit.
7 PRO CAB 44/147.
8 Bright, op. cit.
9 PRO CAB 44/147.
10 Fox, op. cit.
11 R. M. Burdon, *24 Battalion. Official History of New Zealand in the Second World War 1939–45*.
12 Talk with Professor Bergonzini in Bologna.
13 Gilbert, op. cit.
14 Talk with Ludwik Lubienski.
15 Talk with Edmund de Rothschild.
16 Talk with Arnold Graves near Lake Trasimene.
17 Anders, op. cit.

Chapter 21

1 Nicholson, op. cit.
2 PRO CAB 44/148.
3 John Strawson, *The Italian Campaign*.

4 PRO CAB 44/148.
5 Quilter, op. cit.
6 Suzanne Lassen, *Anders Lassen V.C.*
7 Marek Swiecicki, *Seven Rivers to Bologna.*
8 Hudson MS in India Office Library.
9 Macintosh, op. cit.
10 Italian Partisan Publication: *Bologna nella resistenza.*
11 Talk with Susanna Boltonelli and Magli Umberto in Bologna.
12 Tiziano Costa, *The Bologna Story.*

Chapter 22

1 Strawson, *The Italian Campaign.*
2 P. B. Shelley, *Lines Written in the Euganean Hills.*
3 Colonel A. Kearsey, *The 10th Royal Hussars in the Second World War 1939–1945.*
4 Hastings, op. cit.
5 PRO CAB 44/148.
6 Robin Keay, *Italy. Official History of New Zealand in the Second World War 1939–45.*
7 James Morris, *Venice.*
8 Keay, op. cit.
9 Peniakoff, op. cit.
10 Gilbert, op. cit.

Chapter 23

1 PRO FO 371/48827.
2 PRO FO 371/48827.
3 Keay, op. cit.
4 Report by Lieut-Colonel Peter Wilkinson.
5 Talk with Mietta Shamblin in Trieste.
6 PRO FO 371/48827.
7 Report by Lieut-Colonel Wilkinson.
8 Cody, op. cit.
9 Gilbert, op. cit.

10 Union Jack, 8 May 1945.
11 Talk with Ludwik Lubienski.
12 Anders, op. cit.

Chapter 24

1 John Keegan, *Daily Telegraph*, 24 Sept. 1988
2 Nikolai Tolstoy, *Victims of Yalta*.
3 Research carried out on my behalf in the Public Records Office by Lieutenant-Colonel Jerzy Szymanski.
4 Talk with Denis Hills.
5 Tolstoy, op. cit.
6 Talk with Denis Hills.

Part 6

Chapter 25

1 Report by Lieutenant-Colonel Wilkinson.
2 PRO FO 371/48827.
3 Report by Lieutenant-Colonel Wilkinson.
4 PRO FO 371/48827.
5 PRO FO 371/48827.
6 Stella Musulin, *Vienna in the Age of Metternich*.
7 Talk with Ernest Harrison in Pörtschach.
8 Talk with Dr Anthony Clayton and letter from H. T. Shergold.
9 Talk with Dr Gruber in Vienna.
10 PRO FO 371/50815.
11 Ray, op. cit.
12 Hugo Portisch and Sepp Riff: *Die Wiedergeburt unseres Staates*.
13 Talk with Joseph Anderson.

Chapter 25

1 Official Report: *Public Safety in Austria*.
2 Tolstoy, op. cit.

3 Macmillan, *War Diaries*.
4 Tostoy, op. cit.
5 Papers researched by Lieutenant-Colonel Szymanski.
6 Tolstoy, op. cit.
7 Bright, op. cit.
8 PRO FO 371/46599.
9 PRO FO 371/46617.
10 PRO FO 371/48827.
11 PRO FO 371/46617.

Chapter 26

1 Talk with Sir Peter Wilkinson.
2 Portisch and Riff, op. cit.
3 PRO FO 371/46617.
4 Talk with Sabina Eggar in Vienna.
5 Talk with John Reid in Vienna.
6 Exhibition '1938' in Vienna.
7 Talk with Denis Hills.
8 Talk with John Reid in Vienna.
9 Gordon Brook-Shepherd, *The Last Habsburg*.
10 Hilde Spiel, *Vienna's Golden Autumn*.
11 Musulin, op. cit.

INDEX